HANK & JIM

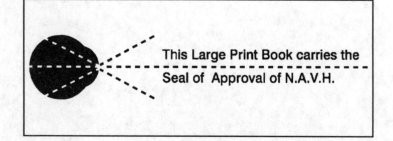

This Large Print Book carries the
Seal of Approval of N.A.V.H.

Hank & Jim

THE FIFTY-YEAR FRIENDSHIP OF HENRY FONDA AND JAMES STEWART

Scott Eyman

THORNDIKE PRESS
A part of Gale, a Cengage Company

GALE
A Cengage Company

Farmington Hills, Mich • San Francisco • New York • Waterville, Maine
Meriden, Conn • Mason, Ohio • Chicago

Copyright © 2017 by Paladin Literature Inc.
Photo on page 556: Courtesy L. Tom Perry Special Collections, Harold B. Lee Library. Brigham Young University, Provo, Utah.
Thorndike Press, a part of Gale, a Cengage Company.

LIBRARY OF CONGRESS CIP DATA ON FILE.
CATALOGUING IN PUBLICATION FOR THIS BOOK
IS AVAILABLE FROM THE LIBRARY OF CONGRESS.

ISBN-13: 978-1-4328-4420-2 (hardcover)
ISBN-10: 1-4328-4420-2 (hardcover)

Published in 2017 by arrangement with Simon & Schuster, Inc.

Printed in the United States of America
1 2 3 4 5 6 7 21 20 19 18 17

For John Sacret Young,
who got me into it.
And for Robert Osborne,
who got me through it.

CONTENTS

PROLOGUE

In the end, as in the beginning, they didn't need words.

Hank's health broke first. The pacemaker had been implanted while he was playing Clarence Darrow in 1975, and that was followed by a tumor the size of a grapefruit in his diaphragm. The tumor was benign, but the surgery resulted in a troublesome staph infection.

Prostate cancer was diagnosed in 1979 when he was appearing in *First Monday in October*. The cancer had moved into the bone, but doses of estrogen sent the disease into remission. After that came various hip and back problems.

His frailty was obvious. In 1980, when he wanted to make *Gideon's Trumpet* for television, the only way he could be insured was to pay part of the premiums himself, which he did without much complaint. Clarence Gideon was a good part, and a good part meant more to Hank Fonda than bread, than air.

"Retire? I wouldn't know what to do," he said, dismissing the very idea.

Finally it rounded back to the heart again, which was descending into congestive failure. Before, he had always rallied, if only because dying was bound to interrupt acting. But this time the doctors and his family weren't so confident.

He was in intensive care. His wife, Shirlee, remembers that things were looking grim until Jim Stewart came for a visit. Fonda had been in a deep sleep, but when he heard Jim's unmistakable voice he began to stir.

"Stewart, is that you?" he said, his eyes still closed.

Assured that it was, Hank opened his eyes. It was definitely Jim standing there.

"Where's my root beer float?" Fonda asked.

At that point, everyone in the room knew he was going to live for a while longer, because Henry Fonda took root beer floats very seriously. Another thing he took seriously was Jim Stewart, his best friend.

By the time Fonda won his ridiculously overdue Oscar for *On Golden Pond* he was in a wheelchair. He had acted right up until his body failed him. Between completing

10

On Golden Pond and getting his award, he made a TV movie with Myrna Loy called *Summer Solstice,* then appeared in a play. He had to be carried onto the set and placed in position before the curtain rose, but he didn't care. Acting was not a job to Henry Fonda. It was, rather, his identity.

"If I go," he told his wife, "I go with my boots on."

By the early summer of 1982, he was clearly spiraling down. On May 16, he celebrated his seventy-seventh birthday. It had been precisely 139 days since his release from Cedars-Sinai Medical Center, where he had resided for seven endless weeks. Shirlee had been keeping track — Cedars had been his thirteenth hospitalization since their marriage in 1965. If anybody noticed the unlucky number they didn't mention it.

He hadn't left the house since his daughter, Jane, had brought him his Oscar right after the ceremony. Some days he didn't leave his bedroom. The skin around his face had begun to tighten and fade, which had the effect of making his startlingly blue eyes loom even larger. The rest of him had aged terribly, but his eyes remained radiant and fierce with life.

Every day Stewart would leave his house on North Roxbury in Beverly Hills and visit

11

his friend up the hill in Bel-Air. Most days he would bring flowers in one hand and a bag of vegetables in the other, harvested that morning from the garden he and Gloria, his wife, had planted next to their house. If Fonda was awake and in the mood for conversation, they usually discussed gardening, and the pleasure it gave them.

When Jim wasn't around, Jane would sit by her father's bed. Her hope was that he would talk, say something that might dispel the aura of silence and grudge that had plagued their relationship since she was a little girl. But in his dying, as in his living, Henry Fonda kept his own counsel, reserving his thoughts about death to himself.

"When I die, put my ashes in the compost pile," he had told Shirlee. It was the sort of defiant, I-don't-give-a-good-goddamn statement people often make, but Fonda meant it. If there's anything an organic gardener understands, it's the importance of quality fertilizer.

As Jim sat with Hank that long summer, they figured out that the fall of 1982 would mark fifty years since they had thrown in together, two starving young actors in New York City. Since then they had been inseparable, emotionally if not physically.

On the surface, their friendship was a

match of opposing personalities. Henry Jaynes Fonda was an agnostic trending toward atheist who had been raised in a Christian Science household on the plains of Nebraska. James Maitland Stewart was a churchgoing Presbyterian from the archetypal Midwest town of Indiana, Pennsylvania. Hank was an ardent New Deal Democrat, Jim an equally serious conservative Republican. Hank had had five wives — a fact he found mortifying — and often difficult relationships with his children, while Jim had one wife and was adored by his children.

Stewart had been finishing his architecture degree at Princeton when he was diverted into the least likely career ever attempted by a citizen of Indiana, Pennsylvania. Fonda was introduced to the craft by Dorothy Brando, whom everybody called Doe, an Omaha wife and mother with a bad marriage and a drinking problem who also nudged her son, Marlon, into the profession.

Hank lived most of his life like a tightly wound spring, and his acting followed suit. As one critic noted, he tended to project "anger over affirmation . . . he is almost always more convincing, attractive and memorable when at odds with something

— the situation, the community, himself." He could relax only with a few select friends — for a long time with John Ford and his roster of reprobates, always with Jim, Johnny Swope, or Leland Hayward.

Stewart was apparently comfortable in life or at work. One actress said that if you happened to turn your back and just listened to him talking, you couldn't tell if he was playing a scene or having a conversation with someone on the set. He was that natural, that at ease.

What set Stewart apart from the other leading men of his generation was his embrace of emotional extremes — pain connected to nothing less than unmediated agony.

Stewart was regarded with open affection by the communities of Hollywood and movie fans alike. He was practically a member of the extended family of man. Nobody called Fonda "Hank" except close friends, but millions of people who never met Stewart referred to him as "Jimmy."

In spite of their many differences, these unusually tall, skinny, gifted young actors had bonded immediately over their shared passion for their work, and for an ethereal young actress named Margaret Sullavan. Both of them worked with her. Fonda loved her, married her, then lost her. Stewart pined for her.

Through all the vicissitudes of the world, through career ups and downs, through their mutual jettisoning of their careers to go to war and the difficult adjustment that came after, they had stayed close, taking care to steer carefully past the shoals of their differing politics.

And now Jim was doing the only thing he could for his pal — be there while Hank struggled to stay awake, struggled to breathe, struggled to stay alive for one more hour, one more day. Dying is hard work, and Hank was exhausted.

Besides discussions of gardening, and periods of companionable silence, there was occasional yelling about episodes from their shared youth. Stewart was mostly deaf, while Fonda's hearing loss was about fifty percent. Each of them had to shout in order to be heard by the other. This scene that had unaccountably not appeared in a play by Samuel Beckett struck Hank as hilarious — his sense of humor encompassed the bleak, while Jim could manage only a thin smile at their shared decrepitude.

Once or twice they reminisced about the time Stewart had played his accordion in Times Square at three in the morning, gradually gathering a crowd and passing the hat. It was a story they had been haggling over for decades, each of them secretly delighted by the fact that they could not agree on the particulars.

Stewart said the assembled multitude amounted to at least a dozen, and maybe more. Fonda, who insisted that Stewart's stories were always embroidered, weakly asserted that the assembled group involved no more than eight people. Stewart said they had raised 26 cents; Fonda insisted it was 18 cents.

Ah yes; they remembered it well.

Sometimes they talked about the model of the Martin bomber they had built together in New York, and that Jim had dragged across the country so that they could fly it together in Hollywood.

What was missing from the conversations was any discussion of acting, at which they both excelled, or the movies, which had granted them immortality. "People say Hank and I are living in the past when we get together," Stewart had said a few years earlier. "But it's not that. It's fun to remember things."

In so many ways, these men had parallel lives. Each was an actor before he became a star, and they remained actors after they became legends. Each of them embodied America's geographic as well as moral center — integrity mixed with a bloody-minded obstinance that wasn't acting.

Beneath his placid surface, Stewart's emotions churned, while Fonda had the stillest center of any American actor — as eloquent in his isolation as a painting by Edward Hopper. He adamantly refused to show the machinery at work, which constituted his triumph as an actor as well as his blockage as a husband and father.

Fonda would always be indelibly identified with Tom Joad, the idealistic, dispossessed ghost in the American darkness. That said, he was equally expert at playing bastards. He lunged for the part of a martinet in *Fort Apache* because Pappy Ford wanted him. And sometimes, as in *The Wrong Man* and *Once Upon a Time in the West,* Fonda created something truly startling — an impassivity that barely masked crushing existential guilt in the case of the former, bottomless evil in the latter.

But for most people he was Abe Lincoln defending an innocent man charged with murder, Wyatt Earp cleaning up Tombstone, Mister Roberts coping with a restless crew and a petty tyrant, juror number 8 endlessly arguing about the guilt or innocence of a

Puerto Rican boy.

What distinguished Fonda's acting from the beginning was watchfulness, beneath which was an equally perceptible attitude of "Don't push me." It's there in his Lincoln, where he comes across as gentle and unassertive, except for the fact that he always wins, always gets his way.

And it's certainly there in *The Grapes of Wrath,* when Tom Joad tells a truck driver how he knocked a man's head "plumb to squash." There's no regret in his voice, just a statement of fact salted with a certain satisfaction that says the son of a bitch had it coming.

"A black friend of mine," wrote James Baldwin, "swore that Fonda had colored blood. You could tell, he said, by the way Fonda walked down the road at the [beginning] of the film: *white men don't walk like that!*"

Baldwin's friend might have been right, psychologically if not genetically, for Hank Fonda was a man apart, in life as surely as in his work. He held himself aloof from the reflexive glad-handing of show business, the cheap embraces, the ecstatic cries of "Darling!" He was as wary of cheap compliments as he was of cheap people; he knew how hard it was to build a performance that lasts, let alone a career . . . or a friendship.

Stewart was gentler with people but equally fearless in his work. Stewart played a sly voyeur in *Rear Window,* a haunted necrophile in *Vertigo,* a furtive circus clown in *The Greatest Show on Earth,* tenacious, driven cowboys in *Winchester '73, Bend of the River, The Far Country,* and *The Man from Laramie,* a Mitteleuropa clerk in *The Shop Around the Corner,* a middle-class banker driven to desperation in *It's a Wonderful Life,* a swozzled bachelor with an invisible friend in *Harvey,* a grizzled old pilot in *The Flight of the Phoenix,* a crafty small-town lawyer in *Anatomy of a Murder,* a cynical reporter in *Call Northside 777,* a senator in *Mr. Smith Goes to Washington.*

Superficially, they were different people. Beneath his often dour exterior, Hank had an antic gift for mimicry and physical humor that convulsed his friends. Jim was puckish, a little vague, more intrinsically relaxed. Perhaps it was the war that gave him a certainty about himself, the war where he had commanded men and flown B-24 bombers over Germany.

Fonda went to war, too, but as with so much else in his life, it was just one more irritating burden whose rewards seemed insufficient compared to the hope that had preceded it and the effort he had put into it.

Fonda was a closet intellectual and perfectionist, which inevitably meant he carried around a residual sense of disappointment with himself and others that could quickly ascend to seething impatience. If he attempted something, even if it was only a hobby, he had to achieve excellence. He did it with his gardening, his needlepoint, and especially with his painting. Stewart was far more easygoing; he didn't read much, was outwardly affable, rarely lost his temper.

But on the deepest level, they shared one crucial characteristic: they were both loners, extremely sparing with the gift of intimacy, reserving themselves for themselves. Once, an actor complained to John Ford that although he'd worked with Stewart several times, he still didn't know the man.

"You don't get to know Jimmy Stewart," replied Ford. "Jimmy Stewart gets to know you."

Another similarity involved the essentials of their craft — neither of them had ever had an acting lesson. They were united in the belief that the best way to learn how to act was to act. Know the lines; don't be afraid to think; above all, don't talk about it, do it.

And now, suddenly, incomprehensibly, they were two hard-of-hearing old men who cherished their differences every bit as much as their shared memories.

Hank had good days when he was fully present, followed by bad days when his energy faded and he stayed inside himself. He had grown a beard out of pure defiance: "I made a pact with myself that only when I am well will I shave it off, which I am almost ready to do." The beard, which had been perhaps an inch long when he got his Oscar in March, was now bushy.

When he felt up to it, he would sit in his favorite chair with a large sketch pad in his lap and draw. In the morning light he looked uncannily like the elderly, emaciated Auguste Renoir.

It was only right that Jim be there while Hank was dying. He had been there when Hank was acting, been there when Hank was courting his wives. They had lived together, double-dated together, starred in movies together, designed immeasurably complex practical jokes together.

There was so much to remember.

■ ■ ■ ■

BEGINNING

■ ■ ■ ■

ONE

In Hank Fonda's telling, the earliest years were the most important.

He was born in Grand Island, Nebraska, 150 miles southwest of Omaha, in a rented house of six tiny rooms. The date was May 16, 1905, and the next day the local newspaper carried an announcement: "Dr. Roeder reports Uneeda Biscuits for sale at any old price from salesman William Brace Fonda this morning, a bright baby boy having arrived at the home of Mr. and Mrs. Fonda on West Division Street yesterday."

When Henry was six months old, the family moved to Omaha, where his father continued working as a salesman, a successful one — the census for 1910 lists a servant named Minnie Stout living in the Fonda family's home. A few years later William Fonda opened a reasonably successful small business: W. B. Fonda Printing Company, on Farnum Street. There were two employees, four or five presses. By that time, William Fonda owned his own home.

Henry Fonda's last wife would say that the key to his often difficult life was that he never really liked himself, and that is borne out by a fragment of autobiography that dates from the 1970s. "For the first quarter of my life I had no real direction at all. I think it's safe to say I was without ambition and I don't say that proudly. As a boy, if someone patted me on the head and asked me what I was going to be when I grew up, I probably looked at them so idiotically that they lost interest in my future."

All that began to change when Fonda was in the sixth grade. The class was asked to write a short story of a page or two. The best story would be printed in the local paper. Fonda, who described himself as "a good boy [who] always did my lessons," titled his story, "The Mouse," and told it from the point of view of the title character. It involved a burglar, and a mouse who alerted the house and became a hero. Henry won first prize — $1! — and also got his name printed in the paper right on top of his story. His mother bragged to her father and from that point on Grandpa Henry assumed that the boy would become a writer. Grandpa Henry had worked on the railroad, said Hank, "but he was a poet at heart, and I treasure the letters he wrote to me, his grandson and namesake, from his home in St. Paul.

"I was assigned to an ambition," he would write. "I don't remember being thrilled by it, but I accepted it, and by the time I was ready for college it was assumed that I would major in journalism."

Along with a full ration of youthful indecision, in most respects Henry was a typical kid of that time and place. He lost his virginity in a house of prostitution. The price was $2, and he hated every minute of it. "It was just 'wham-bam.' I was repulsed. It turned me off for quite a while."

In other respects, he had unusual talents — by the time he was an adolescent it was obvious that he could draw quite well. Violence sickened him, as he discovered when William Fonda took the fourteen-year-old Henry to courthouse square to witness the lynching of a black man. The poor unfortunate's name was Will Brown, and he was accused of raping a white woman.

The date was September 28, 1919.

It was a full-scale race riot. After Brown was dragged from his jail cell, stripped and probably castrated, he was lynched. After that, the mob filled his body with bullets

27

and dragged it through the streets of Omaha. Finally, the body was burned in a bonfire, while pictures were taken of the jubilant population in front of the flames. Omaha's mayor, who tried to stop the lynching, was also strung up but cut down just before he strangled.

William Fonda said nothing about what they were watching. "He didn't preach, he didn't make a point, he just made sure I saw it."

Henry Fonda never explained why his father made him witness something so horrifying. "When it was all over, we went home. . . . I would like to think he realized it would be a lesson," he said as an old man. "I had to grow up and move away from Omaha to appreciate that my father was a liberal Democrat in a hotbed of Republican reactionaries."

It was the beginning of Henry Fonda's fierce hatred of bigotry and intolerance. It was also the beginning of what his daughter would describe as his "land-based morality" — a sense of right and wrong that derived, not from the arbitrary structures of men, but from the rhythms and verities of the natural world, which he strove to be a part of all his life.

Henry Fonda always trusted seasons, soil,

and seed; he trusted people infrequently.

As a young man, Fonda's passion for the movies was a sometime thing; other than an enthusiasm for the weirdly babyish Harry Langdon, he gave the impression that movies didn't play a huge part in his life. He studied journalism at the University of Minnesota, but dropped out after two years, making vague noises about going back in a year or two. He marked time for a couple of years doing itinerant labor — iceman, mechanic. In 1925 he began hanging around the Omaha Community Players, doing whatever needed doing, from dressing stages to cleaning up the place after performances.

His acting began as the idea of a young wife and mother named Dorothy Brando, who thought Hank might have the makings of an actor. By September 1925, it became clear that Fonda wasn't going back to college, and Doe Brando asked him to play the juvenile lead in Philip Barry's *You and I.* "They had rehearsed it for a few days and the boy playing it had decided to go back to college," said Fonda decades later. "I was the guy who didn't go back to college, so I was available and I got pushed into it."

That was the beginning; as Fonda put it, he "got the smell of this thing." He began hanging around the theater doing whatever needed to be done. His father was not happy — young Mr. Fonda was twenty years old and earning precisely nothing at the Omaha Players. He grudgingly took a job as a clerk with a credit company in June 1926, but in September Doe Brando called again. The theater was putting on *Merton of the Movies,* an extremely popular 1922 play by George S. Kaufman and Marc Connelly, and Fonda was perfect for the title role of a green country boy who lucks his way into a Hollywood career.

William Fonda hit the roof. "My mother was the diplomat who kept me home, instead of [my having to move] into the Y so that I wouldn't have to argue with my father." Fonda was up early, went to his job at the credit company, then went straight to the theater to rehearse. "By the time I got home, he was in bed, so I never saw him."

If William Fonda was not pleased by his son's lack of definition, or his habit of hanging around the theater, he was not unalterably opposed. He attended a performance of *Merton of the Movies* and liked what he saw. When one of Henry's sisters ventured a criticism of Hank's performance, William Fonda lowered his newspaper and said, "Shut up. He was perfect." Henry Fonda remembered this moment of parental approval all his life, although he would only rarely be able to give his own children similar praise.

"Well, from that moment, I couldn't make a mistake as far as my father was concerned, and when I decided a year or two later that I wanted to quit my job overnight and go to New York, not a word. Boy, he was great."

A few years later, a friend of Fonda's was introduced to the extended family, and his impression was of a studied normalcy. "I remember his father being a very lean, swarthy Italian type of man, and [the father and sisters were] all three of them interested and supportive and wanted to do anything for [Hank] that they possibly could."

Merton of the Movies garnered a lot of local attention, as did Fonda. In October 1926, his first newspaper interview appeared. "I don't intend to make acting my profession," he said. "It is just my hobby. It was thrilling at first, but the glamour has worn off. From 7:30 a.m. to 7:30 p.m. I am a businessman."

Brave words, foolish words. Much like Merton, Fonda was hooked, and for very specific reasons. "As far as I can remember," he said, "I was shy and self-conscious and I'd cross the street rather than pass some-

31

body just to say hello. . . . That's why I'm an actor. I discovered . . . that [with] acting I could put a mask on and I wasn't self-conscious."

It went deeper than that, though. "The thing that I was getting fascinated by was not acting, but . . . *theater.* This strange new atmosphere and people that I was meeting. The life backstage." This man who would spend much of his life in emotional isolation responded to the camaraderie, the band-of-brothers aspect of theater the way most people respond to being on an athletic team.

Although Fonda would always embody as well as project a great deal of internal conflict, he never blamed his parents for any of it. His mother, Herberta, was "angelic," his father was "wonderful." William Fonda built kites for his son, who loved flying them all his life; the father built toys and radios in his basement. The son loved the father's unassuming competence at everything. "Only when I grew up and moved away did I realize exactly how much I loved him, how much he meant to me and what an unusual man he was."

By the time he was a young man, Fonda had developed very specific emotional tics. Emotional displays were anathema. He liked girls, liked them a lot, but he wouldn't pursue them. At all. Girls had to pursue him.

Henry Fonda first came to New York in the late spring of 1927, helping an Omaha friend drive a new Packard back home. He went to the theater and saw nine plays in six days — "three matinees and six nights." He specifically mentioned seeing Helen Hayes in *Coquette,* but that show didn't open until November 1927, so it might have been wishful thinking. But whatever he saw changed his life.

Slowly, Hank was becoming accustomed to the wider world. Take bootleg whiskey. Fonda learned that the one sure way to see if it was okay to drink was to pour a small amount on the running board of a car and light it. If the flame burned blue, it was good to drink; if it burned red, it was poison.

When Hank got back to Omaha, he worked as an assistant director at the Playhouse, acted in *The School for Scandal, Seventeen,* and, opposite Doe Brando, in Eugene O'Neill's *Beyond the Horizon.* For the first time, he was drawing a salary from the Players. It was minute, but it was money.

The next few years were occupied with auditions, performances, jobs from acting to stage managing — the itinerant, semipro life of a young actor who will take any job in order to eat and work in the theater at the same time.

For a summer he worked with a Lincoln impersonator named George Billings, who toured small cities and towns doing a canned show of the great man. Fonda played John Hay, Lincoln's secretary, who would come onstage and deliver exposition that would lead to Billings reciting selections from Lincoln's correspondence and speeches.

The bookings were the smallest of the small time — two days in Montana and the same in Iowa, lower even than vaudeville's lowly Gus Sun circuit. Imbued with the time-honored optimism of youthful actors, to Hank it was only a question of time until Broadway was bowled over. "Prospects for future work are brighter than ever," he wrote home, in steadfast but blissful ignorance of reality.

It soon became obvious that Billings was a drunk, and it was a 50-50 proposition as to whether he would show up, or, if he did show up, would be able to remember his lines. Still, if he made the performance, Billings could cry real tears at the same moment, in every performance. Hank marveled at his skill, and also marveled at the $100 a week that Billings paid him. But Hank's internal Calvinism was already formed, and working with a drunk was just too dodgy. He moved on, not without regrets: "I didn't make $100 a week for ten [more] years."

In 1929, Joshua Logan was recently graduated from Princeton and helping to run a group called the University Players. It was an apt description of the company — a bunch of stagestruck kids from the Ivy League and Seven Sisters. Logan had been born in Texarkana, Texas, in 1908, the son of a lumberman who committed suicide when his son was two years old. Josh was raised in Louisiana by his mother and stepfather, a military man who had taught at Culver Military Academy in Indiana and rode the boy hard. The neighborhood kids and his stepfather all regarded Josh as effeminate. The kids called him a sissy and his stepfather ordered him, "Don't swing your ass like a girl."

Logan enrolled at Princeton mainly because he had read about the Triangle Club theatricals that toured the country during Christmas vacation. Princeton students wrote the shows, composed the music, and starred. "I had to be in that club," remembered Logan.

He visited New York City for the first time and saw *What Price Glory* with Louis Wolheim, and just like that, Joshua Logan found his tribe. He stayed on for weeks, seeing *The Ziegfeld Follies* with Will Rogers and W. C. Fields, *George White's Scandals* with Willie and Eugene Howard, listened to Harry Richman sing "The Birth of the Blues." He didn't neglect straight plays either; shows with impeccable provenance such as Walter Huston in Eugene O'Neill's sultry *Desire Under the Elms,* as well as the equally sultry but less pedigreed *White Cargo.*

The University Players had been founded in 1928 by Charles Leatherbee of Harvard and Bretaigne Windust of Princeton. Leatherbee came from money; his grandfather was Charles Crane, of Crane Fixtures, while his stepfather was Jan Masaryk, who would die under mysterious circumstances during the Communist takeover of Czechoslovakia.

The precipitating event was a Manhattan cocktail party for Vladimir Nimirovich-Danchenko, who, along with Constantin Stanislavsky, founded the Moscow Art Theater. Danchenko must have been mightily charismatic, because meeting him led to Windust and Leatherbee kicking around a general idea that undergraduates in their respective theater programs ought to be able to continue their theatrical training in the summers, whether the school facilities were available or not.

Leatherbee's family had a house in Woods Hole, Massachusetts. He anted up the money to form a Moscow Art–style theater that would be headquartered at the Elizabeth Theater in nearby Falmouth. The Elizabeth was the town's movie theater, but the management was amenable to renting the place out on Monday and Tuesday nights, when hardly anybody went to the movies.

At Princeton, Logan had played football, boxed, acted, and directed. When he wasn't suffering from depressive twinges, he was a buoyant, gregarious man. He and Hank Fonda would have a long friendship that extended into their professional lives, and Logan added a little something extra to that mix by developing something of a crush on Fonda. "He was the best looking human being I ever saw," he would assert.

Actually, Logan may well have just been objective. Some early portraits of Fonda from his first days in the theater have survived, and he was indeed breathtaking, with much of the dark beauty of Tyrone Power but more masculine.

The atmosphere at the University Players

was chaotic, because it was basically a theatrical collective. "Benign anarchy might describe it," wrote Josh Logan in his memoirs, "with everyone fighting for his own ideals. . . . The energy of two dozen undiscovered stars, the mixture of grand and poor, mostly poor, the fact that everyone was nearly the same age, the lack of a principal or teacher to shake fingers or teach 'academic precepts' — all of this made for a kind of hell. Only the strong could live through this criticism because it was as hot as a baptism of fire. . . . Physical fights were nonexistent, but belligerent stand-offs could last for days.

"But always we were totally involved, ecstatically alive."

That first summer, the University Players put on A. A. Milne's *The Dover Road,* Eugene O'Neill's *Beyond the Horizon,* and George Kelly's *The Torch Bearers.* The girls lived in a nearby cottage, the boys lived in a converted subchaser that was owned by Leatherbee's father. The result of all this ferment was an entirely unexpected profit of $1,200.

While all this was going on, Henry Fonda had taken the money he'd saved working for the alcoholic Billings and agreed to drive the wife of a friend of his father's to Cape

Cod. He tried to get a job with the Province-town Players and failed, but succeeded at the Cape Playhouse, where he was taken on as an assistant stage manager, which inevitably led to his being assigned small parts. Fonda began canvassing the other theater companies around the area.

It was the University Players production of *The Torch Bearers* that brought Henry Fonda to Josh Logan and the University Players. Logan never made any claims for his acting, but his performance as a foolish old man named Huxley Hossefrosse struck young Hank as the funniest thing he had ever seen, and his hysterics carried the rest of the audience along and made the performance sing.

"I can't imitate it," Logan would say of Fonda's laugh. "It was like a sob, and it went way up in the air and then there was a strangulation of some sort. But it was every kind of sound that could possibly come. . . . It's a little bit like trying to imitate Fonda singing. He sings very well, really, and it's always on key. He just hasn't got anything to do with the way the song really sounds."

After the performance, Fonda went backstage. "We looked around and saw this boy standing there," said Logan. "He was lean and lanky and he had an extraordinary chest

— his chest was caved in and his pelvis stuck out, and his lower thighs went back and his knees stuck out. He just wasn't as well-conditioned as he should've been. But he was also in a black sweater pullover, and the typical golf pants of the day, which were supposedly plus fours, but his were minus two."

Logan realized there were only two possibilities: either Fonda was dressed in the height of fashion but was incompetent at mixing and matching, or he was poor. Logan's first impression was little short of love at first sight: "His extraordinarily handsome, almost beautiful face and huge innocent eyes, combined with that roughhewn physique, made for a startling effect."

Fonda asked if Logan had played Huxley, and when the answer was in the affirmative, Fonda once again let out his strange laugh. "I loved him from that minute on," said Logan, "and nothing has ever shaken that love. And there have been some good shakes, too."

Also in the cast of *The Torch Bearers* was a young man named John Swope, the son of the president of General Electric and the nephew of Herbert Bayard Swope, the legendary editor of the *New York World*. John Swope would graduate from Harvard in 1930 and become a boon companion of Hank's.

It was one of the great two-fers of twentieth-century theater. In one night Fonda met two lifelong friends who would in turn lead him to a half dozen more, including Jim Stewart. As Jane Alexander, one of the children of the University Players would note, "First loves are so strong."

Unlike Logan and Fonda, John Swope's theatrical career didn't last long; he had a strong, booming voice, but he was a terrible ham and was always on the verge of breaking character. He was eventually told in no uncertain terms that acting was not his métier. The young man would have to find another artistic vocation.

Leatherbee was properly encouraged by the first summer of the Players, and began to make plans to build a theater. He managed to extract a loan from some Cape Cod bankers, and chose a site at Old Silver Beach in West Falmouth. The structure was to be constructed of equal parts wood, Celotex, and vaulting ambition, and would connect to an already existing tearoom and bathing pavilion.

Hank first went to work for the Players as a carpenter, then an actor, where, Logan said, "Fonda wiped us all off the stage

41

simply by seeming to do nothing,"

Around this time, Hank went back to Omaha to do a benefit for the Playhouse. The show was *A Kiss for Cinderella,* and one of the actresses was a young girl named Dorothy McGuire, who described herself as "very shy," but stagestruck. She was always making up plays and directing them. Her teacher thought she should try out her enthusiasm on a larger stage.

McGuire tried out for the play opposite Fonda, who was "very giving." She got the part, and after the glorious experience was over — "I could scarcely look at him when I was in the play, because he was so handsome" — Fonda asked her if she'd given any serious thought to being in the theater. Having planted the seed, he would always support McGuire in her career; in time, he would introduce her to his friend John Swope, who would marry her.

It was April 1929 and Fonda traveled back to the East Coast and his future. Young Mr. Fonda was about to fall irrevocably in love with an actress named Margaret Sullavan.

"She was not exactly beautiful," wrote Norris Houghton in his memoir of the University Players. "She was a little shy. She had a husky voice with a strong southern accent. She was about 18, slight, with sandy blonde hair." But if nature had not endowed Sullavan with spectacular physical gifts, it had compensated with something else: "There was electricity here, a wonderful arresting magnetism."

Sullavan was effervescent, entrancing, one of a kind, utterly charming and completely conscious of it, with one of the great voices — warm and throaty, as if she was getting over a bad cold. And although the University Players were made up of Ivy Leaguers, Sullavan somehow wormed her way in despite a lack of any meaningful experience. But then Maggie Sullavan always had a way of getting what she wanted.

She was born in Norfolk, Virginia, in 1909, the daughter of a wealthy stockbroker. She began acting during her final year at Chatham Institute, rehearsing her debut part as instructed, then turning all the director's instructions on their head during the actual performance. The result was that her interpretation of a debutante transformed into a brutal parody of her flightier classmates. It was her debut as an actress and it was also her swan song at Chatham. She wasn't asked to join the drama club. After that, she studied dance at the Boston branch of the Denishawn studio, followed by an appearance for the Harvard Dramatic

Society, where Charles Leatherbee saw her.

Joshua Logan had already developed that instinctive sense of appraisal that every good director needs, and Sullavan knocked him out: "She had from the very beginning that kind of incandescence, that magic, that indescribable quality that is just extremely rare. . . . She had a pulsing and husky voice which could suddenly switch, in emotional moments, to a high boy choir soprano. Her beauty was not obvious or even standard. It showed as she tilted her head, as she walked, as she laughed, and she was breathtakingly beautiful as she ran. . . . We were all in love with her."

Logan wasn't kidding. Charlie Leatherbee was in love with her, Johnny Swope was in love with her, and Fonda . . . Fonda was beset by waves of interest mingled with justified wariness. At first Fonda was merely intrigued with the woman everybody called "Maggie," but whom he insisted on calling "Peggy." Then he fell deeply in love and lust. "Hank was much in love with Peggy," was the way Norris Houghton remembered it, "and Peggy thought she might be in love with Hank."

It was not any one thing, it was everything — her honey-colored hair, her trim figure, the way she threw back her head when she

44

laughed. As for Sullavan, she seems never to have gotten past the intrigue stage. She adamantly refused to call him "Hank" as his friends did; all her life she called him "Fonda."

Things moved slowly between them. "I think by the end of the summer I had kissed her," Fonda said, but then he went on to explain the circumstances. One night someone in the Players passed Hank a marijuana cigarette. Emboldened by his first high, he asked Sullavan if she would be interested in a moonlight swim. After that, and, perhaps, something more, they fell asleep in the sand dunes. Hours later they were awakened by the early morning sun. That moonlight swim sealed it; from that night on, Sullavan was Fonda's girl.

"She was a character even the first time I met her," Fonda would say as an old man, shaking his head at all that fire and how it had first captivated him, then nearly killed him.

Two

In 1930, a young man named James Maitland Stewart was a sophomore at Princeton when the drama club put on a show that featured Margaret Sullavan. "Hank wasn't in the show," remembered Jim, "but he came down to Princeton and I met him at that time." Stewart was an architecture student, and Fonda had undoubtedly traveled to Princeton to keep an eye on Sullavan.

Nothing much happened; the two young men met, shook hands, exchanged pleasantries, and went about their business. Sullavan did the show and left with Fonda. Stewart returned to his architecture studies. Life went on.

In the summer of 1931, as the University Players were in the middle of their season in West Falmouth, John Swope began moving toward his own art when he picked up a 16mm movie camera and documented the

Players' backstage life in home movies, complete with titles written on plate glass placed between the lens and the natural backgrounds of Falmouth.

The atmosphere Swope photographed was of a windswept, eroticized summer camp. We see the group communally building sets, darning costumes, lining up for dinner. The Hank Fonda captured by Swope's camera is a revelation — not just gleamingly handsome, but animated, exuberant, utterly carefree. We even see an early example of Fonda's penchant for art, as a witty drawing of a Chinese man is credited to "HANK." (Josh Logan would characterize Fonda's artistic style at this time as "Gauguinesque" but the existing evidence points to a young man with a natural gift who was leaning toward caricature.)

The reason for Fonda's exuberance is clearly Sullavan. Swope's camera shows Hank and Maggie busily at play and quite obviously falling in love as they paint signs or nuzzle in profile. Josh Logan is lurking around on the perimeter of the shots, and there are even some scenes of the Players onstage, bravely performing in front of sets that would have not been out of place in a high school play.

Swope's documentation of this crucial

developmental stage of people who would be major players in the American theater was typically prescient. He was always an energetic man, playful yet patient, with a sense of humor that could smooth over nearly any disagreement — his children would see him angry precisely twice in their lives. Swope was one of the few exuberant personalities that didn't irritate Fonda; rather, he energized him. Swope liked everybody, and, because of his fundamental warmth and humor, everybody liked Swope.

"Hank Fonda could be a very reticent man," said Norman Lloyd, the actor/manager/director whose career spanned the twentieth century and part of the twenty-first. "And Jim Stewart was similar in temperament. But John was able to bring them out of their shells; you simply couldn't resist John. He had this energetic way of approaching you that enveloped you. With John, everything was going to be exciting and *fun*."

Swope would become D'Artagnan to Jim's and Hank's moodier musketeers; as their careers grew and flourished with an eerie simultaneity, their lives became bound together in a warmly encompassing weave.

If the physical standards of the University Players were low, the acting talent stood out. "In a company where there were no stars, Fonda shone," was the way Josh Logan put it. One of the lesser lights circling the brilliant constellation formed by Fonda, Sullavan, and Logan was a young man named Bart Quigley, who had been a few years behind Fonda at Omaha Central High School. Bart's father had been Buffalo Bill Cody's personal physician in North Platte, Nebraska, years before, and in time Bart would become a distinguished orthopedist, but at this point he was a stagestruck kid relegated to small parts. He and Fonda also became lifelong friends and grew to have a lot in common: both would father famous actresses.

Fonda's character was already defined: "He had great convictions, even at that time, about what was good, what was right, what was wrong," said Logan with the perceptible philosophical sigh that infects a lot of his reminiscing about his friend. Socially he was shy, but only up to a point. Before and after Sullavan, he didn't fend off the women who flocked to him. "He had them," remembered Logan. "He was sort of a dreamer. He was an artist."

At this remove, it's hard to gauge just how good the University Players were. Given the level of talent involved, they had to have

49

been considerably better than most summer theater troupes, even though that's essentially what they were. Josh Logan told stories of production catastrophes, the sort of actor-laddie stories that old theater folk love to regale friends with.

But he was always serious about the level of performance. Logan directed *Coquette,* with Sullavan as the title character and Fonda as her doomed lover, and his memory focused on the "poetically tragic quality of the star-crossed lovers." Logan loved Sullavan's portrayal of an impulsive, destructive young woman, and Fonda's intensity and masculinity. He also claimed that the University Players had better actors than the Group Theatre. Certainly, they must have been less mannered. Fonda's Plains pragmatism meant that he never had any use for the Group: "I didn't like them. I didn't like the way they talked. They intellectualized too much, used words that [didn't] mean anything to me."

Logan realized that the experience of the Players was transforming him, transforming all of them. Logan had migrated to theater as "a half-assed opportunist," a young man in search of praise. But living with actors, getting plays on their feet, he began to be aware of his own taste. As he put it, "to appreciate the furnishings of a room, or shape of a house, or the designing of a set. I was stimulated by the choice of one color over another for a costume, or the perfection of a prop, or the subtlety of lighting.

"I turned into a visual animal. I became acutely conscious of the way an actor stood, or moved, or stopped, or sat. . . . I felt actors should capture the relaxed anticipation of an outfielder: living anatomy in repose but with a promise of instant action."

Other than Charlie Leatherbee, the Players didn't have any money, but they had possibilities and that made all the difference. The kids were self-absorbed, on fire with the secular religion of the theater, and the perennial urges of the young. Josh Logan would marry Barbara O'Neill, one of the Players, although that ended in divorce, and Fonda and Sullavan would form one of the most tumultuous double acts in theater history.

As Frederick Lewis Allen would write, the period between 1923 and late 1929 represented "nearly seven years of unparalleled plenty; nearly seven years during which men and women . . . believed that at the end of the rainbow there was at least a pot of negotiable legal tender. . . . For nearly seven years the prosperity bandwagon [had] rolled down Main Street."

But outside of the young person's bubble, things were suddenly terrible. An interesting statistic: between 1865 and 1920, a total of 3,108 banks failed in the United States. In 1930 alone, 1,352 banks failed, which was only a fraction of the 26,355 businesses that collapsed in that one year — the highest rate of business failures in history. And it got worse. In 1932, there were 31,822 business failures.

What this meant for the theater was a corresponding rate of disaster. Between 1928 and 1933 the number of Broadway productions dropped by half and the number of working New York theater employees, actors as well as crew, plummeted from 25,000 to 4,000. Across the country, untold numbers of repertory and stock companies folded.

"Seven or eight years ago," wrote James Thurber in *Fortune* magazine in 1932, "a just-average comedy or drama often had a fairly good run — two or three months, let us say, anyway; the same kind of play nowadays is likely to close in a week." Irving Berlin's *As Thousands Cheer,* which opened in September 1933, would be the only significantly profitable show of the entire 1933–34 theater season.

On the streets of New York, there were more than 15,000 homeless, wandering the streets, said one historian, "like particles in liquid suspension, seeking shelter however they could." Many of them eked out an existence in shantytowns that were dubbed Hoovervilles, along the Hudson River, below Riverside Drive.

On the streets of Hollywood, things were nowhere near as bad because Hollywood is a company town, and the companies were muddling through . . . after a fashion. Between 1930 and 1933 the combined market value of the five major studios — Warner Bros., RKO, Paramount, MGM, and Fox — declined from about a billion dollars to $200 million. Warners had to sell $60 million in assets in order to stay in business. Paramount had profits of $25 million in 1930 and filed for bankruptcy protection in 1933. MGM stood alone as the only movie studio to stay in the black during the Depression, even if their profits were reduced to about a quarter of what they had been. But nobody went out of business.

Throughout the financial debacle, God was watching out for the University Players. They weren't starving, weren't homeless, were making a slender go of it. "Working in Falmouth was not exactly a constant reminder of how tough the nation as a whole had it," remembered Norris Houghton. "Roughing it aboard a yacht, like we did the first year, might not have been as luxurious as some people believe, but it wasn't sleeping on a Manhattan sidewalk or park bench, either. Above that, though, I'd be tempted to say that the company as a whole was less aware of the social, economic, and political trends of its times than any other intelligent, educated group of young people in America."

Life with Sullavan was up and down, in and out. Fonda and Sullavan played opposite each other in James M. Barrie's *A Kiss for Cinderella* in the summer of 1930, and audiences came from all over the Cape to see Fonda in *Outward Bound* and Sullavan in *The Constant Nymph.*

Onstage, they meshed beautifully; offstage Sullavan turned him every which way but loose. "Offstage she was a true Southern rebel," said Fonda. "Peggy was Scarlett O'Hara before Margaret Mitchell ever dreamed of her. In fact, at times she made me feel a little like the Leslie Howard character. All that girl needed was a hoop skirt. She had everything else Scarlett had, particularly her temperament."

They took out a marriage license as early

as June 1931, just about the time the University Players moved to Baltimore in search of a year-round audience. Sullavan kept the license for the rest of her life. Fonda declared himself to be white, twenty-six years of age, living at 5 Prospect Park. His occupation? "Artist."

But they didn't marry that month. They finally did the deed on Christmas Day 1931, in a ceremony performed in the dining room of the Kernan Hotel in Baltimore by one Horace Donegan, the rector of the Episcopal Christ Church. Everyone drank cheap champagne and Bretaigne Windust sang "Ah, Say Not So," from *The Constant Nymph.*

Josh Logan was there, and he remembered that Fonda and Sullavan joined in the song, which would have been charming except for the fact that "Sullavan had an atrocious voice. . . . The only way she could get on key was to kind of memorize the steps up to the next note."

Johnny Swope's 16mm camera once again documented priceless moments in time. Fonda is sporting a boutonniere in his lapel, there are bouquets scattered around, and Fonda and Sullavan share one long kiss while some other University Players hover in the background.

What rivets is the behavior.

With the exception of the wedding kiss, Sullavan is focused on the task at hand — signing the wedding license, or carefully cutting the cake. Fonda looks at her constantly, trying to get her attention, which she gives only in brief flashes. She's not exactly indifferent; it's more as if her new husband is simply far down the list of the things she has to attend to. She knows he's there and she's not particularly concerned about keeping him there. It was a preview of coming attractions.

Fonda and Sullavan headed out on their honeymoon, but felt sorry for the Players, who were presumably crippled by their absence. They turned back, but instead of going onstage, they disappeared into their hotel room, where they remained incommunicado for days, occasionally sending out messages beneath the door rebuking the company for the indifferent quality of their production of *Lysistrata*.

Aristophanes was followed by James M. Barrie — the Players were nothing if not eclectic. Barrie's *Mary Rose* was marred by Sullavan throwing a fit about the set. Fonda had indicated that Sullavan was prone to tantrums, but this was the first time Josh Logan encountered one directly. He decided to face the situation squarely: he told her that if she hated the set that much she should go home and he would recast the part.

Sullavan promptly changed her mind about the set. The play after that was by S. N. Behrman, and was to be directed by Windust, but he came down with tuberculosis and Logan was called in. He didn't know the play, so began instructing the players to follow the directions in the script, at which point Fonda protested: actors shouldn't move if the director doesn't know why. Logan persisted, and finally Fonda spoke up again and said that he was speaking for the entire company. They had, said Fonda, sent for Charlie Leatherbee. They expected him to get an experienced director from New York.

When Leatherbee showed up he refused to acquiesce to mutiny. Logan settled down and so did the actors.

They were a contentious bunch. Fonda tended to bridle at Logan, whose authority he didn't particularly respect — "We've got many people more talented than he is," Fonda had snorted when Logan was named one of the company's directors. Fonda's dissatisfaction spread to about half the company.

"He was my friend . . . but not when I was in charge of him," was the way Logan put it. "When Fonda is against you, look out. It's very rough. He just avoids you. Argues violently in public. . . . He felt that I had let him down, that I had gone over to the directors, and he and I were kind of revolutionaries before that, and now suddenly I've joined the Lenin side, and he's still on the Trotsky side."

Yet Logan understood that Fonda was not using his considerable supply of anger in pursuit of personal aggrandizement. He simply refused to go along with anything he regarded as cheap or expedient. "He was the most outstanding young egotist I'd ever met in my life. He had a way of willing you to go with him."

Then there was Mrs. Fonda, whose charm was generally deployed when she wanted something, and who wanted something most of the time. Periods of docility were rare. "I think she probably was the most difficult woman I've ever met in my life," remembered Logan, who knew thousands of actresses. "She was so attractive, and so beautiful, and she had so many little Southern tricks . . . to win you, but she was willful as all get out."

To which Fonda could only reply Amen.

"I never knew I had a temper until I got married. Time after time that slender girl's words stung me like a wasp. It got to the point where we didn't live on love. We were at each other constantly, screaming, arguing, fighting. It's all a big blur now. I don't know whether I stamped out in a rage or whether Sullavan threw me out.

"It was just hot and cold all the time. And fights . . . we would be in desperate fights about anything."

Anything could easily become everything. One time Fonda was collecting spare change from the troupe for fireworks to light up the 4th of July. Sullavan took offense over something and poured a pitcher of ice water over Fonda's head. "I don't remember it," said Fonda when he was reminded about the incident fifty years later, "but I'm sure it's true because that's like her."

"They fought like cats and dogs," said Logan. "About absolutely everything. Both of them were perfectionists, and if [a] possible reading of a line was slightly more subtle than another way, they would go on for days as to how to do that, and what they thought about it. And I guess it was worthwhile because when they did appear they were just as good as the Lunts."

The core problem was that Fonda couldn't

wear Sullavan down, and vice versa. Immovable force, meet irresistible object. They separated by March 1932, and Sullavan quickly segued to the director Jed Harris, who had been living with Ruth Gordon. Fonda heard about it, of course, and he indulged in every young man's right to flagrant masochism: he stood below the apartment he had shared with Sullavan and waited for Jed Harris to leave the building. Instead, the lights would go out.

"I'd stand there and cry and then wipe away my tears so that I wouldn't look like a wino on the subway riding uptown. . . . That just destroyed me, completely destroyed me. Never in my life have I felt so betrayed, so rejected, so alone." There is a strong suspicion that Hank never got Sullavan out of his head, let alone his heart, and didn't really want to. In a letter to his sister about this time, he nicely described Sullavan as "cream and sugar on a dish of hot ashes."

In Jed Harris, Sullavan found someone every bit her equal when it came to emotional turbulence. He had brilliantly directed *Our Town, The Front Page,* and other plays, but he was universally loathed for his wanton cruelty toward his lovers, toward his actors, toward everybody. With Sullavan, Harris was by turns adoring, jealous, abusive, demanding, and then adoring again.

At one point, Harris told his sister that Sullavan proposed a suicide pact. "I'm ready to kill myself out of love for you, say you feel the same way too," Sullavan supposedly told him. "If we killed ourselves, at least we'd be together forever. It would prove how much we loved each other."

Harris's sister told him they were both *meshugeneh.*

Sullavan eventually broke away to go to Hollywood, where she met William Wyler and married him several weeks later. Harris followed her to Hollywood, called Wyler, and told him "You're a weak, untalented man married to a woman who is in love with me." Wyler responded by driving to Harris's house in a rainstorm and beating him up. The marriage didn't last.

For Fonda, it was as if the University Players — and Maggie — had never happened at all. The experience of being desperately in love with someone who doesn't share your depth of feeling can be devastating, and so it was for Hank. It's entirely possible that the Sullavan disaster closed off some part of him forever, made him refuse to give himself completely ever again. Certainly, the beaming, flamboyantly carefree Fonda seen in John Swope's home movies would become a very rare sight, as he slowly began transforming into a more withholding personality.

Sullavan quickly conquered Hollywood, but a stunned Fonda was on his way to nowhere in particular. Between Sullavan and his discontent with the way the University Players were being run, he bailed. "He was a tremendous loss," Logan would write. "He was the heart of the company." But the director had a replacement up his sleeve: the talented beanpole from Princeton whom Fonda had met in 1930 and who was just about to graduate.

Logan called Jim Stewart.

Logan told him that he would be replacing Fonda as the romantic juvenile. "Oh, no," Stewart protested. "Hold on a minute. I couldn't. I promised my father I'd help run the hardware store in Indiana, Pennsylvania, this summer. Besides, I'm not good enough to replace Fonda." Logan persisted, and the architect on his way to being an actor finally capitulated.

James Stewart was with the company by June 1932, when he appeared in Booth Tarkington's *Magnolia* and succeeded in a comic part. Meanwhile, Henry Fonda sat in New York — impoverished, miserable, alone.

The problem Fonda encountered was that

coming to New York after a few successful summers with the University Players really didn't mean anything, simply because the glorified summer stock operation was too far out of town to attract notice from New York–centric producers and scouts. "[New York agents and producers] had to see you," Fonda explained. "It had to be more than your word that you had played *The Barker, Coquette, The Constant Nymph* and so on. That was too far away for producers, and our group didn't attract them."

In the summer of 1932, the University Players were back in Falmouth, in their own theater. (The theater would burn to the ground in 1936; it was never rebuilt.) Shortly after that, they made a sink-or-swim decision and decided to throw in their lot with a character named Arthur Beckhard, a Broadway producer of no distinction whatever. Still, Beckhard had produced Broadway plays, and he undoubtedly conjured visions of a Broadway repertory theater before the assembled Players.

A single disastrous production entitled *Carry Nation,* which opened on October 29, 1932, and closed almost immediately spelled the end of the University Players. At the time of its demise the stock company

63

was quite impressive: Mildred Natwick, James Stewart, Joshua Logan, Myron Mc-Cormick, Kent Smith, Barbara O'Neill, Norris Houghton, and Bretaigne Windust, all of whom were cast onto the turbulent waves of New York City in the deepest pit of the Great Depression.

At this point, Fonda and Stewart knew each other only superficially, but that was about to change. Hank would say of Jim Stewart that "He was swept into the theater almost without his knowing it. All he wanted was a little fun."

He got the fun. He also got a way of life.

THREE

James Maitland Stewart was born in his father's house, and given his grandfather's name. The date was May 20, 1908, the place 965 Philadelphia Street in Indiana, Pennsylvania, about fifty miles northeast of Pittsburgh. He was the only son of Alexander and Elizabeth Stewart, and in time would be joined by two sisters, born in 1912 and 1914.

Indiana, Pennsylvania, consisted of 6,500 hardy souls. The town spawned two famous men with an odd similarity. Besides, Stewart, the writer and naturalist Edward Abbey was also born there — two tall men who were always willing to go their own way.

The Stewarts were among the more prosperous members of the community. Alex Stewart ran the J. M. Stewart Hardware Store in a building on Philadelphia Street that had been built in 1853. The first James Stewart had taken over the store in 1883 and had renamed it in his own honor. Alex kept the name, although it was generally known in town as either "Stewart's" or "the hardware store."

Indiana was and is a conventional American small town, but the Stewart Hardware Store was far from conventional. For one thing, it was three stories tall, and as Jim would say decades later, it was "full to the rafters with everything needed to build a house, hunt a deer, plant a garden and harvest it, repair a car, or make a scrapbook. I could conceive of no human need that could not be satisfied in this store."

The store was the center of Jim's youth. His earliest memories were of its smells — the dry aroma of coiled rope, the sweet smell of linseed oil used to soften baseball gloves, the acid tang of open nail kegs. In 1913, the Stewart family moved to a larger house at 104 North Seventh Street, on top of Vinegar Hill, which afforded a good view of the entire downtown area.

Jim was a shy boy. His father called him Jimbo, his mother called him Jimsy. Jim's mother played the piano, his sister Virginia played harmony while his other sister Doddie played the fiddle.

He built model planes with his buddy Hall Blair, worked up a magic act with Bill Neff.

He took up mechanical drawing and designed airplanes and thought about chemistry — his father was already making noises about the boy attending Princeton, Alex's alma mater. "I wouldn't say he was a loner," remembered his sister Virginia, "but he could spend a lot of time absolutely alone, his own best company, and never mind it."

He worked at the kind of jobs that were available to a boy in a small Midwest town — he helped out at his father's store, ran the movie projectors at the Strand Theatre, painted white stripes on the roads. For a time, he went into business building small crystal radios that cost $20 and could pick up KDKA in Pittsburgh, where he heard live coverage of Warren Harding's inauguration — the first radio broadcast to reach Indiana.

As with many in the early twentieth century, it was not a Mark Twain boyhood exactly; more like something out of Booth Tarkington. "We celebrated Halloween with an *enormous* parade," Jim remembered. "Everybody got dressed up. We celebrated New Year's with actually more noise than the Fourth of July. We saved the firecrackers and the skyrockets and one outfit got on one side of Main Street . . . and we almost had a *battle.*"

He was a shambling, likable boy, with kindness as a keynote of his personality. Jim had a dog named Bounce, who was attacked and killed by a neighbor's dog while Jim was away at summer camp. Jim was more than grieved, he was furious, and he told his father he wanted to kill the neighbor's dog. Alex trapped the offending animal and handed Jim a gun, but he couldn't do it, couldn't kill an animal who had acted like an animal. In the process, he learned something about himself. For the rest of his life, he was a sentimental goner about animals.

The alternating currents of his personality — the gentleness and obstinacy that were primary components of his acting — were functions of his bloodlines. "He came out of two different worlds," was the way Stewart's daughter Kelly would put it.

His performing side came from his mother. Elizabeth Stewart descended from a tradition of free-spirited political liberalism, while Alex's traditions and values were much narrower, more absorbed with matters of duty and honor. Family legend had it that when the Spanish-American War broke out, Alex was in such a hurry to get to the enlistment center that he forgot to turn off the Bunsen burner in his chemistry class at Princeton. He would join the fight in World War I with equal alacrity.

Jim remembered that his mother "was the only person [Alex] would listen to about anything. And there were times when we kids sure appreciated that. He would raise his voice about pretty nearly anything — but never to her."

It was a potentially difficult combination of elements, but Jim managed. Alex was nearly as tall as his son would become, but unlike Jim he was sturdy and muscular, with a personality to match. People who liked Alex thought he was outgoing; people who didn't like him thought he was overbearing.

A small-town businessman had to be resourceful, and Alex was not above bartering his merchandise. The story goes that he once took a ten-foot python in trade from a carnival that went bust, said snake being displayed for a long time in the window of his store for the edification of the citizens who had never seen a reptile of such proportions. Then there was the time Alex took a used accordion in trade, which was all the inspiration Jim needed in order to become reasonably proficient at the instrument. He also learned to play the piano, albeit in a more conventional manner — he took lessons.

"Jimmy had an interesting family life,"

remembered his friend Hall Blair. "They were very close. At every meal they all took hands and said Grace. On Sunday they all went to [Calvary Presbyterian] church. [Alex] was in the choir and [Elizabeth] was the organist. . . . At home they all sang hymns and had musical Sunday evenings. They always had the *New York Times* and magazines like *Atlantic Monthly* and *Scribner's*. They followed theater and opera."

Since Alex's own interests extended far beyond Indiana, Pennsylvania, he made sure that his children would never be insular. He organized regular family outings to Pittsburgh, and in the summer they would head for points east, west, and north: Yellowstone, Washington, D.C., Canada. The Stewarts may have lived in a small town, but their horizons were high and wide. There was a Steinway in the drawing room.

When Alex went to World War I, the family traveled to New York to see him off. When they got back home, Jim set up a little theater in the basement of their house and began producing theatricals with a wartime theme: *Beat the Kaiser* was eventually given the more emphatic title *To Hell with the Kaiser,* and there was another show called *The Slacker.* The admission was one cent; Jim's sister Virginia remembered that her brother "was terribly intense about his plays, just as he is about everything he gets interested in. There are no halfway measures with Jim." It was an early sign of theatrical ambition, but it ended after Alex returned from the war, and didn't flare up again for nearly ten years.

Jim remembered only a few childhood moments of feverish excitement. One of the latter was in 1923, when Jim saw the funeral train taking President Harding from Washington to burial in his hometown of Marion, Ohio. The train passed through Blairsville, about twenty miles from Indiana, at 3:30 in the morning. Alex woke his son up at 2:30 and they drove to Blairsville, where there were only about six people waiting.

"Suddenly the tracks gave off a low hum," Stewart remembered. "The funeral train was coming! Dad shoved two pennies into my hands and said, 'Run, put them on the rails. Quick, now!' "

Stewart put the pennies on the rail, then stood back as the train rolled past. He saw the brightly lit observation car that held the casket of the president, covered with a flag and guarded by two Marines.

After the train passed, Jim retrieved the pennies. Alex kept one and Jim kept the other for decades, even after he left Indiana and moved to New York to become an actor.

Jim's interest in model planes indicated an interest in flight, and that was confirmed when he got his first plane ride in high school. The plane was a war-surplus Curtiss flown by a man named Jack Law, who was barnstorming around the area and who charged a dollar a minute. Alex Stewart came out to witness the event, and insisted on picking up the town doctor first — in case of a crash, he wanted his son to have every chance at survival.

From the beginning, Jim had a strange, circular hemming-and-hawing speech pattern. "The stuttering and the stammering and all of this. This I had when I was a *kid*. I don't try to put that on — I never *did* — in a movie or a play."

Everybody liked Jim, although he had his quirks, and in a small town everybody knew about them. For one thing, he was cheap. Hall Blair's wife, Eleanor, said that "He'd go to a movie with a girl, then afterward go to a soda shop or something. As soon as the two of them sat down, Jim would take out a dime and put it on the counter between them and say, 'OK, this is what we have to spend.' He was so infamous for this that Hall and the others would laugh, even be disappointed if he didn't do it."

When Jim was sixteen, Alex sent him off to Mercersburg Academy, a prep school that would get the boy in line for Princeton — fifty-four of the 104 boys in Stewart's class would move on to Princeton. Jim had a vague yearning for the Naval Academy, but Alex was determined that his son would be like him — it was Princeton or bust.

Jim was home when Lindbergh flew the Atlantic to Paris in May of 1927. He got a large piece of beaverboard, warped it to approximate the curvature of the earth, and drew a map of the North Atlantic on the board. He built a model of Lindbergh's plane, the *Spirit of St. Louis,* then scale models of New York's Woolworth Building and the Eiffel Tower and installed the three structures in the window of the hardware store.

Lindbergh began his flight on May 20, 1927, Jim's nineteenth birthday, which he took as a good omen for both of them. "Every time I got a flash that a fishing boat or a steamer had sighted Lindy's plane, I rushed to the store window and moved my model plane closer to France." When the news arrived that Lindbergh had made it all the way to Le Bourget Airport in Paris, Indiana exploded. Church bells rang, everybody quit work.

At Mercersburg, Jim joined the Drama Club and acted in the winter play, Romain Rolland's *The Wolves.* Surprisingly, he played one of the leads. On February 20, 1928, nineteen-year-old Jim made his stage debut. The director described Jim as a "funny-looking long-legged kid" and his performance as "clumsy."

That fall, Jim trooped off to Princeton as a member of the class of 1932. Although Alex wanted him to come back after graduation and take over the hardware store, Jim had other ideas. His declared major was architecture and he had every intention of practicing.

Drama, in the form of the Triangle Club, was something Stewart was ostensibly doing with his left hand. True, he had spent a summer with Bill Neff working the Chautauqua circuit. Neff was a magician and Jim was the barker, inveigling the audience to come in and see the show. The experience provided anecdotal gold for years, notably a story about a levitation trick that didn't come off because a stagehand who was supposed to operate the apparatus fell asleep.

But the Triangle Club excited Jim more than Frank Lloyd Wright or Louis Sullivan ever could. The accordion provided his entrée, providing onstage mood music for scenes. By the time Stewart was a junior he was friends with Joshua Logan, who was a year ahead of him and producing the Triangle shows. Logan spotted talent immediately. "He was good. . . . I knew deep down he loved acting but was too embarrassed to admit it."

Logan noticed that Stewart had a way of communicating with an audience despite his strange mannerisms. One day Logan asked him if he had given any serious thought to becoming an actor. "Good Gawd, no," he replied. "I'm going to be an architect."

"He walked away as if I had slandered him," Logan remembered.

At this point, Stewart's favorite actress was Norma Shearer. He was especially fond of her performance in Ernst Lubitsch's *The Student Prince in Old Heidelberg.* Jim may have been spending too much time at the movies for his own good; in the summer of 1929, he didn't return home because he had to attend remedial math classes at Princeton — his grade point average was not where it needed to be.

Acting was a time-passer, no different than playing the accordion or some of the drawings he did for the *Tiger,* the school paper. When Logan and Charlie Leatherbee formed the University Players, Stewart observed from afar.

In his junior year he saw Margaret Sullavan, accompanied by Hank Fonda, on campus in a play. Stewart was gob-smacked by Sullavan, and he would stay that way.

In January 1931, Josh Logan and Charles Leatherbee traveled to Russia to pay obeisance to the Moscow Art Theatre. They returned by April, and moved the University Players to the Cape in order to change the course of the American theater — or so they believed.

In Jim's senior year, he and his accordion appeared in a Triangle production called *The Spanish Blades,* which offered him several solos. He also played small parts in two shows put on by the Theatre In-time, a more serious group than the Triangle Players.

The Spanish Blades was seen by a man named Billy Grady, who happened to be a talent scout for Metro-Goldwyn-Mayer studios — the home of Norma Shearer, not to mention other huge stars such as Greta Garbo, Joan Crawford, and Clark Gable. "They were a motley group, and, like all amateurs, accentuated their . . . appearance with excessive mugging and gestures,"

Grady would write years later. "All but the skinny guy at the end. He was six foot four, towered over all the others, and looked uncomfortable as hell. While the others hammed it up, the thin one played it straight and was a standout."

Grady went backstage and introduced himself, then wrote in his notebook that the boy had "an ingratiating personality" but was a type in which the studio would have "no particular interest."

When Stewart graduated in the spring of 1932, the Depression was at its deepest point. Even though he had a scholarship to pursue a master's in architecture, he was understandably dubious about the prospects for a young architect in the middle of a worldwide depression. And then Josh Logan asked him to join the University Players. Hank Fonda had just left and the void needed to be filled.

Stewart remembered that the conversation ran along the lines of, "Why don't you come up and spend the summer with us? . . . You can build scenery and I'll give you small parts and you can play your accordion in the tea room." At this point, Stewart's repertoire consisted of a handful of popular songs, all in the key of C.

The offer was more of a summer job than

a job, and Stewart knew it, but it must have appealed to the romantic in him, as did the communal nature of the theater. "The enthusiasm of Leatherbee, Logan and Windust was catching," he would say in retrospect. "They did their own casting, directing, built scenery, arranged lighting effects, and had unbounded energy in running the theater. It proved to be an ideal training school." Everybody did everything, and for a kid without a strong sense of vocation, the lack of definition was a selling point.

Logan and Jim somehow convinced Alex Stewart that playing the accordion for a summer theater was a preferable alternative to architecture. Undoubtedly Alex had presentiments of the same disaster that led F. Scott Fitzgerald to plead with his daughter to avoid amateur theatricals: "Amateur work is fun but the price for it is just simply tremendous. In the end you get 'Thank you' and that's all. You give three performances which everybody promptly forgets and somebody has a breakdown — that somebody being the enthusiast."

Stewart and Logan probably minimized the commitment involved; possibly they proclaimed that Jim could always return to Princeton and architecture. But by now Jim's commitment to architecture was wavering, even though he would maintain a modest interest in the profession. His favorite building would always be Radio City Music Hall, which nicely combined Art Deco and show business.

After Logan used up his store of eloquence, Jim went after his father as well. "There was a moment of stunned Presbyterian silence," he recalled. "Presbyterians don't actually feel that theater-going, card playing and dancing are instruments of the devil; still, my father couldn't help thinking that the practice of architecture was more respectable than becoming an 'actor fellow.'

" 'If that's the way you want it, Jim,' he said, 'then OK.' "

"Dad was upset. My father didn't like it at all — till the day he died he didn't like it."

The same day he got his degree from Princeton, Stewart took off for West Falmouth, where he became the resident accordion player for the University Players. He was promptly given a small part in a play called *Goodbye Again*.

"That got me into it," said Stewart. "That got me started. The accordion lasted two nights; they said my playing destroyed their appetite."

The moment of mutual realization actually came in July 1932. The play was *It's a Wise Child,* the character was named "Cool" Kelly. "It was clear on that night . . . that, in young Stewart, they had a comedian with special gifts: an all-American drawl, a lanky good humor, an air of bemused naturalness, and an infectious charm." Shortly afterward, the Players threw in their lot with Arthur Beckhard, and shortly after that, they were all unemployed.

James Stewart would wonder about the way life has of disrupting carefully laid plans. Ultimately, he knew why he decided to abandon a career he had spent four years preparing: "I think it was because I'd never been to the seashore."

Hank Fonda was still on the run after the University Players imploded. He moved into a three-room apartment on West 63rd Street, just off Central Park West in midtown Manhattan. "I forget who found the place," Stewart said forty years later. "Seems to me Logan did." Fonda's initial roommates were the intrepid Logan and a dryly amusing young actor named Myron McCormick, who would achieve fame on the stage as Luther Billis in Logan's production of *South Pacific,* and in movies as Paul Newman's wary manager in *The Hustler.*

Josh Logan described the apartment as consisting of "a soot colored bedroom with twin beds, a living room with two sprung studio couches, a bathroom with a mildewed shower and a huge kitchen stove." For reasons nobody could grasp, the stove was in the hallway. All this for $35 a month, the lion's share of which was contributed by whoever happened to be working the most.

The Depression being what it was, they needed a fourth person to help make the rent, so they invited Jim Stewart, newly sprung from his father's expectations, to throw in with them. When Stewart moved in, Fonda was completely broke and had been living on rice for weeks. Work arrived for Fonda in the form of a stock company in New Jersey, which was followed by another stock company near Larchmont, in Westchester County, which was followed by yet another stock company on Long Island.

The wolf was not only at the door, he was in the room and he was ravenous, but it didn't matter. Broadway wasn't exactly a hive of activity, but there was still an audience desperate for escape from the world outside the theater doors, and actors were willing to work cheaply.

"Those were great days when we were getting started," Stewart would say in his old

81

age. Fonda concurred, although for different reasons: "I wasn't smart enough to be discouraged. I keep saying that and I don't think anybody really understands or believes it. . . . I didn't ever think about doing anything else. I wasn't prepared to do anything else. I hadn't any talent to do anything else."

Overflowing with the optimism of youth, the aspiring artists were conscious only of the fact that the world of the theater was intoxicating, and that it was right outside the door of their apartment. This was a blessing, because the smell of mildew thrown off by the shower meant that they spent as little time in the apartment as possible.

"We'd get a job and open but we never expected it to run because they never did run," Fonda said. "So we were out the next day doing the rounds of Times Square. But that was the excitement of the theater to us in those days. I never dreamed then that one day I would be a star. I wasn't thinking in terms of my name being up there. It was just to be in the theater, to make a living at this. I didn't care whether it was a big living. I was perfectly happy to be walking on in *I Loved You Wednesday.*"

Fonda always insisted that he worked the

least of all of them, and that Myron McCormick worked the most, because he was in demand as an actor on radio. Stewart, on the other hand, distinctly remembered that Fonda worked the most. It was the beginning of their highly divergent memories of their shared youth.

The historical record indicates that Fonda's memory was accurate. His Broadway debut came in November 1929, with *The Game of Love and Death,* which closed in January. His next Broadway show was nearly three years later — *I Loved You Wednesday* in October 1932, which closed two months later. Another two years rolled by before *New Faces of 1934* in March of that year, which ran till July. If he hadn't filled in with all manner of work in stock in the tristate area, Fonda would have starved to death.

In contrast, Stewart began to get work fairly quickly after he relocated to New York. His first Broadway show was the ill-fated *Carry Nation,* followed a few months later by *Goodbye Again,* which ran till July 1933. In October he appeared in *Spring in Autumn,* then two months later appeared in *All Good Americans,* which ran little more than a month. That led to *Yellow Jack* in March of 1934, which ran only two months but earned him notice and got sold to MGM as a vehicle for Robert Montgomery.

"Hank just went about his work and was very quiet about what he was doing, about how he felt about it," said Stewart. "And Logan talked about [the theater and] the rest of us sort of listened, I think, including Fonda. . . . Fonda and Logan were the two who were completely committed to the theater. I wasn't. I didn't know what I was going to do."

Fonda dubbed their apartment "Casa Gangrene." Jim struck up a conversation with the doorman of an apartment house a couple of doors down, who told him that Legs Diamond had lived there until the day he was murdered in December 1931. This proximity to illicit fame thrilled Stewart, who rushed back to the apartment to tell his roommates all about it. "Oh yeah," said an unimpressed Fonda, "this whole street's full of gangsters, whores and pimps. But there's a nice clean YMCA across the street with a free gym. We could get in shape and fight 'em off."

The boys took turns cooking, and it turned out that Fonda had a knack, even though he had never tried it before. (It would become clear in the coming years that Fonda could — *had to* — achieve excellence at anything he set his mind to.) He would call his mother for likely recipes, and he grew adept at Swedish meatballs, mashed potatoes, spinach, and Mexican rice, all of which he considered easy dishes, all of which Stewart rated as abysmal.

Logan was impressed, not to mention envious; in his memoirs he sounds as if his mancrush had strengthened: "Anything he touched he mastered: acting, carpentry, painting and now cooking. Lithe as a tiger, he could turn on that young, innocent *Merton of the Movies* look and melt everything in sight."

Fonda had one more gift that drove Logan wild — he could walk on his hands. "Since childhood," Logan reminisced, "my greatest passion was to walk on my hands, but I was always too heavy, too weak, too chicken or too something."

Stewart was attracted to Fonda because Fonda could make him laugh. "Fonda had tremendous humor," said Stewart. "He was very famous around the University Players for this. And a fellow by the name of Alfred Dalrymple who was also from Princeton and who was with the University Players. . . . They had a routine with a beach chair that folds up and you get on, all completely pantomime. And Fonda came by this — it was a natural humor [that] sort of developed."

About half of the theaters on Broadway had closed. Veterans of World War I were selling apples on every other corner. A bedraggled character named Broadway Rose (the original of Damon Runyon's Apple Annie) was allowed to sell flowers in Shubert Alley because decades before she had danced in a Shubert chorus line.

This seems to have been the economic low point in the lives of both Hank and Jim; in later years, flush with money but never self-approbation, they would regale their wives with stories of how they had subsisted on the same diet as Chinese peasants: rice, rice, and more rice. Sometimes they would go to Walgreen's basement, buy a chocolate malted, and sip it for as long as they could.

Somebody once asked Fonda about his experiences in the Depression and he replied, "I was barely aware of it. We were in a depression as actors all the time." Stewart said that "There were periods when all of us together barely had $35 a week. A couple of times we came home to find the place locked because we hadn't paid the rent. I called Indiana more than once. We practically lived on milk toast. It was very cheap and very filling the way we made it. A little of it went an awfully long way."

The boys developed strategies for survival familiar to starving artists of all generations. Besides focusing on low-cost, high-carb foods, they regularly attended art openings and gorged on hors d'oeuvres.

As the winter deepened, things began to change, at least for Stewart. "He had the least experience but the shortest wait for success," grumbled Josh Logan decades later. In December 1932, Jim's three-minute turn as a chauffeur in *Goodbye Again* got attention from the critics. *The New Yorker* said that he walked offstage with "a round of spontaneous applause."

Margaret Sullavan swanned in after a performance and sought out Jim, who was surrounded by his roommates. She kissed the stunned Stewart on the cheek, which stunned her ex-husband Fonda even more. She told them that she was off to California to make movies for Universal Pictures. And then she turned to a new friend of theirs named Burgess Meredith, pointed at Stewart, and said, "That boy is going to be a major Hollywood star!"

Most of the assemblage found this startling; the general line about Stewart at this point was that he was a very long shot for employment, let alone stardom. "She really believed in him," remembered Meredith. "Maybe sooner and much more than a lot of the rest of us, including Jimmy himself."

Shortly after Christmas of 1932, Hank and Jim were on their way to a party when they saw a discarded, bedraggled Christmas tree in an alley. They decided to take it back to the apartment and decorate it. Logan was going through a blue period and they thought the tree might cheer him up.

Lugging the tree across the New York streets and into the elevator of their building removed most of its few remaining needles, but Fonda and Stewart still presented Logan with the remains of the tree. In Stewart's telling, Logan managed to restrain his enthusiasm over the generous gift.

Fonda was in a very special depression all his own. He complained mightily about his roommates, about his lack of work, and he also vented about his ex-wife. As Burgess Meredith would remember, Hank was "letting a great deal hang out."

When things got a little dull, the apartment building would offer up comedy relief. "We'd be sitting there, after the theater, drinking a beer or two and the door would open," said Fonda. "We'd turn around and three characters that looked like they'd just walked in from a Warner Bros. gangster movie would appear. Chesterfield coats with black velvet collars up and white Borsalino hats pulled down, dark glasses and hands in their pockets. They'd walk over to the bedroom, glance around, shrug, never open their mouths, and leave.

"It happened so often, always with different guys, but they all were after the same thing. When they couldn't find the girls, they'd go down the hall or the floor above."

One morning, a hoodlum was shot and killed on the front steps of the building next door. The cops came, the body was removed, the blood was cleaned up. Life went on.

Goodbye Again ran through the winter, moved to another theater in the spring and finally closed in July of 1933. For a while at least, the rent was being paid on West 63rd Street. The boys laughed a lot, listened to jazz — a passion that never left Fonda — and rotated the bed so that whoever stayed out the latest would have to sleep on one of the two living room couches.

That winter, Hank got a job in a stock company in East Orange that paid him seven or eight dollars a week. To help out, the producer gave him jugs of applejack, which in turn kept the crew in the apartment warm through the winter.

In Fonda's memory, there was a lot of drinking going on. "For serious drinking, we'd buy raw alcohol and mix it with gelatin." He remembered that his personal low point came in March of 1933, when he was flat broke and took a job at a florist shop. It lasted two or three weeks, until lugging heavy clay pots around began to hurt his knees. That, and Easter, combined to render him unemployed once again.

It was around this time that someone came up with a fundraising idea that involved renting an old speakeasy on West 40th Street for one night a week. The boys organized a steak and beer party and charged $2 a head. They made hobo steaks — large slabs of beef with salt caked on the sides. Hank would slice the steaks, cover them with butter, and make sandwiches out of them.

Add some beer, and the dish was complete. Years later, Jim would become a devoted patron of Chasen's restaurant in Hollywood, partially because he loved Dave Chasen, partially because Chasen served a great hobo steak.

The old speakeasy was a dive, but the food was good and there were additional compensations. Stewart organized the music.

On the low end, it involved his accordion. On the high end, Benny Goodman, then working as a staff musician at NBC, would bring a couple of guys from the orchestra and jam. Hank remembered that a pretty fair clarinet player named Artie Shaw occasionally sat in.

"When [Benny Goodman] came around," said Stewart, "I tossed my accordion into a corner and listened with the rest. He was truly an artist and after a while became our biggest attraction. . . . There wasn't a person in the place who had any doubt about him succeeding."

Hank was in heaven, and Jim began to develop an enthusiasm for jazz as well. Other people who dropped by from time to time included Katharine Cornell, Helen Hayes, and Ruth Gordon.

After about a year, Stewart and Fonda broke up the party on West 63rd and got a room at the Madison Square Hotel, which was downtown in the 20s, after which they scattered to work in summer stock. To fill in the hours when they weren't pounding the pavements looking for acting jobs, they began to build model airplanes.

Both Hank and Jim would tend a fund of stories about their time in Manhattan, but Fonda insisted that his were accurate while

Stewart's were so full of fanciful narrative additives that all reality was vanquished.

One story involved the aftermath of a closing night party for a play. "I brought my accordion," remembered Jim, "and about 3 o'clock it was over. Fonda and I were crossing Times Square to get the subway to go down to Madison. And we got in the middle of Times Square, and Fonda said, 'I wonder if . . .' Now, it's 3 o'clock in the morning . . . 'I wonder if you'd start playing your accordion now, whether you'd get an audience?' I said, 'Well, I believe there's only one way to find out . . .' "

Stewart started playing.

Suddenly we saw about four men who looked as if they hadn't been awake for very long. And this is where Fonda and I disagree. I say there were about 18 around us; Fonda says there were about eight. I was playing and I suddenly looked around and Fonda was passing the hat. . . . Then we disagree on the other thing. I said that we got 28 cents. Fonda said we got 18 cents. Now they were making requests.

And I suddenly felt a real crack on my . . . on my bottom. And I turn around and, of course, it was a cop. And he said, "What in God's name are you fellas doing? It takes me, every night, two and a half hours to get all these guys asleep in hallways around here, and here you start making this terrible noise and you've gotten them all awake, and it's going to take me another three hours to get them asleep again. Now get out of here. Beat it."

But I remember one of them sneaking up to me and saying, "Go down to 42nd and 8th, and we'll be over and play some more."

This captures a great deal of Stewart's take on their shared youth — Fonda instigating, Stewart following and getting into trouble. It also establishes Stewart's perverse pride in the awful power of an accordion to cause dissension in an otherwise placid environment.

The boys reinstituted the steak and beer parties, this time on a floating basis. One night they both drank far too much beer, and on the way home they simply couldn't hold it anymore. They got off the subway and had four blocks to get to their apartment. They decided to solve the problem with the aid of a snowdrift. Fonda said that it was his idea to see if they could piss their names in the snow. Stewart said that all he was able to form were his initials, but Fonda insisted that Jim inscribed his entire name.

In later years, full of dignity, revered within the industry and without, Jim could grow a little frosty if this story came up. He would deny it with a touch of sorrow, while Fonda always insisted it was God's truth.

In the late winter of 1934, the ice broke and Fonda's fifteen months of Broadway unemployment ended. He appeared in *New Faces,* the first of Leonard Sillman's long-running revues. The cast also featured Imogene Coca, and she and Fonda paired off. "Hank was crazy about her," Stewart said.

New Faces ran for 149 performances, from March to July. After *New Faces* closed, an up-and-coming agent named Leland Hayward told Fonda that he wanted to handle him and suggested he come out to California. Fonda didn't want to go, but Hayward upped the ante with a pep talk and a plane ticket.

"It was very hot," said Fonda, "I had a summer Palm Beach type suit. It was wringing wet and wrinkled and he met me at the airport and took me to the Beverly Wilshire Hotel. I went into the shower, shaved and cleaned up and when I came out, there was another man sitting there. I didn't know him, and Leland introduced me to Walter Wanger."

Leland Hayward was a persuasive man — he was known as the Toscanini of the telephone — but he also had a sharp eye for serious talent. He was tall, slender, had a lot of energy, and immense charm. He was a stylish WASP with a crew cut and a lifelong preference for class. "Names were his priority," wrote Arthur Laurents. "If you had a name, you were talented; vice versa sometimes but not often. He himself had glamour. He drank like a Fitzgerald fan, behaved as though to the manor born and his objective was fun and to make things fun for those around him." When a Hayward employee named William Fadiman was lured away by Sam Goldwyn to head his story department, Hayward idly asked Fadiman what Goldwyn was paying him. When Fadiman told him, Hayward snapped, "Not enough," and got on the phone. By the time the call was over, Hayward had coerced Goldwyn into raising Fadiman's salary.

"He couldn't stand a bad deal, so he automatically became my agent for that particular job," said Fadiman. Best of all, Hayward didn't charge Fadiman a commission.

Hayward would perform similar wonders for Fonda, but then they had a lot in common. Leland was born in 1902 in — wait for it — Nebraska, the grandson of Monroe Leland Hayward, a U.S. senator. He went to Hotchkiss, then Princeton, where he flunked out. From there he went to the *New York Sun* as a reporter, where he flunked out again.

It was back to Princeton, but he quit to marry Lola Gibbs, a pilot who taught him to fly. They divorced, remarried, then divorced for good. He began his career as an agent while drinking at the Trocadero in Hollywood. Business was bad and the owner complained that he would pay $3,000 or $4,000 a week for an attraction that would pull in some crowds. Fred and Adele Astaire, for instance.

Hayward went right to the theater where the Astaires were playing and signed them up, collecting a 10 percent commission for his trouble. A career was born: "The pickings were so easy, I decided this was my line of work."

By the time he met Fonda, Hayward was commuting between Hollywood and New York three times a week by flying his own plane seventeen hours each way. He and his partner Myron Selznick had a standing bet that Myron would kill himself through overwork before Hayward died in a plane crash.

Hank was in Los Angeles for only a couple of days, but that was long enough for Wanger to take the leap and sign him: $1,000 a week, two pictures a year, to be scheduled in the summer so Fonda could go back to New York in the winter and do a play.

It was a whirlwind courtship, and Fonda was uncomfortable. "I kept thinking there's something wrong, it can't be, it's too much, and I said 'How do I get out of this?' "

He went back to New York, where he quickly nabbed the starring part in Marc Connelly's play *The Farmer Takes a Wife,* a story of the pre–Civil War Erie Canal. Fonda was recommended by June Walker, who had the female lead and had seen and admired his work.

"I got in touch with him," remembered Marc Connelly, "and he came here and he read for me and I thought he was amazingly right. . . . Never looked for anybody else. No, no he was right for it." Connelly said of Fonda at this nascent stage that he was "a fine workman. Nice chap to work with. And I just thought a good man."

In October 1934, while the show was in

rehearsals, Fonda's mother broke her leg. On October 5, a blood clot formed and traveled to her heart. Herberta Jaynes Fonda died a very sudden death at the age of fifty-five. Her death notice in a Nebraska paper noted that she was survived by two daughters "and a son, Harry Fonda of New York City." William Fonda would die a year later.

The Farmer Takes a Wife opened on October 30, and Fonda was met with critical appreciation ("A manly, modest performance in a style of captivating simplicity," wrote Brooks Atkinson of *The New York Times*). The play ran for more than a hundred performances.

Nineteen thirty-four was also a good professional year for Stewart. In March, he opened in *Yellow Jack,* about the outbreak of yellow fever in Cuba. Jim had the lead, and the reviews for the play — directed by the eminent Guthrie McClintic — and for him personally were fine. Brooks Atkinson said he was "excellent," and Robert Garland at the *World Telegram* said that his performance was "simple, sensitive and true. And replete with poetic underbeat."

Jim would mark *Yellow Jack* as the beginning of taking the craft of the theater seriously. "Before I had only been playing at it.

But the role of . . . O'Hara was so powerful, the experience such a tremendous one, that my mind was made up, for the first time the thought of eventually turning to an architect's desk was totally erased from my mind."

The show was too depressing to run for long — it eked out seventy-nine performances, closing in May — but McClintic rehired Jim for a play he was directing in the fall, *Divided by Three,* opposite Judith Anderson.

That summer, Jim did stock at the Red Barn Theatre on Long Island, and made a short for Warner Bros. at their studio in Brooklyn. The title of Stewart's first movie was *Art Trouble,* and it was two reels of knockabout starring Shemp Howard (later one of the Three Stooges) and Harry Gribbon as house painters who get mixed up with a couple of rich kids, one of whom was Jim. The job paid $50 a day, which was all the impetus that Jim needed to take the job.

The thing about *Art Trouble,* as well as all of Stewart's early films, is that he's already present at his own creation. Most great stars have a period of psychological and technical apprenticeship, where you can observe them putting together the pieces of their screen personality through the process of dozens of different parts in a dozen different movies — what works, what doesn't?

Not Stewart. He seems shy, but not about the camera. He's assured, has a relaxed demeanor, and he's comfortable with dialogue. And then there were his endless legs that made him look like the brother of tap dancer Hal Le Roy.

Divided by Three opened and closed in October, but Fonda went to see the show and came away amazed. "He was playing the son of Judith Anderson, a formidable actress. But he was standing up there eye-to-eye with her and he was just marvelous. In his dressing room I looked at him and sat there shaking my head, wondering, 'Where did this come from? How the hell did he get to be so good?' . . . But it ruffled my feathers a little. Here I was busting my shoe leather trying to make it in the theater, and this lackadaisical fellow Stewart just stumbled into it."

Not only was Jim good onstage, he was good offstage as well. One of the backstage people who worked with Stewart on *Divided by Three* said that Jim "may have been the least neurotic actor I've ever been around. He was almost too nice. No airs, never demanded special attention, seemed to always to keep his insecurities to himself even when he was a kid in his twenties."

On October 15, the author and photographer Carl Van Vechten had Stewart come to his apartment for a portrait. Van Vechten had an uncanny knack for sussing out great talents just as they were catching the wave of renown. Equipped with a couple of photo-flood lights and some curtains, he made dozens of revealing portraits of New York literati, members of the Harlem Renaissance, and the occasional actor. His shot of Stewart captures the innate dignity of the young man. Jim sits, with his arms folded in his lap, looking with a faraway gaze off to his left. He's impeccably turned out, hair neatly combed, wearing a tie and a good jacket. Except for the startlingly sensual mouth, it could be a portrait of a young banker, a man of contained style. But the mouth indicates he could also be a poet or voluptuary.

The failure of the McClintic play didn't faze Jim; he opened in *Page Miss Glory* in November, and that carried him through to March. Hank and Jim were still rooming together, but things were looking up and they were both making some money. They began indulging themselves with more elaborate model planes.

It was Christmas 1934 when the imperative kicked in — Hank and Jim went out to buy Christmas presents for their families. They found what they were looking for at Macy's. "I saw a model airplane, a Martin bomber," said Stewart. It was made out of balsa wood and was a thing of beauty, assuming you had a passion for Martin bombers with two rubber bands for propulsion. The boys got so excited they ended up buying the bomber as their Christmas present for themselves.

Their modus operandi was to come home after their respective plays and shed the excitement of the performance by working on the model. Each would carve a separate piece of the model by hand, with the finished pieces being glued together.

"By then," said Hank, "Stewart and I were so into model airplane building that we wouldn't allow any of the hotel maids into our rooms. It was ankle deep in balsa shavings and we were afraid if they came in to clean, they'd wreck our plane. . . . It looked like a storm had hit.

"We finished the framework and covered it with silk, and the instructions called for us to paint it. The paint came with the kit."

Stewart's memory of the building of the bomber made it sound like a close cousin to the construction of the Panama Canal.

"After a while, the places we had . . . had begun to stink of glue, and you couldn't look anywhere around without seeing balsa wood shavings. The Martin bomber was really something special, though."

Before they could finish the bomber, the phone rang. It was Walter Wanger's office. "Hollywood wanted me, so I left the decorating job to Stewart," Fonda remembered.

In the mid-1930s movie studios were in the market for replicas of Gary Cooper: tall men with a touch of the prairie. But Hank's first picture wasn't going to be for the producer who had signed him. Wanger had loaned him to Fox, a studio with a genetic knack for Americana — Will Rogers coexisted with Shirley Temple as their biggest star until Rogers' death in 1935, and John Ford flourished at the studio for more than twenty years. Fonda had some of Rogers's rural quality, with the added benefits of being tall and romantically gorgeous.

The Farmer Takes a Wife closed in January 1935, and Hank left for Hollywood a month later. He remembered that he went grudgingly. "I had no ambition to be a movie actor," he would say, and from his lifelong eagerness to get back to the stage, and lengthy long-term residences in the East, there's no reason to doubt him.

Stewart walked his friend to the train at Grand Central Terminal. Fonda was wearing three hats piled on his head, so his limited supply of headware wouldn't be crushed in his luggage. Besides his suitcase, he was traveling with a kitten named George that he had adopted from a New York saloon. He smuggled George onto the train and weaned him during the time it took to get to Los Angeles, soaking napkins in cream and milk.

After Fonda left, Stewart puttered with the Martin bomber for a few months, apparently unable or unwilling to finish it without his pal. "He called me every once in a while, but he wouldn't tell me what was going on *there,*" said Stewart. "He'd say, 'How are you getting along with the bomber?' " Since Fonda had abdicated his responsibilities, the bomber was Stewart's to finish, but the issue was complicated. On some level, Fonda felt the model was his intellectual property and Jim seems to have gone along with that proposition. "He wanted me to wait and not paint it . . . because he had an idea of how he wanted to paint it," said Jim.

About three months after Fonda had left for Hollywood, Jim's ship came in — a contract with Metro-Goldwyn-Mayer. Stewart's screen test had been shot in New York and involved the talent scout telling him, "Imagine that I have a large horse in the palm of my right hand. I'm going to release him so he can gallop up to you. He goes obediently, but the path he chooses is to go up the wall, across the ceiling, and down the other wall. After that, he will come back to me and climb into my hand." A few weeks after the test, Jim was offered a standard beginner's contract from MGM, options every six months, extending outward for seven years. Stewart remembered his starting salary as $350 a week, good money for an unproven kid in 1935.

Stewart's last Broadway play for almost ten years was called *A Journey by Night,* which opened on April 15, 1935, and closed a week later. Atkinson of the *Times* said that it was "hackneyed to the core," and clobbered Jim as "wandering through . . . like a bewildered Austrian tourist just off the banks of the Danube."

After that, Jim wrote Hank to tell him he was on his way west. Hank quickly wrote back to tell him to bring the Martin bomber and make sure to pack it securely so it wouldn't break in transit.

Stewart took the bomber home to Pennsylvania so he could take it with him to

California. "My dad made a box for it; it looked sort of like a machine gun." Stewart painted the box black — he could never remember why — and lugged it onto the train west with him, even sleeping with it in his upper berth. Porters would ask him what he had in the case. "It's a model airplane," he would answer. There was never a follow-up question.

When Stewart got off the train in Pasadena, he was lugging two suitcases and the packing crate. Fonda was there to greet him. "Is that the airplane?" was the first thing out of Fonda's mouth. Assured that no newborn baby was ever treated as gently as their beloved bomber, Hank relaxed. They were walking to the car when Fonda looked Stewart over and told him that the hat he was wearing was out of place. Everyone in New York wore hats, but in Los Angeles it was unnecessary.

Jim stopped to admire the 1935 Ford Cabriolet convertible that Fonda had bought. It sure beat any transportation they had had in New York. On the other hand, Fonda was still Fonda — he hadn't bought a Cord, he'd bought a Ford. Jim tossed his hat next to his suitcase and carefully placed the crate in the backseat. Fonda drove them to the house in Brentwood he had been renting. Jim looked around and liked what he saw. He decided to stay.

From here on, things were going to be different. Mainly, they were going to be busy. Fonda was already making a movie, and Stewart was about to be thrown into the maw at MGM, so for several months the Martin bomber stayed in its crate.

Eventually they opened the crate and Stewart painted it just the way Fonda wanted. A few days later, after the paint had dried, they wound up the rubber bands tight and flew her, and she was every bit as impressive as they had hoped. The boys were thrilled beyond measure. An encore was clearly called for, but on the second flight, something went wrong and the bomber crashed. The damage was extreme; the boys gazed sorrowfully at the deceased model.

It doesn't seem like a great deal of payoff for all the delayed gratification, but Jim thought it was worthwhile. He cherished the Martin bomber's brief soaring for the rest of his life, calling its single successful flight "Glorious. Amazing."

FOUR

Fonda's first film was an adaptation of *The Farmer Takes a Wife*. He found a part for George the cat, a scene that needed a cat drinking milk on a boat. George played his part as if he'd been in the movies all his life. Fonda's costar was Janet Gaynor and his director was Victor Fleming, an effective all-arounder who could direct pretty much anything, make it emotionally believable and keep it moving, as he would prove when he directed both *The Wizard of Oz* and *Gone With the Wind* in one year.

Typically, Fonda was horrified by the resulting film. "He didn't look like me, he didn't sound like me," he said of his character. "I was ready to take the first plane back to New York." Fonda would never develop much enthusiasm for watching himself in the movies. He never saw the majority of his pictures unless they jibed with his belief system or he had a sneaking feeling that he just might have nailed it. "*Grapes of Wrath* I saw," he would grumpily admit, "I saw *Ox-Bow*, I saw *Twelve Angry Men*."

For Fonda's second picture, Fox gave him a remake of the D. W. Griffith wheeze *Way Down East,* directed by Henry King. The original's distinctions had been the performance of Lillian Gish and the thrilling climax, in which Gish is rescued from going over an icy waterfall by her loyal country swain, played by Richard Barthelmess. Hank had the Barthelmess part.

The remake is not a particularly good picture — Rochelle Hudson is no Lillian Gish — but it's not negligible. King shapes a couple of moving sequences, and Ernest Palmer's camera recaptures some of the rapture that fills his work for Frank Borzage and F. W. Murnau; a sequence of a runaway horse in a wheatfield summons some of the headstrong sensuality of *City Girl.*

Hank was cast as a virtuous hayseed, a talkie version of Charles Ray or the aforementioned Barthelmess. This would be Hollywood's go-to positioning of him for years, and it would even encompass some good pictures — *Chad Hanna,* and, if you weren't afraid of oversimplification, you could categorize Tom Joad that way as well. But the repetitive casting would chafe

Fonda in a very personal way. He may have sounded like a hayseed, but he was in fact well-read, ambitious, and driven.

Jim's first batch of pictures weren't distinguished either, but unlike his friend, in whom the studios obviously saw potential and took some trouble to position, MGM just tossed Stewart in the water to see if he could swim. They put him to work in the trenches of screen tests, coming in bright and early to work with actresses the studio might be interested in. The different scenes Stewart appeared in constituted an ongoing process of definition; they could look at the young man and figure out his affinities.

The publicity department was also called in. "Was he a comedian, or a romantic leading man?" asked the MGM still photographer Ted Allan. "We tried photographing him outside, leaning over fences, working with a shovel, with a tennis racket. But while that worked with Robert Taylor in helping to make him more athletic, it didn't work with Stewart."

Jim's first movie for MGM was entitled *The Murder Man,* sixth-billed beneath Spencer Tracy, Virginia Bruce, and a seriously miscast Lionel Atwill. It's a tight little seventy-minute B movie, a hard-bitten newspaper saga that's a precursor of Fritz

Lang's *Beyond a Reasonable Doubt,* and not at all bad. Stewart plays a young police reporter called Shorty.

Aside from the plot, and Tracy's typically intense, modern performance, the interesting thing about *The Murder Man* is the fact that it's really a Warner Bros. movie that happened to be made at MGM. The pace is fast, the characters disreputable, the prevailing attitude bitter. Although Stewart would become famous for his hesitant speech pattern, he copes perfectly well with the rat-tat-tat of the dialogue.

MGM didn't stand on ceremony. Jim was then tossed into a short called *Important News,* opposite Chic Sale as a small-town newspaper editor who sees a wanted criminal shot down by the FBI. Instead of putting the story on the front page, he goes with a story about a frost warning that is far more important to his readers. (Louis B. Mayer's stars may have been primarily attractive to urban audiences, but his values skewed rural.) Stewart is his young assistant and the close-ups emphasize his youth. Although he was twenty-seven years old at the time, he seems barely out of adolescence.

What's clear from these first halting castings was that Jim already possessed the emotional transparency of the star — the way they have of communicating character and personality directly to the audience even if the writer and director aren't being much, or any, help. These early pictures could not remotely be categorized as showcases for Stewart, but he acquitted himself well in all of them.

Coming to the rescue was Margaret Sullavan, who asked for Stewart to costar with her in Universal's *Next Time We Love,* a charming love story about a workaholic journalist and his actress wife. Sullavan worked hard in rehearsals to nudge Jim out of some of his stage habits, and he gives a relaxed, apparently casual performance of great charm.

Written by an interesting assembly of talent — among the uncredited writers were Rose Franken and Preston Sturges — and shot in a leisurely fifty-four days, it cost $460,000, with Sullavan getting $1,750 a week and Stewart earning a modest $500 a week.

It's a good picture that lacks a convincing conclusion, but it was noticed both by critics (*Time* gave Stewart a particularly strong notice) and by MGM. Billy Grady, the studio's casting director and a fan of Stewart's, told reporters that "The boy came back from Universal so changed I hardly recognized him. . . . Sullavan had taught him to march to his own drummer, to be himself, completely."

The boys were getting used to Hollywood — Fonda warily, Stewart enthusiastically. In May 1936, they gave their first joint interview, to gossip columnist Sheilah Graham, just a year away from her liaison with F. Scott Fitzgerald. Fonda told her that they would love to go back to Broadway and do a play, but Stewart wasn't so sure. "There's a feeling of permanency we didn't get on the stage," he said. "Life is very pleasant here — and they pay you well."

They showed Graham around their rented house and the surrounding half-acre, including a group of cats yowling in a shed. "If only we could catch them," murmured Stewart. They put on an impromptu musicale — Stewart played the piano and accordion and manfully grappled with the saxophone and flute. Fonda did the same with the violin, then tried the drums and even did some of his unmusical singing. After that they treated Graham to some home movies in which Stewart played both hero and villain — Stewart the hero shot Stewart the villain.

Graham seems to have been well disposed

toward Fonda ("He is even better looking off screen than on"), not so well disposed to Stewart, whom she described as "thick-lipped" and "not handsome."

The piece caught the young men reflecting the same attitudes they would maintain for the rest of their lives: Fonda pining for the theater, Stewart content with Hollywood.

"I was just wrapped up by the whole idea of this place where make-believe took place," said Jim. "Every once in a while you'd look and there was Garbo and there was Gable . . . and the whole thing was a wonderful experience for me.

"I don't ever remember saying, well, now I'm going to do this and I'm working towards this. I was so busy and so wrapped up in what I was doing that things just seemed to happen. . . . It was all a learning process for me and I enjoyed every minute of it."

But Fonda held himself psychologically aloof. If Stewart was a curious puppy, Fonda was a cat — contrary, somewhat disgruntled, and perfectly content to walk by himself.

Jim pegged Hank's issue as one of thwarted self-determination. "He had this sort of way he planned to do his acting and continue with his craft — he had this pretty well worked out, and he objected to the idea of getting a message from the front office saying you'll be with so and so and so and so. He liked the idea of picking his own vehicles. He just felt he'd rather be independent and be able to choose his own thing, which in Hank's case I can understand because of this absolute devotion to his craft that he has had all these years. He was capable of making the right decisions for himself."

Hank and Jim had moved their friendship to a different city, one where the sun shone all the time. They were living in a rented house at 233 Carmelita, which was next door to Greta Garbo's (also rented) house. It was also home base for a slew of feral cats. Since Stewart and Fonda were both fond of cats, they decided to try to domesticate the ferals, with predictable results. Not only did the cats resist everything except food, they begat more cats. After a year or so, the population had grown to more than thirty cats. Since naming them all would have been impossible, Fonda called each of them "George."

Years later, Josh Logan mentioned, very much off the record, that there were a few occasions late at night, when they all would come home after an evening of strenuous drinking to find the cats lined up in the driveway. At those times, the gas might accidentally have been hit and the surplus feline population slightly decreased. Since Fonda liked cats, and Stewart was partial to anything on four legs, the finger of guilt is probably directed toward Logan.

One day Fonda and Stewart were looking over the household bills presented to them by the couple who took care of the house for the owner. They noticed a large charge for milk. Since they had vowed not to feed the cats milk — that way lay madness — the charge was most curious. They decided to investigate the housekeeper's quarters. Fonda opened the door to the maid's bathroom and found the bathtub filled with milk with — by actual count — thirty-seven cats gorging themselves. When Fonda told this story, he would add a coda that may or may not have been strictly factual. He said that the sight of a tub filled with milk reminded him of Claudette Colbert's milk bath in DeMille's *Cleopatra*. Curiosity aroused, he stripped and climbed into the tub of milk. He didn't say whether the cats appreciated the interloper.

The problem demanded a solution. What

to do? Stewart ruled out poison because "that'd be mean, and they'd crawl under the house and die, and then it *would* stink." Finally he suggested the ASPCA, but the boys couldn't figure out how to trap thirty-seven cats that didn't want to be caught.

They finally decided to share the wealth by knocking a hole in the base of the fence that separated their yard from Garbo's. Stewart's version of the resulting mishap was that the operation was going well until their shovel severed a water pipe and flooded the backyard. Fonda refused to admit that anything like that ever happened. "What Stewart doesn't remember he invents," he grumbled. Off the record, he would simply say, "Bullshit. We never got out of the house. We sat there drinking beer [and talked] about it."

Whatever happened with Plan A, there was no Plan B. What did work were the fleas, which rapidly infested the yard, the rugs, the house, and Hank and Jim. Between the cats, the fleas, and her obstreperous neighbors, Garbo thought it wise to move.

The story of the cats and Garbo achieved primary status in Hank and Jim's personal mythology of their misspent Hollywood youth, but there was an objective third party to confirm the saga. John D. Stewart was a cousin of Jim's who came for a visit in the summer of 1936, and his memory was that

Jim said . . . I had to figure out a way of getting rid of the cats without hurting them. . . . Every time we'd grab one of the cats, and they weren't the easiest animals in the world to get your hands on, the housekeeper would come running and say, "You can't get rid of that one because he's Mr. Fonda's favorite." As far as she was concerned, they were all his favorites.

Well, one day we finally caught one and decided to paint it purple, figuring that the other cats would be frightened by such a bizarre creature and leave on their own. Just as we finished, who arrived but Fonda, who'd been out of town for a few days. We handed him the cat, and he gave us one of those long, slow looks of his that seemed to go right into your soul, up, down and every which way. From that day on, whenever I'd see him give one of those looks to someone in a movie, I'd think that someone had just handed him a purple cat.

Having created a monster, or, rather, dozens of monsters, Fonda and Stewart decided to move. They went to a rental

118

agent to sublet the house so they could make a clean getaway. "One of the first people to look at the place was Jeanette MacDonald," said Fonda. "And I can remember walking around outside with her and you could literally see black clouds of fleas jumping up onto her stockings." Mac-Donald rented a house four doors down from Fonda and Stewart, who soon moved to another house *sans* cats.

When they weren't battling cats and fleas, Stewart and Fonda were living a life they had never dared to dream. They were regular visitors at the home of the director H. C. (Hank) Potter, who had been a college friend of Stewart and Logan's. There would be tennis in the afternoon, followed by cooling off with a lot of Cokes, followed by a buffet supper, followed by music.

Hoagy Carmichael would stop by regularly, and Fonda remembered with wonderment times when Carmichael and Johnny Mercer would both be sitting at the piano. Back in New York they had enjoyed listening to a group called the Merry Macs that specialized in five-part harmony. The Macs had moved to California and they too would drop in and harmonize while Carmichael and Mercer backed them up.

They were in paradise, and they were

smart enough to know it.

In 1936, MGM worked Stewart like a rented mule. He made nine widely varied films. He played, variously, Jeanette Mac-Donald's errant brother (*Rose-Marie*); Eleanor Powell's boyfriend who serenades her with "Easy to Love" (*Born to Dance*); Janet Gaynor's would-be boyfriend in hot competition with Robert Taylor (*Small Town Girl*); Joan Crawford's would-be boyfriend in hot competition with Franchot Tone (*The Gorgeous Hussy*); the long-suffering boyfriend of Jean Harlow (*Wife Versus Secretary*); and, just for the sake of variety, a crazed killer (*After the Thin Man*). The last featured one of Jim's few inadequate performances — at this stage of his development, crazy wasn't in his bag of acting tricks. He even tested for a part in *The Good Earth,* but was spared the ignominy.

None of these were great movies, but that wasn't the point. Generally speaking, people went to see stars, not specific movies. The films were all learning experiences, especially with Jean Harlow, who didn't wear a bra and who kissed Stewart as if they weren't in front of a movie camera but in a bedroom.

Jim didn't seem to have a handle on any

specific style or technique other than the one he was working out for himself. Spencer Tracy had told him to forget that the camera was there, which was easier in theory than in practice.

All this was classic MGM: First, find an actor who has a connection to the camera and, beyond that, to the audience. Then throw him into every kind of picture there is, opposite every kind of actor and actress on the lot, to see if he can hold his own against experienced competition. With any luck at all, at the end of that process, you might have a star. The last time the studio had worked a young leading man that hard, his name was Clark Gable, and the result was the primary leading man of the 1930s.

The result of this flurry of pictures was that by the end of 1936, the studio understood that Stewart was a different kind of actor from Gable, Taylor, or Montgomery. Actually, he wasn't one kind of actor, but several. Stewart was the brother, the sweetheart, the nice guy next door with a bias toward doing the right thing, always decent but never a pushover.

He was Jimmy Stewart.

By 1937, and *The Last Gangster*, MGM was awarding him second billing beneath Edward G. Robinson. Stewart plays a reporter who falls in love with the wife of the title character, who takes it amiss when he gets out of prison and finds his ex-wife married to Stewart. Complications ensue.

The studio's inability to figure out what kind of specific actor Stewart was is indicated by the ridiculous pencil mustache they pasted on his upper lip for the picture's later stages, which he manfully refuses to be embarrassed by. It's not much of a part, or much of a picture, but Stewart is likable and holds the camera. He always would.

Stewart was not a fan of his early work. "I was all hands and feet," he remembered. "Didn't seem to know what to do with either." Whenever he looked at his first pictures he was appalled, although he's really bad only in the climactic scene of *After the Thin Man,* when he is shrill and overwrought.

Hank and Jim's new address was 255 Chadbourne in Brentwood. Joining the glorified frat house was Johnny Swope, as well as a revolving troupe that included, at various times, Josh Logan, Myron McCormick, and Kent Smith. Swope had been working for the National Recovery Administration, where he was evaluating the effectiveness of various housing programs by taking photographs as part of the documentation process. He traveled all over the country, including the coal mines of West Virginia, and when Hank and Jim suggested he come out to visit, they didn't have to ask twice.

The more time Fonda spent with Swope, the better he liked him. "In a way, he was one of the ugliest men you've known," Hank said, "and in another way the most beautiful. It was not the traditional handsome face, and yet if you knew John you couldn't but adore him."

Fonda remembered the specific moment when he and Jim realized what Swope should do with his life. "John was invited to help crew the *Paisano* in the Los Angeles–Honolulu Yacht Race," remembered Fonda. "He took a Leica with him. I know that within a few days after his return he spread out before our popping eyes the most beautiful display of sailing pictures I had ever seen. They were breathtaking. I would like to think that our enthusiasm then had a lot to do with the direction his life was to take."

But not quite yet. Leland Hayward, who would always play benevolent godfather for the entire University Players clan, hired Swope as an assistant producer and publicity photographer. But Swope promptly went off into a personal project, documenting the concentric circles of the subculture of 1930s Hollywood.

Hayward was indulgent, but only up to a point. After Swope had been working for him for some months, Hayward cut him back to twenty hours a week, leaving the other half for the project that would become *Camera Over Hollywood*. But Swope didn't really put in his time with Hayward, so he was finally let go. No matter — Bennett Cerf published *Camera Over Hollywood* in 1939, which led directly to Swope becoming one of the most prestigious freelancers in the *Life* magazine stable.

"My father had a big personality, but not over the top," said Mark Swope. "His great gift was the ability to step into a stranger's space, put them at ease, and photograph them. It's the most marvelous ability, and all great photographers have to have it."

With the Martin bomber carried to its just reward, the boys needed a new pastime, and for a while they focused on their home movies, using Fonda's 16mm camera. By now, they had also talked Leland Hayward into bringing Josh Logan into the fold, a decision, Logan remembered, that Hayward "wavered about for years."

When Logan got off the plane in Hollywood, Fonda was there shooting the arrival with a 16mm camera, with Jim and Maggie Sullavan forming the rest of the welcoming party. Logan moved into the house, which now featured four, count 'em four, bachelors of varying degrees of randiness, focus, and ambition.

They dreamed up a movie melodrama in which Stewart played the villain. When the plot called for him to be shot, they looked through the kitchen for something that might replicate blood. Catsup being a cliché, they decided on beet juice. Unfortunately, some of the beet juice went up Stewart's nose and sinuses, which caused a visit to a nose and throat specialist.

The doctor ascertained a problem, but couldn't figure out what was causing it. "Beet juice," said Stewart. The doctor nodded and stalled for time by cleaning his glasses, but he couldn't summon the will to ask just how beet juice had gotten up Stewart's nose.

Then as now, people wonder about grown men living together. Generally, they come to one conclusion, as Cary Grant and Randolph Scott would find out. (Errol Flynn and David Niven managed to dodge the implications.)

Orson Welles arrived in Hollywood to

make a screen test, and heard the rumors about Hank and Jim. "I thought these two guys were either having the hottest affair in Hollywood, or were the two straightest human beings I ever met in my life," Welles said. After he met them, Welles "came to the conclusion that they were the two straightest human beings I'd ever met in my life."

The boys were still painfully skinny, so they began a regimen involving morning eggnog. A friend told them to add a little brandy, but, as Jim would remember, "We noticed that the eggnog kept getting darker and darker, and by eleven a.m. we were both pissed!"

After the catch-as-catch-can casting of Stewart's first couple of years, he finally got into some good movies that strongly indicated he carried something special within him.

Of Human Hearts was made by MGM's graceful house director Clarence Brown. The part of a rebellious preacher's kid in small-town Ohio on both ends of the Civil War undoubtedly carried echoes of Stewart's matriculation in Pennsylvania. Most of the film focused on his character's rebellion, while the doubtful climax, where Lincoln (John Carradine, under a ton of makeup) takes time out from waging the Civil War to tell Stewart he should write home to mother, focuses on his momentarily mislaid sweetness.

More to the point, Stewart was second-billed behind Walter Huston, a great actor who could work in either broad theatricality or absolute naturalism. In *Of Human Hearts*, Huston switches back and forth, depending on the scene, and Stewart matches him step for step.

That same year, MGM threw him into *The Shopworn Angel*, a remake of a film that had originally starred Gary Cooper and Nancy Carroll. Stewart's costar was Margaret Sullavan. With any cast, it's a moist confection about a young Texas soldier in World War I who falls in love with a spoiled music hall soubrette. It was directed by Jim's friend Hank Potter with a hard hand but it was nevertheless a good-sized hit, even if Stewart plays an undifferentiated cornpone saint. Louella Parsons wrote that "Jimmy Stewart's boyish appeal and ability to win audience sympathy are one reason he is beginning to be box office plus. He has an irresistible attraction for the young people, and the older folk also share this admiration."

The boy next door was moving in.

Aside from the considerable independence Jim had shown by sidestepping Alex's plans for his life, there was no trace of rebellion in his relationship with his father. So it followed that he was quite happy at his home studio, and always spoke of that era in the most glowing terms.

I've always felt that the studio system is the *ideal* way to make pictures. Everybody calls them the moguls — the Harry Cohns and the L. B. Mayers and the Warner Brothers . . . and there's been terrible books written about these terrible people. . . . This is just a *lie.* This is not true. These men were completely in love with the motion picture. And they *believed* in the motion picture. And worked for quality. They didn't *need* censorship. They did their own censoring and were very good at it.

You worked six days a week. You got there every morning at 8 o clock and you left at 6. And if you weren't making a picture — a big part in a small picture, or a small part in a big picture — you were working out in the gym, you were doing tests with other people that they were thinking about signing. You were out on the road with a picture you weren't even in, plugging it from the stage. . . . And there was a *feeling* of sort of. . . . You were a part of a . . . you were a part of something that was *excitement* all the time. . . .

I've always been very grateful; I've had great good fortune in my life. But I've always been very grateful that I had a *chance* to benefit by the big studio system.

Of course, Stewart grew up with a bossy father, and had been able to defuse any number of possible confrontations with the old man, so a bossy father figure — Louis B. Mayer for instance — held no fear for him. "If you detested some idea that a boss had, or detested that he was a boss period, you were in for a lot of aggravation," said Eddie Albert, who broke into movies just a few years after Stewart. "Jimmy was never like that. Nobody struck up friendships or put people at ease faster than he did. And that goes for executives, other actors, people on the crews." It was really very simple. Jim liked most people, or pretended to, so most people liked him.

He was also helped in developing his sea legs by the fact that his agent was Leland Hayward, the same man guiding Hank's career. Hayward was now the agent for

Greta Garbo, Edna Ferber, Ginger Rogers, Dashiell Hammett, Lillian Hellman, Myrna Loy, Boris Karloff, Kurt Weill, and Helen Hayes. And just to keep everything in the family, Leland was also the new husband of Margaret Sullavan, who had married him almost immediately after divorcing William Wyler — her husband following Fonda — in 1936.

Hayward got Josh Logan a job as a dialogue director on David Selznick's production of *The Garden of Allah.* Logan dined out for years on his tales of that garbled production — the clashing egos of Marlene Dietrich and Charles Boyer, the even larger ego of Joseph Schildkraut, who styled himself as the only appropriate lover for Dietrich, and the overwhelmed director Richard Boleslawski, who was from the Moscow Art Theatre, for God's sake.

Stewart's priorities had undergone a 180 degree shift. The tentative commitment to architecture had been obliterated by, first, acting and now — gaining fast — flying. He began taking lessons at Mine Field, later Clover Field, still later the site of Los Angeles International Airport. He wasn't the only one. Leland Hayward had been flying long before Fonda and Stewart came into his life, as had Johnny Swope. Among the rest of the movie colony, Tyrone Power, Robert Taylor, and Robert Cummings also had pilot's licenses, as did some actresses, among them Ruth Chatterton, Joan Fontaine, and Margaret Sullavan.

Leland Hayward owned a Waco and when he entered a race between Los Angeles and Cleveland in 1937, he asked Stewart to serve as copilot. The Waco was leading for most of the race, but engine trouble grounded it before the finish line. After they got back to Los Angeles, Stewart wrote his agent and friend:

> I'm going to begin to feel like a real flier. I haven't had a chance to thank you for the whole trip. I got a kick out of every minute of it and it was sure swell of you to ask me to go along.
>
> Here are some pictures, not as good as I'd hoped for — Hank took a lot the day he left and I'll send you some prints of those as soon as they're developed.
>
> Thanks again . . . Jim Stewart.

Hayward then enlisted Stewart as an investor in an airfield in Phoenix.

By 1938, it was clear that Stewart was a rising star, and MGM did much better by

131

him than they did with a lot of their stars. For one thing, they loaned him to premium talents that were better than the homegrown product. Stewart made *You Can't Take It with You* and *Mr. Smith Goes to Washington* at Columbia, *Destry Rides Again* at Universal. It wasn't until 1940 and *The Mortal Storm, The Philadelphia Story,* and *The Shop Around the Corner* that MGM equaled the efforts of their competitors in formulating vehicles for their new star. It took five long years, but MGM finally figured out what to do with him.

By the time he started to work with Frank Capra, Stewart had already settled into a specific professional groove, which never really changed. Edward Bernds, Columbia's best soundman, worked on all the Capra pictures and noted that "Jimmy was respectful toward Capra, but hardly worshipful in the way that, say Clark Gable was during *It Happened One Night.* Same thing with regard to the crew. He was professional and friendly, but always a little removed. . . . Jimmy already had his own center in his work even back then. I think he came to work, and everybody, from a lighting man to Capra, was there only to aid in that."

Beyond that, there was the matter of his

acting, which amazed even experienced pros. He projected a man who was unworldly but possessed of an unbreachable inner strength revealed in climactic moments, when he would unleash an emotional torrent. Frank Capra said that, "He grabbed you as a human being. You were looking at the man, not an actor. You could see this man's soul."

"He was the most naturally gifted actor I ever worked with," said the distinguished character actor Thomas Mitchell, who shared the screen with him in *Mr. Smith Goes to Washington.* "I don't think it came from training or technique . . . it came from forces deep within him."

There were those who felt that Stewart might have cherished his emotional scenes a bit too much. "Now, don't paw the ground," George Cukor told him just before a big scene with Katharine Hepburn in *The Philadelphia Story.* The same film provided Stewart with one of the few times when he was visibly flummoxed. During his drunk scene with the radiantly alert Cary Grant, Stewart hiccupped, which he hadn't done in rehearsal. Grant promptly said, "Excuse me." Stewart just looked at him for a second, then went on with the scene. Game, set, match to Grant.

Jim didn't come close to pawing the ground in Ernst Lubitsch's *The Shop Around the Corner,* one of the most exquisitely balanced movies ever made, perfectly judged in comedy, sentiment, and performance. Jim's costar was again Maggie Sullavan. Two people are working together who are unknowingly each other's lonelyhearts pen pals. Smitten on the page, they can't stand each other in the flesh.

The key emotional scene comes when Sullavan is bedridden by romantic grief and is heartened by a letter from her correspondent. Stewart, the correspondent, is sitting next to her. A clumsier actor or director would have allowed a touch of triumph to pass across the man's face, for he knows the score and she doesn't. Instead, as Andrew Sarris wrote, "an intensely sweet and compassionate and appreciative look transfigures the entire scene into one of the most memorable occurrences in the history of cinema."

Stewart not only loved Sullavan, he observed her closely, and he understood what she brought to the party. "Humor. She had great humor. It wasn't mechanical with her. It was a part of her. This was one of the things that made her great. When you'd play a scene with her, you were never quite sure, although she was always letter perfect in her lines, what was going to happen. She had you just a little bit off guard, and also the director. I've always called what she did planned improvisation — she could just do moments that would hit you, maybe a look or a line or two, but they'd hit like flashes or earthquakes; everybody'd sort of feel it at the same time."

In years to come, Stewart would play all manner of neuroses, through bitterness and into madness. But the audience willingly followed him into the darkness, because they understood that this was a man whose natural personality was centered around tenderness, never more nakedly than in *The Shop Around the Corner.*

Unlike Stewart's slower ascent, Fonda became a star immediately. In 1936, he was cast by his ex-wife to appear opposite her in a comedy entitled *The Moon's Our Home,* made while Sullavan was in her brief inter-regnum between William Wyler and Leland Hayward. The locations were at Lake Tahoe, and Sullavan greeted him with "Hello, Hank."

"Hello, Peggy," he answered.

"They call me Maggie out here."

"Maggie? I'll still call you Peggy. OK?"

"OK."

In a few days, they were more or less back where they had been shortly before their marriage. When they got back to Los Angeles, they started house hunting. At that point, Fonda, Sullavan, Stewart, and Swope went to a party at the West Side Tennis Club. Hank made the crucial mistake of asking another girl to dance, and Sullavan blew sky high. Someone else took her home. On Monday, they were back on the set, and she told him, "This is a mistake, Hank. The thing between us — it's not going to work."

At that point, Maggie met Leland Hayward, who had been having a fling with Kate Hepburn until he was suddenly struck by a case of the Sullavans. Decades later, their daughter Brooke would be in an elevator with Hepburn. They were introduced and Hepburn looked Hayward up and down.

"*You* are Maggie and Leland's daughter?" she inquired with raised eyebrows, in the appalled manner of Edna May Oliver.

"I remember thinking, 'This is a nightmare.' " Hayward said. "She was wearing trousers that were six inches too long and she hadn't pinned them up or hemmed them. A very strange woman."

Hank liked to talk about Jim's strange

136

power over women, how he would escort a star to a premiere and the morning after the lady in question would stop by to personally deliver candy, flowers, or records as a token of delight in his company.

As for himself, Fonda indicated a fatal lack of popularity. In his telling, he was almost a recluse, while Stewart was . . . *besieged.* "Women wanted to — I don't know how to say this — mother him," Fonda said. "They were the aggressors. They showered *him* with flowers."

Stewart would take great delight in pricking Fonda's affectation of isolation, often by enumerating chapter and verse. He noted Fonda's infatuation with the actress Shirley Ross, and said that, "We both dated Virginia Bruce." And he seemed particularly fond of one dating foursome — Fonda with Lucille Ball, Stewart with Ginger Rogers. They started out at the Trocadero, followed by Barney's Beanery. By the time they came out of Barney's, it was dawn. Fonda looked at Ball, who was made up for evening light. He didn't like what he saw. "I reacted badly. And that was the only date we had. If I'd behaved myself, just controlled myself, they might have named that studio Fondalu instead of Desilu." Stewart would also point out that poor, lonely Fonda spent a brief period with Janet Gaynor, followed by Loretta Young. "He had his share, without question," Stewart said with grudging respect. "He had his share and then some."

Hank met his second wife in England in the summer of 1936, where he was shooting *Wings of the Morning,* the first Technicolor film shot in Europe. The lady's name was Frances Seymour Brokaw, and she was a young patrician widow. The late Mr. Brokaw had been the first husband of Clare Booth, who was later to write *The Women* and marry Henry Luce. The late Mr. Brokaw was said to have been a wife-beater and was definitely alcoholic. He had conveniently died in a sanitarium in 1935, leaving his twenty-seven-year-old widow with a million dollars.

Just before he met Frances, Hank was residing in the state of romantic limbo where Sullavan had placed him. She preserved several letters Fonda wrote her that summer, the first written on July 1, 1936, just after he arrived in England.

Peggy My Dear,
    There's so much to tell you about I can't possibly write it. I've gone very English country — taken a home near

the studio — with a fantastic address —

Brook Cottage
Station Parade
Gerrardin Cross
Bucks
England

I'm going to have stationery made up just to perpetuate that address . . .
This is the first letter I've written you for six years.
I don't really believe you're coming over here . . .

The next letter Sullavan kept was sent from New York and is postmarked September 9. It captures Fonda backtracking furiously and trying to calm Sullavan down.
This is not in the nature of an explanation, he writes, "just a few statements."

I am sincerely sorry that I have been so stupid and unthinking. You know how I feel about you — I can't tell you those things now — Frances knows too, and understands.
I care more about you — your health and what happens to you — than I do myself.

. . . I've been such a blundering fool. I wanted you to be as happy as I am. I hate to think I've spoiled my chances of caring about your happiness.

We are going to be married here in New York before I leave . . .

My thoughts are with you,
Hank.

Reading between the lines, it seems clear that Sullavan had reacted badly to Fonda's temerity in falling in love with somebody else. Jane Fonda, Hank's daughter with Frances, knew Sullavan well and said that "She was always in love with my father . . . she just couldn't stand thinking that she didn't control [him]."

Clearly, Sullavan still had a good deal of leverage where her ex-husband's life is concerned, and always would. For Fonda, Sullavan would always be the one who got away.

Wings of the Morning is narratively erratic — the Irish tenor John McCormack suddenly appears and sings three songs for no apparent reason — but visually bewitching. The light in England and Ireland is softer than in Los Angeles, so the images have a luscious softness to go with a subdued pastel hue. Fonda's dark coloring and blue eyes were particularly striking in three-strip Technicolor, which was a difficult process to work in. It required unnatural makeup that looked ghostly gray to the naked eye, and the rushes were usually in black-and-white and looked as though they had been shot through milk.

Technicolor required a huge amount of light, and arcs would be used even on outdoor locations, directing fill light to any dark areas. It was hard on the eyes, and when Fonda wasn't blinking, his eyes were watering. "My baby blues didn't like it," Fonda said. "I had a lot of trouble just keeping my eyes open."

Hank's costar was Annabella, a stunning French blonde whose beauty doesn't date. *Wings of the Morning* was her first picture in English, so she was learning the language as she was making the movie. Fonda seems to have been willing to help in his own way.

Josh Logan remembered that when Fonda got back from England, it was clear that something had happened. "I went to pick him up and he said, 'Oh, I had a wonderful time, we walked along the streets together, we'd take the last bus and then get off and walk home like two kids.'" Logan made some innocuous remark about Frances, and Fonda said, "Frances? I'm talking about

Annabella." And when Logan asked, "What about Frances?," Fonda said, "I'm marrying her on Thursday." Logan was the best man.

Fonda never directly replied to the implications — he and Jim were both circumspect about their sex lives — but his late-life feelings about Annabella ("Delightful . . . wonderful. A dear, dear, dear woman. I'm still very close to her.") were startlingly ardent for his cool personality. Annabella would marry Tyrone Power in 1939, while Fonda and Brokaw married two months after they met.

Fonda was a riveting presence on-screen from the beginning, if only for the tension between his inner stillness and the vocal urgency that made everything he said sound important. His career picked up steam when Walter Wanger loaned him out to Warner Bros. to costar with Bette Davis in *Jezebel*. Davis and Fonda had made an indifferent picture together in 1937 called *That Certain Woman*, but that had been directed by the efficient Edmund Goulding, whereas *Jezebel* was being made by William Wyler, a perfectionist who took his own sweet time.

Jezebel ended up going five weeks over schedule, driving both producer Hal Wallis and Fonda to distraction, the latter because he had a stop date of December 17 so he could travel to New York for the birth of his first child. Wyler released Fonda in time for the birth of Jane, but Bette Davis had to shoot her close-ups without the off-screen presence of her leading man.

Fonda struggled manfully with a mediocre Southern accent and having to pretend that George Brent was a reasonable rival. Wyler's dilatory pace made Hal Wallis wonder if the director — Sullavan husband #2 — was trying to break the spirit of Fonda — Sullavan husband #1. "Do you think Wyler is mad at Fonda or something, because of their past?" he asked associate producer Henry Blanke in a memo. "It seems that he is not content to okay anything with Fonda until it has been . . . ten or eleven takes."

Actually, Fonda and Wyler liked each other, if only because they were both perfectionists unwilling to compromise where the work was concerned. One of them devised an elaborate practical joke to be played on Leland Hayward — Sullavan husband #3. First, Fonda called Hayward and told him to get out to Warner Bros. as quickly as possible. "Get me out of this picture," demanded Fonda when Hayward showed up. "That son of a bitch Wyler, I don't want to work for him another day."

Hayward then scheduled a meeting with Wyler, who came in bellowing, "Get me another leading man. I want him out of this picture." A nervous Hayward pointed out that the picture was almost finished, and replacing the leading man would be prohibitively expensive.

"I don't give a damn," said Wyler. "I'd rather reshoot the whole thing. Get him out!" Hayward went into overdrive and managed to calm the bogus rage. Fonda and Wyler agreed to a meeting, where they surprised Hayward by bringing in a photographer to take their picture. "Welcome to the Maggie Sullavan Club!" announced Wyler. Luckily, Hayward had a sense of humor.

Jane Fonda was born on December 21, and that same day her exultant father wired Wyler:

I ADMIRE YOUR PICTURES AND I WOULD LIKE TO WORK FOR YOU. I AM EIGHTEEN MINUTES OLD BLONDE HAIR BLUE EYES, WEIGHT EIGHT POUNDS AND I HAVE BEEN CALLED BEAUTIFUL MY FATHER WAS AN ACTOR SIGNED JANE SEYMOUR FONDA.

Wyler wired back:

144

MY DEAR MANY THANKS FOR YOUR KIND
WIRE. HEARTY CONGRATULATIONS ON YOUR
ARRIVAL AND HEARTFELT CONDOLENCE ON
YOUR CHOICE OF FATHER HOWEVER WE
FEEL IT OUR DUTY TO CORRECT ANY ILLU-
SION YOU MAY HAVE BEEN UNDER IN THE
PAST AS WE FEEL YOU ARE OLD ENOUGH
NOW TO BE TOLD THE HAPPY NEWS YOUR
FATHER NEVER WAS AN ACTOR . . . WYLER
WANTS TO MAKE A TEST OF YOU SOON AS
POSSIBLE . . . AND HEREWITH REQUESTS
YOU CALL HIM UNCLE BECAUSE HE FEELS
THERE IS AN UNDEFINABLE BUT NONETHE-
LESS DEFINITE RELATIONSHIP SOMEWHERE
SOMEHOW.

When Fonda got back to California Walter Wanger cast him in *Blockade,* where
Fonda played a partisan in the Spanish Civil
War outgunned by Franco's Fascists. In the
end, Fonda turns to the camera and explodes in a passionate speech. "Where can
you find peace? The whole country's a
battleground. There is no peace. There is no
safety for women and children. Schools and
hospitals are targets. And this isn't war, not
war between soldiers. It's not war, it's
murder. It makes no sense. The world can't
stop it. Where is the conscience of the

world? *Where is the conscience of the world?"*

For Fonda, these pictures were marking time — *Jezebel* was primarily a vehicle for Bette Davis, and *Blockade* was a tract. It was John Ford who turned him into something more than an attractive leading man. Fonda had watched Ford shooting interiors for *Stagecoach* when they were both working for Walter Wanger. Fonda's response to John Wayne was more or less identical to Josh Logan's initial response to Fonda: "I thought he was the most beautiful hunk of man I'd ever seen."

It was clear from even a brief time on the set that Ford was . . . *different.* Immensely self-contained, indifferent to other people's opinions, occasionally cruel, with an unmatched eye for composition and dramatic accent.

"He didn't shoot a hundred thousand feet of film that an editor played with for four months to put it into shape," said Fonda. "He just shot what he wanted and he cut it in the camera, so there wasn't any film to play with and there wasn't the problem of what scene do we use, any of that shit, not with Ford." Hank understood that working for Ford could be emotionally dangerous, but he also intuited that it could change his career and, possibly, his life for the better.

The first film Ford offered him was *Young Mr. Lincoln,* which Fonda shyed away from, saying it was "like playing Jesus." This only irritated Ford. "What the fuck is all this shit about you not wanting to play this picture? You think Lincoln's a great fucking Emancipator, huh? He's a young jack-legged lawyer from Springfield, for Christ sake."

A cowed Fonda changed his mind, but as the film moves along Ford does in fact treat Lincoln like Jesus — a man who uses parables to hide his disassociation from the common man. In the end, he walks toward a gathering storm and ascends to myth.

Ford was enraptured with his new leading man and, shockingly, didn't hesitate to say so: "What a performance, Toots," he wrote Fonda after they finished *Lincoln.* "You're a great artist."

Ford hadn't seen anything yet.

He promptly slotted him into his next picture, *Drums Along the Mohawk,* opposite Claudette Colbert. It's a more conventional part in a more conventional picture, but it works for Fonda, perhaps because it involved some aspects of his family history — the Fondas were originally Dutch settlers who settled in upstate New York. As Devin McKinney wrote, "All that ties the film to a pioneer's pain is Fonda . . . the flat surface of a deep man."

The locations for *Drums Along the Mohawk* were in a remote part of Idaho thousands of feet above sea level — twenty-eight days of shooting with no place to go. "John Ford was smart enough to know you could get rock happy there after a while," Fonda said. Ford had the crew move some big logs into a circle around the camp fire. "Twenty to thirty foot logs, and [we'd] sit on them and there was entertainment every night."

Fonda was put in charge of said entertainment. There were comic sketches, somebody would play the guitar, and Fonda, Ward Bond, and a couple of other men worked up a barbershop quartet. At the end of every evening, Ford would have someone play "Taps." Ford seamlessly created the atmosphere of a summer camp where they happened to be making a lavish Technicolor adventure movie during the daytime. "We became such a family that you cried a little bit [when it was over]," Fonda remembered.

The picture's climax was a long chase scene as Fonda is pursued by Indian warriors for miles on end as he races across the wilderness toward reinforcements. Ford didn't shoot the chase as a self-contained segment, but in short bits and pieces during the month of location work. "Every now and then, where we happened to be, he might say, 'Here's a hell of a spot for a run-through.' So he'd holler to wardrobe, and I would be changed into another costume. I would be filmed jumping over a log, and then the Indians would come and then I'd change back to my other wardrobe and continue the other scene."

Fonda was learning how crucial the attitude of a director was to filmmaking, not to mention in stimulating the creativity of the actors. Ford's sense of community marked him as different from Henry Hathaway, "who yelled a lot," but who was also

a sensitive man. On *The Trail of the Lonesome Pine,* [Hathaway] would come to me and Beulah Bondi and use some words that would get both of us so excited about playing the scene, more than we had thought of when we learned our lines.

Henry King [who directed *Chad Hanna*] didn't have that quality. . . . He was not a great director, but he was a big picture director. He was so involved with flying that I could say to Slim Summerville, "Watch this. I bet I can stop production for 45 minutes." A plane would go over, and I'd say, "Henry, what is that?" and he would stop and talk about that airplane and the size of the motor and the kind of wings. A nut about flying. It was Henry King, not Ford, not [William] Wellman, Henry King who said about John Carradine that he could "ride in a buggy in the whip socket." It wasn't like Henry to say amusing things, but this was the funniest comment he ever made.

Drums Along the Mohawk was successful, but *Young Mr. Lincoln,* lost more than $100,000. Neither Ford nor Darryl Zanuck cared: this young man had a special quality that needed to be cherished and developed.

Ford invited Fonda into his social circle, which revolved around Ford's yacht *The Araner.* At Ford's right hand was John Wayne, and below him were characters like Ward Bond, a warm, expert character actor universally regarded as not very bright but genuine and somehow endearing — Ford's version of the class clown.

Fonda was not a heavy drinker, but he liked Ford, he liked the *Araner,* he liked to fish, and, like Ford, he didn't particularly like Hollywood. For Ford, that was enough; Hank was accepted as a member in good standing of a loose — very loose — confederation. There was serious drinking interspersed with serious fishing, mainly bonitos, dorados, and marlin, which Ford admired for their strength, endurance, and beauty.

One Christmas Ford and his friends took a cruise to Mazatlán, complete with a Christmas tree in the salon, but the primary purpose of the trip was drinking, as was attested by a waggish captain's log Ford kept by hand:

1:18 pm. Went ashore — got the owner, Fonda, Wayne, and Bond out of jail. Put up a bond for their behavior.
9:30 pm. Got the owner, Fonda, Wayne and Bond out of jail again. Invited by Mexican officials to leave town.

The next day, usually designated for hangover recovery by lesser men, was more of the same:

Owner went to Mass — brought priest to Araner — purpose to sign pledge [to give up drinking]; pledge signed — celebrated signing of pledge with champagne, later augmented with brandy.
Arrived Muertos — great time, 14 hours — 35 minutes. This would never have been possible without the advice and help from Mr. Bond, a great navigator who is

sneaking drinks. Gave lessons on fishing to Mr. Fonda.

Fonda had never encountered a character quite like Ford, but then nobody else had either. "He cast actors if they were good [card] players," Fonda would say with wonder. Damned if the card players didn't turn out to be good actors.

For Hank and Jim, these years constituted a time of of constant pleasure. Sullavan and Hayward were living at 12928 Evanston Street in Brentwood, a block or two away from the house where Jim and Johnny Swope were living. Hank and his new wife were within a couple of blocks of Sullavan, Hayward, and Jim.

The feelings Stewart had for Sullavan were always contained, perhaps because Fonda's feelings for Sullavan were always raw. Stewart may not have known that Swope also had fallen for Sullavan, and she may have fallen right back. Swope saved some notes from Sullavan, brief, scrawled sentences ("Where did you go in the middle of the night?") that indicate the relationship may have gone beyond the speculative.

Swope's function within the group was to document the good times. In 1936, he sent out a Christmas card that showed various permutations of Fonda, Stewart, Logan, and Swope celebrating, arguing, playing the accordion with airplane goggles on. In the corner of one shot were Fonda and Frances, with Hank blowing a celebratory trumpet. It is highly doubtful that Stewart or Fonda would have posed for such pictures without the encouragement and kinetic personality of Johnny Swope to egg them on.

"John would extract a little more gregariousness out of them," said Mark Swope. "Stewart and Fonda could get together and not say a word, and have a fine time just being in each other's company. But my dad wasn't constructed like that. He would charge up the room."

They were all having a great time, going to parties, gala premieres, two young men about town and their recently married pal. "They were as close as friends can possibly be," said Mark Swope. Once, someone asked Fonda what he was thinking about in the moments before the director said "Action!" It turned out to be a laundry list of actor's issues, any one of which was enough to provoke extreme anxiety. Mark Swope wondered how Fonda could live like that, and then he realized how important Jim and his father were to their friend.

One party in particular stood out in their memories — a gala birthday party for William Randolph Hearst that Marion Davies threw in 1937. "She asked everybody to come in the Spirit of Seventy-six," remembered John Swope, "so we decided to come as the Marx Brothers. We went down to Western Costume and rented the uniforms and the equipment. . . . We rehearsed and decided how we were going to make our entrance. All the time we were rehearsing . . . I'd say, as Harpo did, 'I chase blondes!' "

As the boys were getting dressed for the party, they would take a sip of their favorite libation for every new piece of clothing. By the time they got to the party, they were lit up like a night game at Yankee Stadium. They made their entrance marching around the room playing the fife and drum, with Swope as Harpo, Fonda as Groucho, and Stewart as somebody other than Chico — he looked just like Jimmy Stewart, but then he always did.

"I saw this blonde," said Swope, "so I just dropped the drumsticks and went and wrestled the blonde to the floor. [When I got back to playing] Fonda leaned over to me and said, 'Well, you dumb son of a bitch, that was Marion Davies!' "

It was a momentous evening in all sorts of ways. Jim had already perfected what Josh Logan called a way of protecting himself "so that he won't get locked up with any woman" — always cordial and attentive, never emotionally naked. He was listening to someone talk about how rude it was of Norma Shearer to wear one of her costumes from *Marie Antoinette* to the party. Shearer was wearing her MGM makeup, and the MGM hairdressers had done her hair, while everyone else was just having fun playing dress-up. Stewart had had a crush on Shearer since boyhood and was standing up for her when he turned around to find her gazing at him. "You're gorgeous," he blurted out.

"From then on," said Josh Logan, "she followed him everywhere he went."

Marion Davies was not one to hold a grudge about either Shearer or the boys from Brentwood; she gave them second prize for their efforts, while awarding first prize to Hearst.

Jimmy Stewart was a peculiarly innovative actor, but because he was so apparently casual and unprepossessing people took his originality for granted. "Jimmy had the same effect on pictures that Marlon Brando had some years later," Cary Grant said. "Jimmy had the ability to talk naturally. He knew that in conversations people *do* often interrupt each other and that it's not always easy to get a thought out. It took a little while for the sound men to get used to him, but he had an enormous impact. And then, some years later, Marlon came out and did the same thing all over again — but what people forget is that Jimmy did it first."

Jim was stealthy in other ways too. He might have been from a small town in Pennsylvania, but he had an attitude about women that verged on the sophisticated and could be encapsulated in two words: enjoy them.

The affair with Norma Shearer came during her Merry Widow period after the death of Irving Thalberg. Josh Logan estimated the affair lasted six frenetic weeks, during which "she took royal possession of him."

Jim traveled in her limousine to restaurants and screenings. Shearer gave him a gold cigarette case sprinkled with diamonds so he would always be able to give her a cigarette when she asked for one. "The long, shy, former architecture student was shuffling and stuttering his way through the gaudy glamour of movie city," was the way Logan put it. It was a glimpse of Hollywood from heights so lofty he could never have imagined them, and it began to show.

Stewart began to talk like a stockholder instead of an actor; he would dismiss a movie because "it won't make a nickel," which made Josh Logan irate: "How could you change so quickly from a man of ideals? You sound like a crass distributor who can only think in picture grosses." The argument led to a temporary estrangement.

As far as Stewart was concerned, all other romantic relationships were short-circuited when he made *Destry Rides Again* with Marlene Dietrich, who began the picture by calling Jim "that mumbling baby-faced beanpole." A few weeks into the movie, Dietrich had changed her tune. "Stewart has something. I don't know exactly what it is, but there is something so sweet about him."

Stewart was less circumspect. "After a week's work on the picture, I fell in love with her. She was beautiful, friendly, enchanting and as expert at movie acting as anyone I'd ever known. The director, cameraman, cast and crew felt the same way. We all fell in love with her."

Once, during a close-up, Dietrich instructed him in how to handle problems of focus. "You're trying to look me in the eyes, but you're trying to look at both my eyes with both your eyes — which is impossible. Always look at the downstage eye and it keeps your eyes from going off, photographically."

Dietrich instructed him in other ways as well. One thing led to another, and Marlene got pregnant. Fifty years later, Dietrich's daughter Maria Riva would assert that Stewart was informed of the situation on a dance floor in Hollywood and that he walked away without a word. It was a response that might have militated against the two ever working together again, but they did, on a rather good movie called *No Highway in the Sky* in 1951. The pregnancy was quickly terminated, but not before word got around town. By then, Jim had moved on to a serious relationship with Olivia de Havilland.

According to a close friend of de Havilland's, she knew about the affair with Dietrich and the pregnancy. Nevertheless, by the middle of 1939, she was falling in love with Jim and thinking about marriage. She even accompanied him and Hank as they headed out to Lake Mead to experiment with a new permutation of their favorite hobby: radio-controlled model airplanes.

John Swope would occasionally go along for the ride, and his photographs of the two men with their heads bent low over their planes confirm that they were very serious about play, although not so serious that they couldn't enjoy the sight of de Havilland's shapely body as she bent over to get into the car.

But there was something bothering de Havilland that came to a head when Stewart escorted her to the New York premiere of *Gone With the Wind* on December 19, 1939. As the limousine proceeded down Broadway, they passed a theater playing *Destry Rides Again,* which had opened at the end of November. The sight of the marquee for the Dietrich picture dampened what would otherwise have been an exultant mood for de Havilland.

It crystallized her realization that, if she married Jim, she would always be no better than the third woman in line. It wasn't Dietrich that was the problem — that was a fling, plain and simple, easily dismissed. The problems were, respectively, Margaret Sullavan and Jim's mother. It had become obvious to de Havilland that Sullavan had him wrapped tightly around her little finger, and enjoyed having him there. Jim would invariably drop everything to attend to her emotional needs, which were incessant. De Havilland could put up with Jim's devotion

159

to his mother — she was, after all, two thousand miles away — but not to Sullavan, not to another actress.

Beyond that, there was the question of Jim's essential diffidence, his way of preserving his core for himself. Burgess Meredith understood perfectly: "The main thing about Jimmy's relations with women, including Olivia, was that it was very, very difficult to light him up. They were there or they weren't there. He could always show them a good time, but it was never the center of his universe to do so."

Stewart's explanation of the breakup with de Havilland was typically evasive, not to mention unemotional: "I had to stop going with Olivia because I never could say her name right when I had to introduce her."

Burgess Meredith had replaced Fonda as Jim's roommate. He lived in New York and stayed with Stewart and Swope when he came west to make a movie, and when they needed to be in New York, they stayed with him. When Meredith was having an affair with Paulette Goddard that preceded their marriage, Jim and Swope would obligingly clear out of the house for the evening. Meredith had a more turbulent personality than Stewart, but they got on well because Meredith was cheerful. He particularly enjoyed

Jim's habit of finishing a meal, then assisting the digestive process by pulling out his accordion and serenading his companions.

Jim wasn't much more forthcoming with his roommates than he was with the MGM publicity department. "He was a press agent's nightmare," remembered Meredith. People who judged Jim as a country bumpkin, a more articulate version of Slim Summerville, found that the truth was diametrically opposed to that image. Stewart may have taken a long time to get a story out, or to cross the street, but he got things done, albeit at his own speed.

Meredith came to admire Jim's discipline, his attention to detail, his expertise in handling money, and the sense of detail that would also be a primary feature of his characters. Before Jim took off on even a rudimentary Sunday afternoon flight, he put his aviator's maps down on the living room floor and carefully studied his route. "Anticipation," he told Meredith, "that's the key to flying. The only other thing you need is luck."

By this time, Jim had logged over three hundred hours in his Stinson 105 two seater. His feeling for flying was not unusual in its articulation, but it was in its passion: "You're like a bird up there. It's almost as if you're not part of society anymore. You have a feeling of real power up there — that we human beings aren't really altogether helpless, that we can be completely in control of an amazing machine, that we do have some control over our destiny. And, of course, it's the only place where one can really be alone."

Stewart was hungry for a deeper immersion in flying. He got it when Leland Hayward started up an outfit called Southwest Airways. Johnny Swope was the treasurer, and Jim contributed some capital, along with Hank, Cary Grant, Brian Aherne, Hoagy Carmichael, and producer William Goetz. Swope plunked down $15,000 of the money on a patch of land near Phoenix. More money was spent on converting the weeds into what Hayward called Thunderbird Field, which gradually spawned Thunderbird Field II and Falcon Field nearby.

Years later, Leland Hayward estimated that this particular caprice lost something in the vicinity of a million dollars. On the other hand, Thunderbird Field trained thousands of pilots for World War II, and served as an occasional film location as well. Southwest Airways cut some of its losses after the war by operating a successful commercial route between Los Angeles and San

Francisco. Hayward and his investors cashed out in 1958, when the company was sold and renamed Pacific Airlines.

Meredith found that Jim was a man who circled carefully before coming to a final conclusion. When the boys went to a play, Swope and Meredith would be chattering about the show's success or failure at intermission, but Stewart would contemplate things for an hour or two after the performance before coming to a final judgment, which was rendered with finality in a sentence or two. "He likes to chew his cud a little before he talks," was the way Maggie Sullavan described his thought processes.

Ah, Sullavan . . . If Jim knew exactly what he thought about movies or plays, he was always slightly tongue-tied when talking about Sullavan. "She was wonderful. Very special," is an unhelpful sample of his accumulated wisdom on the subject. On the other hand, he was quite articulate about Dietrich's savvy and helpfulness. "She knew the camera and knew what lighting was right for her. She knew it so well that she could look up before a scene, and say, 'Would you move the key light up about two inches?' They'd look at each other and say, 'Geez, she's right!' "

These were busy years for Hank and Jim,

but also for John Swope. He had found a place within the artistic Hollywood community, straddling both the movie and photographic worlds, and was regarded as a full-fledged talent, as well as a full-fledged character.

Swope commandeered the darkroom of the *Life* photographer Peter Stackpole for *Camera Over Hollywood.* "Once you got to know Swope you learned to expect the unexpected," said Stackpole. "He'd drive a weather-beaten old convertible and arrive wearing old clothes. If he'd arranged to use the darkroom, he'd be in there for hours on end until the phone rang for him. I'd have to call him, then suddenly the darkroom door burst open and John would shout down the hall 'Who is it?' so loudly that it would cause the person on the other end to start speaking before he reached the phone.

"Something was bound to happen causing some consternation, but you never knew what or when. He'd take my wife flying at the Santa Monica airfield and ask her to let him know if she saw any planes getting too close. What was he supposed to be doing?" Another time, when Stackpole was flying with Swope, Johnny put the plane into a falling leaf dive while singing a Strauss waltz. There was nothing to do with Johnny but hang on and hope that he knew what he was doing.

When *Camera Over Hollywood* was published in 1939, it proved a kaleidoscopic portrait of his adopted town that echoed the observational power of Nathanael West's *The Day of the Locust.* There were ninety-six images in all, loosely organized by theme: "Introduction to Glamour," "The Studio — A World in Itself," "The Paths of Glory."

Swope reinvents himself every couple of shots. A close-up of a showgirl with her face locked in a laugh that might be a scream segues to other images that are pure Walker Evans — an elderly matron walking by a sign that says "SEX: Expose the Flesh," or an extra washing out her laundry in the sink of a mean little apartment. Other images seem like takes on Dziga Vertov, and some are straight photojournalism, for example, W. C. Fields and Mack Sennett on Oscar night, 1938.

Swope's proximity to Hank and Jim bore fruit in some charmingly intimate candids that were interspersed with his predominantly constructivist approach — Stewart lying on a couch cracking nuts while reading a script; Stewart and Norma Shearer in a canoe during their brief dalliance; Stewart

165

and Olivia de Havilland lying on the grass napping with a phonograph by their heads; Fonda playfully blowing a trumpet while Frances embraces him.

The overall effect is heightened, clamorous; you can almost hear the tumult. The volume's importance as a record of the early Hollywood years of Hank and Jim pales besides its importance as a documentary portrait of the Hollywood studio system at high tide, a world that, as Graham Howe wrote, involved "very real people . . . in the business of creating an elaborate unreality."

By 1938, Fonda was not only a father, he was a homeowner. The house on Monaco Drive in Pacific Palisades was a few doors from the home of Sullavan and Hayward, which couldn't have made Frances feel very secure. When Fonda wasn't working, he was prone to what his daughter would call "Protestant rages," which seem to have centered on a terminal lack of patience. "Dad was so emotionally distant," Jane remembered, "with a coldness Mother was not equipped to breach." Fonda felt that the first several years of the marriage were "beautiful years in our lives," but after that things got rocky.

Perhaps as a means of extracting attention

from her husband, Frances slowly became a hypochondriac. By the time they moved away from Sullavan to nine acres of land located at 600 Tigertail Road, in the hills above Sunset Boulevard, Frances was swallowing less food and more pills. In 1940, she entered the Scripps Clinic in La Jolla for three weeks in the hope that her pyramid of symptoms could be alleviated.

The property on Tigertail — so named because of the way the street wound around the mountain — was originally owned by Alphonzo Bell, the founder of Bel-Air. Fonda paid $27,000 for the land, and another $80,000 to build the house, which was customized to look as much like an old Pennsylvania Dutch farmhouse as possible, with an accompanying pool and playhouse.

Fonda set to work cultivating the land, and built a chicken coop and rabbit hutches. He used the eggs from the chickens and also grew his own vegetables. Over the years he would add numerous dogs, including a Dalmatian, a Great Dane, and a Kerry blue that liked to intimidate the other dogs.

The land was beautiful and the house was homey, but not quite home. The marriage would increasingly be compromised by Frances's illnesses, which were in turn exacerbated by Fonda's stony silences.

When he would retreat, Frances would plead, "Talk to me, Hank, tell me what I've done wrong. Say something, anything." He wouldn't respond, would just walk away.

If the Capra pictures of 1938 and 1939 constituted Jimmy Stewart's breakout, then 1940 was the year that he solidified his hold on the public and the industry. Besides his performance in Lubitsch's *The Shop Around the Corner,* there was his romantic role in Frank Borzage's *The Mortal Storm,* also opposite Sullavan. And then came *The Philadelphia Story,* which finished shooting in mid-August 1940, and made Jim the most in-demand young leading man in Hollywood.

Before the next round of picture making, he sandwiched in a trip to Texas that August to raise some funds for England's solitary fight against Nazi Germany. Accompanying him were the usual suspects: Hank and Margaret Sullavan. In Houston, Stewart and Fonda did an impromptu magic act, then played a duet, Jim playing the accordion, Fonda hacking away at the cornet.

In September, Stewart began shooting *Come Live with Me* for MGM, *Pot o'Gold* for United Artists, and for several weeks that overlapped with *Pot o'Gold, Ziegfeld Girl.*

Success agreed with Jim, although he managed to disguise most of it. There was some tension within his family at what his sister Ginnie regarded as his arrogance. "Jim's spoiled and always has been since he was little boy," she groused in a letter, "but I love him and appreciate his talent so it doesn't matter." Jim had taken a dislike to Ginnie's fiancé, a penniless painter whom he regarded as a phony. This could have been a case of sibling rivalry, or it could have been Jim's latent snobbishness about artsiness that Josh Logan had noticed a few years earlier.

Hank reached his apotheosis simultaneously with Jim. *The Grapes of Wrath* matches actor, character, and directorial approach with a rare precision. John Steinbeck's novel had given the millions of dispossessed a literary dimension and sold 430,000 copies in its first year. John Ford's film gave the story a spare, honest visual representation and became an instant classic without ever quite becoming a commercial hit. Fonda plays Tom Joad as wary, with his temper close to the surface, which is how Ford liked his leading men when he wasn't in a bucolic mood.

Many other actors went after the part, including John Garfield, who was probably

169

disqualified by his New York accent. Darryl Zanuck gave some thought to Tyrone Power, although with what degree of seriousness is impossible to guess. In any case, the part came with a high tariff — Zanuck refused to give Fonda the part unless he signed a seven-year contract with 20th Century-Fox. Fonda swallowed and signed.

Fonda had played downbeat before, in Fritz Lang's *You Only Live Once* and *The Trail of the Lonesome Pine.* In particular, the Lang film is an early example of the paranoid style in American movies — Fonda plays an ex-con, edgy, often angry, and he finds the bad end he's always expected. Fonda disliked Lang and intensely disliked the way he used actors as props for his compositions. But you could argue that *You Only Live Once* gave Fonda the psychological key for Tom Joad. Certainly, Fonda's knack for troublemakers, men who nurture their resentments — a trait with which Fonda was familiar — gave his prairie beauty an undercurrent of pulsing life, as well as that sense of potential danger that every great star possesses.

You didn't have to love Fonda's Joad — he embodied obstinate dissent a little too fully for that — but you couldn't dismiss him. As Andrew Sarris wrote, "The physical and spiritual stature of his Joad is not that of the little man as victim, but of the tall man as troublemaker. His explosive anger has a short fuse and we have only his word for it that he is tough without being mean."

No other actor could have played Tom Joad as well. During the location work around scrubby Pomona and Needles, Ford came to a full understanding of the core of Fonda's gift: do less, suggest more. The two men didn't talk much; they didn't have to. Each of them understood the story and Tom Joad on the cellular level. Ford felt that the Okies were the dispossessed equivalent of his Irish forebears, while Fonda's sense of moral injustice formed the bedrock of the performance, and of his acting life.

Fonda carried the weight of Tom Joad for the rest of his professional life; Tom's integrity as filtered through the actor playing him would be recalled time and again, usually to the benefit of both picture and actor.

It was the part and the performance of Henry Fonda's life, and he knew it. Woody Guthrie saw the film in its New York run, and composed "Tom Joad," his ballad version of the story and the man. "Tom Joad" became the centerpiece of *Dust Bowl Ballads,* the Guthrie album that came out in

May 1940 and became an essential document of the period and its people.

That year, Jim Stewart won the 1940 Academy Award for Best Actor for his well-played but conventional part in *The Philadelphia Story,* historically regarded as a make-good for being overlooked for *Mr. Smith Goes to Washington* the previous year. Fonda would confide that Stewart fully expected to win an Oscar for *Mr. Smith,* and went so far as to prepare an acceptance speech. Unfortunately, Robert Donat played spoiler and got the award for *Goodbye Mr. Chips.* Leland Hayward wrote Fonda that Stewart was "stricken for weeks afterward that he hadn't won."

As happy as he must have been to get the Oscar, Jim knew his pal had just gotten one of the royal shaftings in movie history. "I never thought much of my performance in *The Philadelphia Story,*" Stewart would say. "I guess it was entertaining and slick and smooth and all that. But *Mr. Smith* had more guts. Many people have suggested that I won it as a kind of deferred payment for my work in *Mr. Smith.* I think there's some truth in that because the Academy seems to have a way of paying its past debts. But it should have gone to Hank that year."

Still, a win is a win. The night of the

Oscars, Jim stayed out all night roaming around Hollywood, accepting the town's congratulations. When he finally got back to Brentwood, he woke up Burgess Meredith to show him his Oscar.

"Look what I won," said Stewart.

"So you've been to Ocean [Amusement] Park again," Meredith groggily replied.

Word got back to Indiana, Pennsylvania, so Alex Stewart called his son. At 5 a.m., West Coast time. ("My father never had any time sense," Jim observed.)

"I hear you won something," Alex said. "Now explain to me here what exactly did you win? Is it a plaque or a medal? Or what kind of thing is it?"

Jim wearily told his father that it was a statue, gold-plated and heavy.

"A statue? So that's what it is. Well you better send the damn thing back here and I'll keep it for you in the store."

Jim dutifully sent the Oscar east, where Alex displayed it in a bell jar on top of the knife counter in the hardware store for the next twenty-odd years.

Just to prove that life not only isn't fair, but piles on, Charlie Chaplin got the 1940 Best Actor award from the New York Film Critics for *The Great Dictator*. Hank didn't seem to care all that much — his infrequent satisfaction in his own work was reward enough. He hadn't bothered to attend the Oscar ceremony, opting instead to ship out with John Ford on his yacht and fish for marlin off Mexico.

"I was too embarrassed to go," Fonda explained. "If I'd won, I'd have been speechless. If I'd lost . . ." He was just following Ford's lead. Ford won six Oscars, and always contrived to be someplace else the night of the ceremony.

When they were both old men, Jim would confide that he had voted for his friend Hank for Best Actor over himself, as he should have. He then pointed out that he had also voted for Alf Landon, Wendell Willkie, and Thomas Dewey.

After *The Grapes of Wrath,* Hank became friendly with John Steinbeck and they stayed close for the rest of the writer's life. "My impressions of Hank," wrote Steinbeck, "are of a man reaching but unreachable, gentle but capable of sudden wild and dangerous violence, sharply critical of others but equally self-critical, caged and fighting the bars but timid of the light, viciously opposed to external restraint, imposing an iron slavery on himself. His face is a picture of opposites in conflict."

Part of that conflict was Hank's fury over

the seven-year contract with 20th Century-Fox. Fonda respected Walter Wanger, but he didn't particularly like Darryl Zanuck, and the fact that Zanuck had leveraged one desirable part into a seven-year deal never ceased to irk him. Zanuck wasn't any crazier about Fonda than Fonda was about him. Years later, casting for Zanuck's production of *The Sun Also Rises* was proceeding when someone suggested Fonda for the part of Jake Barnes. "Fonda has no sex appeal," Zanuck snapped. "The women will stay away in droves if we take him." Tyrone Power got the part.

The only other picture Hank did for Fox that he liked was William Wellman's *The Ox-Bow Incident,* which, he would invariably point out, Zanuck had to be harassed into making. He acknowledged that Zanuck would occasionally lend him out for something of quality — *The Male Animal,* which, for inexplicable reasons, Fonda liked, or Preston Sturges's magnificent *The Lady Eve.*

Ah, *The Lady Eve.*

Sturges originally wrote the script ("CLOSE SHOT — AN ANNIHILATING PAIR OF FEET AND ANKLES WITH SOME LEG THROWN IN") with Claudette Colbert in mind, but she dropped out and Madeleine Carroll dropped in. The

prospective male lead was either Joel Mc-
Crea or Fred MacMurray. Sturges thought
Carroll would be all right, but he wanted
better than all right: he wanted Barbara
Stanwyck. "I told him that I never get great
comedies," said Barbara Stanwyck, "and he
said, 'Well, you're going to get one,' and, of
course, he followed through."

Sturges settled on Fonda for the male
lead, while Paramount, with incomparable
obtuseness, preferred Brian Aherne. Sturges
refused to consider anyone but Fonda, and
Paramount spent the money to borrow him
from Fox.

Fonda plays the terminally befuddled
scion of a famous brewing family ("The Ale
That Won for Yale") who runs afoul of a
father-daughter pair of con artists on a
cruise ship. Hank might have been taking a
page or two from his long-ago portrayal of
Merton of the Movies. Like Merton, "Hopsie" Pike is a dope. Decent, sweet-natured,
but a dope nonetheless, preoccupied to the
point of obliviousness, his eyes revealing a
vast, empty plain. He's a herpetologist and
has been up the Amazon for years in search
of rare specimens. "Snakes are my life," he
tells Stanwyck, who gazes at Fonda as if he's
an ice cream soda on a scorching day.
"What a life," she says.

There's a long, delicious scene that captures Hopsie's mortal fear mingled with arousal. He's resting in her lap, she tousles his hair. He looks petrified, but something is stirring that feels good, and he doesn't try to flee. Stanwyck kept breaking up at Fonda's expert wobble between fear and desire, but what he brought to every well-written part was the ability to play more than one thing at a time — the more obvious casting of Eddie Bracken would have been limited to a lavish display of comic panic. Hopsie may be the finest in-over-his-head deadpan comedy performance since Buster Keaton. The truly odd thing is that, having demonstrated a mastery of the *genus* dimwit, complete with pratfalls, Fonda would get comedy offers so infrequently.

Sturges would write that he was "scared to death about *The Lady Eve,*" simply because he liked rowdy and he liked pratfalls and he wasn't at all sure that the audience shared his enthusiasm for the mixture of high and low comedy. But the picture flowed. "Barbara Stanwyck had an instinct so sure that she needed almost no direction," Sturges wrote. It was a happy shoot — the actors hung around the set when they weren't on call. Fonda said that Sturges "wasn't a director, really, he was an audience. He'd sit under the camera and spoil take after take by laughing."

Fonda had liked Stanwyck when they worked together on *The Mad Miss Manton,* a mediocre entry in the screwball comedy sweepstakes in 1938, and undoubtedly the film she was thinking of when she said she never got good comedy scripts. But his feelings seem to have deepened on the Sturges picture — there's a hint of something more than a working relationship in his memories. "I adore that woman," he would say. "I loved her then. We had a dream time. . . . Who do I love and admire? Barbara Stanwyck."

Near the end of his life, he would muse that "If she hadn't been married, I think my life might have taken a different direction." Left curiously unspoken was the fact that he was also married, with, by that time, two children (Peter was born in February 1939). Clearly, on some level Frances had become dispensable, at least in theory.

Hank was now matching Jim stride for stride in drama (*The Grapes of Wrath/Mr. Smith Goes to Washington*) and comedy (*The Lady Eve/The Shop Around the Corner*). But fate, in the person of men and forces larger even than Louis B. Mayer and Darryl Zanuck, was about to bring their good-natured competitive striving to a screeching halt. In September 1940, the Selective Training and Service Act, better known as the draft, was signed into law. American men between the ages of twenty-one and thirty-six were compelled to register for the first peacetime conscription in American history. A month later, Stewart was drafted.

When Jim showed up for his Army physical he was rejected because he was ten pounds underweight. Over the years, Stewart insisted that he went home and embarked on a studious regimen of milkshakes and carbs in order to gain the ten pounds. In fact, he did no such thing. As Robert Matzen proved in his book *Mission,* Stewart appealed to a military doctor to write a letter on his behalf stating that his weight was a family trait — not strictly true, as pictures of Alex Stewart attest. The letter went on to state that Stewart was otherwise a shining example of healthy American manhood. That letter, along with the Army Air Corps' pressing need for experienced pilots, overwhelmed niggling objections about weight requirements. He inducted March 22, 1941, almost eight months before Pearl Harbor. Straining at the studio leash was one thing, but breaking the leash in order to get into the service at a time when almost nobody was happy to get in the service but the occasional Englishman and an ardent interventionist like Robert Montgomery was something else again.

But Stewart had issues pressing him toward service. For one thing, Alex Stewart had served in both the Spanish-American War and World War I, and he expected no less from his son. For another, there was Jim's own passion for flying, which he believed would be far more valuable for a nation at war than acting. (The Air Corps was part of the Army and would not become the separate Air Force until 1947.)

Hank and Burgess Meredith threw a going-away party for their pal. They plundered the prop department at MGM for decorations. Rubber snakes and dummies were hung from trees, stuffed alligators patrolled the driveway. There was a sign in front of the house: "Anti-Military Headquarters." A fine time was had by all, but the party was over much too soon. Meredith drove Jim to the induction center.

On April 4, Leland Hayward sent Jim a letter that indicated his own solid connections with the Air Corps: "It looks like you are definitely going to Wright Field (in Dayton?)." He then took time out to chide Stewart for not paying enough attention to him. "You find time to write Billy Grady, and Ginger Rogers gets a fan letter. What do I get? Collect telephone calls. Nevertheless, call me again."

Stewart was in the Army now, and Fonda would undoubtedly have followed in short order but for the man he invariably referred to as "Darryl Goddamn Zanuck."

Zanuck had other plans.

■ ■ ■ ■

WAR

■ ■ ■ ■

FIVE

On the first Sunday of December 1941, the newspapers were full of enticing presents suitable for Christmas. *The New York Times* carried an ad from W & J Sloan that offered crystal seahorse bookends at $3.95 a pair. On the opposite end of the spectrum was a $160.00 coffee table made out of a drum used in the War of 1812 — repurposing! The Liberty Music Shop was promoting the Deluxe Capehart radio-phonograph, which could play up to twenty 78 rpm records, on both sides, for three hours of uninterrupted music. Cheap at $595.00. A more economical method for listening to music was the Emerson "Miracle Tone" table radio, for $34.95. You could listen to the day's football game on that radio, not to mention Sammy Kaye's orchestra in *Sunday Serenade,* an adaptation of Gogol's *The Inspector General,* and a concert with the New York Philharmonic and Arthur Rubinstein.

Long before December 7, 1941, Stewart had gone through basic training, which must have felt pointless for a man who was already a skilled pilot. He had also sat through lectures such as "Why Condoms," "She Could Be a Carrier," and "What You Need to Know About Venereal Disease" — also pointless for a man accustomed to squiring Hollywood starlets.

Stewart had already logged the minimum of three hundred air hours to meet the requirements for his commission. He took his check ride in a 400 horsepower BT-14 basic trainer with Captain Bobby Heilpern. The test consisted of a few takeoffs and landings, some basic air maneuvers, and a simulated forced landing. Stewart passed with flying colors; Heilpern recalled that Stewart was "shy, intense, not much of a talker, and a very competent pilot."

On December 7, Jim Stewart was pulling guard duty as a corporal at Moffett Field near San Francisco. It had not been an easy few months. Nobody was used to seeing a movie star in uniform, and Stewart felt like a caged cat. "You know when I felt really lonely?" he asked years later. "It was when I first entered the Air Corps. . . . I was older than everyone else and on top of that I was a famous movie star; and no matter how I acted, I was treated as an anomaly, and I was automatically apart whether I liked it or not.

"I remember when I first got in I was a private and five of us were sitting in our tent in the rain one day and suddenly someone swung open the entrance and shouted out, 'There he is, guys,' and eight fellows stood looking at me as if I had 16 heads."

He had complained to Colonel George Usher, the commanding officer at Moffett Field. "How can I help you, Stewart, to get off the spot you're in?"

"The biggest help, sir, would be no publicity. No interviews. No publicity stills, no radio appearances."

"I can fix that," said Usher, and with few exceptions, his word was good. There would be many official Air Force stills taken of Stewart on the ground with his crews, but the only meaningful journalism regarding Stewart's flying career was a two-part article by Colonel Beirne Lay Jr., later the author of *Twelve O'Clock High,* in *The Saturday Evening Post* in December 1945. Stewart was never quoted directly but clearly co-operated with Lay. He never spoke about the war in any detail on the record.

At 2:26 p.m. Eastern time, news of the Japanese attack on Pearl Harbor stopped the world dead. The radio networks went into crisis mode and abandoned their scheduled programming, offering up airtime to the president and his government. Military personnel and plane spotters all over America were told to report back to their units. Soon, recruiting messages filled the air. The war Stewart had sensed was coming had finally arrived.

The tally of the disaster included 18 warships sunk or crippled, 188 fighter and bomber planes destroyed, with 159 damaged. Fatalities totaled 2,400, nearly half of them from the battleship *Arizona.* Another thousand were injured. The only possible bright spot was the fact that the Japanese hadn't destroyed any American aircraft carriers, which had been out to sea at the time of the attack.

The Army finally had a use for Stewart, who had heretofore been primarily a show pony. In the chaotic days after Pearl Harbor, he fronted a recruitment short called *Winning Your Wings,* starring "Lieutenant James Stewart," which was released in May 1942. Stewart climbs out of an airplane in a snazzy flight jacket and pretends to be caught unawares by the camera. "Looks like I'm back in the movies again, doesn't it," he says.

The positive aspects of enlisting in the Air Corps are illustrated, including a salary "as high as $245 a month," not to mention the way girls respond to a man with wings on his uniform. The film also communicates a subtle but unmistakable sense of a serious manpower shortage — several times Stewart stresses that no college diploma is necessary for the Air Corps.

The film was hurriedly shot in two weeks and was nominated for an Academy Award for Best Documentary in 1942. More importantly, it was estimated that it helped funnel more than 150,000 enlistees to recruiting offices.

A little over a month after Pearl Harbor, on January 19, 1942, Stewart was guarding a balloon hangar when a lieutenant walked up and handed him a long white envelope — his commission as a second lieutenant.

The commission didn't relieve Stewart's tension — nothing could. "The possibility of damaging a wing tip while taxiing, ground-looping on a landing or some other minor screw-up which would have excited little comment if committed by another instructor gave him nightmares," wrote Beirne Lay. "He couldn't afford to make a single mistake."

But he never really made a mistake. "A

fundamental trait of character helped him," continued Lay. "He was conscientious — deliberately and painfully conscientious. Putting himself in the place of a student was easy because his own frame of mind was that of a student."

Stewart was transferred as a flying instructor at Mather Field, where he stayed until August, then flew at Kirtland Field in Albuquerque until December. He flew students in twin-engine Beechcrafts, but he also learned the vicissitudes of the Norden bombsight and various bombing techniques. Time at Hobbs Field in New Mexico qualified him to fly the B-17 Flying Fortress. He spent the spring and summer of 1943 at Boise as operations officer at Gowen Field.

At this point, the war had been going on for a year and a half and all Stewart had done was train other pilots. He was not a happy man; one of his letters to Margaret Sullavan refers to "goddamn Boise." There was a war on and Stewart was far from the action. He didn't want to train pilots, he wanted to fly bombers. But there was a problem.

"There must be some hitch about your going into combat," his CO told him. "I've got instructions to classify you as 'static personnel.'"

The problem was simultaneously proce-
dural, bureaucratic, and psychological —
movie stars in the service were powerful
propaganda, but if they started getting
killed, or taken prisoner and paraded as
POWs, that good example could deteriorate
in a hurry. So Stewart trained pilots. And
stewed.

Among the pilots he trained was Nick Radosevich, who arrived in Boise for multi-
engine bomber training, which at that point
meant B-17s. Stewart flew with Radosevich
maybe a hundred hours in total. "He was a
super pilot and always very cautious,"
remembered Radosevich.

One day Stewart told Radosevich that the
B-17s "were going overseas," and asked if
the younger man wanted to go with them
or get broken in on the new B-24s. Radosevich asked Stewart what he was going to
do.

"I'm going to stay for the B-24s."

Radosevich decided to stay for the new
plane. To the dismay of both Stewart and
Radosevich, the B-24 proved much harder
to handle than the B-17. "The 17's would
almost fly themselves. However, the 24 was
a hands-on plane that had to be flown at all
times."

■ ■ ■

In July 1943, Jim returned to Hollywood for Johnny Swope's marriage to Dorothy McGuire on the 18th of the month. They had met at a party at — where else? — Leland Hayward's house, where they were introduced by — who else? — Hank Fonda. McGuire had just made *Claudia* and would soon star in *A Tree Grows in Brooklyn, The Enchanted Cottage,* and *The Spiral Staircase.*

McGuire had idolized Fonda since 1929, when he had returned to Omaha for a benefit for the Omaha Community Play-house. The play was James M. Barrie's *A Kiss for Cinderella,* and Fonda thought the thirteen-year-old McGuire was "frighten-ingly talented." After giving some thought to becoming a nun, McGuire opted for the logical alternative of show business, and found her way to Hollywood.

The marriage ceremony took place at the Hayward-Sullavan house in Brentwood. Stewart wangled a pass so he could serve as best man.

Although Swope had been a member in good standing of the Brentwood bachelor household, he settled into domesticity as if he had pined for it all his life.

"Part of the meshing between my parents was my father's tending of my mother," said their son, Mark. "Most actors, if they're not acting, go kind of nuts. They were able to take care of this, as well as his need to take pictures, by traveling. They had the finances, and she loved to fly, and trips kept her mind off those periods when she didn't have a job. She always knew what she wanted. She was structured around her work, and when there wasn't work, she was a fish out of water. She needed work in front of her."

For a time, the Swopes lived in Phoenix, because of greater access to gas during rationing. John wanted to get a sidecar for his motorcycle, but Dorothy let him know that was not what she meant by "travel." Soon, he would join Edward Steichen's Naval Aviation Photographic Unit. After the Japanese surrendered in August 1945, Swope went ashore in Japan, refusing to wear a gun despite possible hostility directed at a representative of the conquering power. He walked around for days, snapping pictures with his Rollei, compiling the profoundly human document he called *Letters from Japan,* observing the Japanese with a sympathy shared by few in the Steichen unit.

While visiting Hollywood for the wedding,

Stewart appeared in the famous group photograph marking MGM's twentieth anniversary. Louis B. Mayer sat centered in the front row, with Kate Hepburn and Greer Garson on either side of him. The six tiers of stars included William Powell, Mickey Rooney, Spencer Tracy, Robert Taylor, Gene Kelly, Lionel Barrymore, Irene Dunne, and Hedy Lamarr (Clark Gable was missing because he was already off to war). Jim looked as if he'd rather be someplace else, even with Maggie Sullavan sitting right next to him.

He did manage to work in some flying while in Hollywood. He was dining at Chasen's, then and for decades afterward his favorite restaurant, when he ran into a test pilot he knew named Jimmy Mattern. He asked if Stewart would be interested in trying out a brand-new P-38 fighter that just happened to be sitting at Mines Field, and the next day Stewart put the P-38 through its strenuous paces.

After he returned to "goddamn Boise," Jim wrote a letter to Sullavan. "I have been to your house so many times — I know it has been so many times because I can remember almost every one of them. I think this was just about the very best of all. Nothing was strange and a little different, like some things were when I left the house. I've often wondered if you know that you and Leland are the nicest things that ever happened to me . . . Love, Jim." Sullavan kept the letter she catalogued as "Letter from Jimmie" for the rest of her life.

Stewart was now openly chafing at what seemed like endless time spent in military backwaters. He had, after all, enlisted with the express purpose of putting himself in harm's way — his father expected no less. Later he would tell a friend that this was most frustrating period he ever faced, but he had made up his mind that he would not ask for any favors or try to pull any strings; he was in the Army, and would play it the Army way. In any case, training fliers was not a chore to be sloughed off; Stewart's roommate was killed when a student trying an instrument takeoff made a mistake. In one week alone, his squadron sustained three fatal accidents.

Stewart took his students up to test three-engine performance, two-engine performance, and one-engine performance. One night he was taking a new commander out and gave his copilot's seat to the navigator, who wanted to observe operations in the cockpit. There was a flash of light and an explosion on the pilot's side; the number one engine had blown up, and Stewart had to get the navigator out of his chair so he could turn on the fire extinguisher, get control of the other three engines, and set the plane down.

But by July 1943, Stewart was too restless to care about decorum or the chain of command. He finally decided to use what leverage he had and went to his commanding officer, who called up Colonel Robert Terrill, commanding officer of the 445th Bombardment Group, which flew B-24s. Terrill was in need of a top-notch squadron operations officer, as the 445th was scheduled to head overseas in about three months. Stewart leaped at the offer and went to Sioux City, Iowa, for a few months, during which he became expert at the B-24. Within nineteen days, he was appointed squadron commander. In the second week of November 1943, Stewart headed for Tibenham, England.

As he began the long — two weeks — trip to England, (the route: Sioux City to Lincoln to Palm Beach to San Juan to Georgetown to Belem to Natal to Dakar to Marrakech to England), Stewart opened a letter from his father.

My dear Jim boy,

Soon after you read this letter, you will be on your way to the worst sort of danger. I have had this in mind for a long time and I am very much concerned. . . . But Jim, I am banking on the enclosed copy of the 91st Psalm. The thing that takes the place of fear and worry is the promise in these words. I am staking my faith in these words. I feel sure that God will lead you through this mad experience. . . . I can say no more. I continue only to pray. Goodbye my dear. God bless you and keep you. I love you more than I can tell you.

Dad

The 91st Psalm reads,

I will say of the Lord, He is my refuge and
  my
  fortress. . . .
His truth shall be thy shield and buckler.
Thou shalt not be afraid for the terror by
  night; nor for
  the arrow that flieth by day;
For He shall give his angels charge over
  thee, to keep
  thee in all thy ways.
They shall bear thee up in their hands, lest

> thou dash
> thy foot against a stone.

On his first night in England, Stewart and his ten-man crew were sitting in a Nissen hut when the traitor Lord Haw-Haw came on the air. "Good evening," he began in his usual tone of braying sarcasm. "Allow me to be the first to welcome the 445th Bomb Group to England."

The men looked at each other uneasily. For Stewart, the real war was about to begin.

The horror of the Omaha lynching Fonda had witnessed never left him, and he badly wanted to make *The Ox-Bow Incident.* So did William Wellman, who bought the movie rights for $6,500 of his own money and was promptly turned down by nearly every studio in Hollywood. All the studios Wellman had made money for listened to his pitch, then maneuvered him toward the door. The only positive response he got came from a producer who suggested he introduce a moment of respite in the otherwise continuously grim story — have Mae West come out and sing a song to all the exhausted cowboys.

Wellman was getting punchy from rejection and briefly considered casting her. Crazier things had happened in Hollywood.

In desperation, Wellman finally turned to Darryl Zanuck, for whom he had worked when Zanuck was running production at Warner Bros. in the early 1930s. They had been friendly, but a fistfight on a camping trip in the late 1930s had interrupted the friendship, and they hadn't spoken since.

Zanuck didn't greet Wellman with open arms — he knew an art movie coming to bite him on the ass when he saw one — but he finally relented. "It won't make a dime," he told Wellman, "but I want my name on it." Lest anyone accuse Zanuck of dangerously infectious idealism, he extracted a promise that Wellman would direct two movies of Zanuck's choosing in return for making his passion project.

Zanuck was always short on leading men, and neither Tyrone Power nor Don Ameche was a likely candidate for *The Ox-Bow Incident*. Fonda was always Wellman's first choice, but the director did his due diligence anyway. He talked to Joel McCrea about the part, as well as Robert Livingston, who was working at Republic doing serials and the Three Mesquiteer series.

While Wellman prepared his film, Zanuck left to go into the service. William Goetz, who ran Fox in Zanuck's absence, tried to scuttle the project, but Wellman wouldn't be diverted. He shot the film quickly — Wellman always shot quickly — for short money. The reviews were better than good, but Zanuck was right about the film's commercial appeal, at least for the initial theatrical run. Years later, the film had a rebirth on television, and has never stopped showing. Both Fonda and Wellman were deeply gratified by the movie's gradually ascending reputation. Fonda was a particularly tough critic of his own performances, and his own career, but he always put *The Ox-Bow Incident* on the list of his good films.

Wellman and Fonda hadn't met before collaborating on the film, and they quickly became friends. Fonda's house on Tigertail Road was only a few streets from Wellman's house on North Barrington, so there was a fair amount of family fraternizing. William Wellman Jr. quickly developed a crush on Jane Fonda and noticed that Jane's mother had a way of absenting herself from social gatherings. She was not in evidence around the house when Hank was the host and never accompanied her husband on his trips to Wellman's house.

"Henry Fonda was not an extrovert," remembered young Wellman, "but my father could work on him until he was acting like a fraternity boy. He could do the same thing with Gary Cooper. When Fonda came over to the house, my father would always put on a record that featured two comedians doing a doubletalk routine, and the two of them would laugh themselves sick. My mother got very sick of it."

Wellman Senior appreciated Fonda for his acting, his sense of humor, and for his strong stomach. "Fonda," he told his son, "is the only man I ever knew who could drink Scotch and eat chocolate at the same time."

Fonda wrapped *The Ox-Bow Incident* on August 23, 1942, then told his wife he was going to enlist in the Navy, possibly because of John Ford's enthusiasm for that branch of the service. Fonda told no one at 20th Century-Fox, probably because he didn't trust them. He drove himself to the Navy enlistment facility and told the officers there that "I'd like to be with the fellows who handle the guns." He would remember that he was "a typical eager-beaver" who wanted to be a hero and kill the enemy. Other people thought there might be a subtler motivation; Jane Fonda would say that "He was genuinely patriotic and hated Fascism, but I think it was also about him wanting to get away."

Two days after filling out his enlistment papers, Fonda arrived at boot camp in San Diego, only to be yanked away by the Shore Patrol. Fox had gotten wind of what their star was doing and buttons were promptly pushed. Fonda's induction would be deferred until he made one more picture, *The Immortal Sergeant,* during which, he would say sardonically, "I won World War II single-handed." Fonda hated the picture, but more than that, he hated being at the beck and call of 20th Century-Fox, or, for that matter, anybody.

The marriage to Frances was now in a rocky phase — on location Fonda launched into an affair that eventually resulted in a paternity suit. "I think everybody in the company was fucking her," he would say dismissively — not exactly a ringing endorsement of monogamy.

It was November by the time he finished *The Immortal Sergeant.* Jane remembered the night when her father finally left for induction.

He had his uniform on. And it was bedtime and I was in bed and he came into my room. And he sang me a song. [He

202

had] a terrible voice. Even worse than mine. And the song went like this:

"My doggy's name is Guess, is
    Guess.
My doggy's name is Guess, and he
Wags his tail for yes, yes, yes.
And he wags his tail for yes."

And he got up and he went to war. And I've never forgotten that because it's the kind of thing he didn't do very often. He was very often an impersonal father . . . so the moments that were really personal and intense meant a whole lot, and that's one of them that I remember.

Fonda entered the Navy as an ordinary seaman, third class. In May 1943, he was ordered to spend sixteen weeks on the USS *Satterlee* training as a quartermaster. Lieutenant Charles Cassell, who was executive officer on the *Satterlee,* remembered that Fonda "had already, on his own, set up shop in one of the ship's offices and was hard at work checking inventory against allowance . . . and beginning the endless task of making corrections. He also checked regularly on shipyard work on the bridge area and took custody of the navigation equipment when it arrived. . . . Fonda *was* the navigation department."

Cassell said that Fonda was a bear for work, but, typically, tended toward being aloof. After the *Satterlee* headed for San Diego, it was discovered that one crewman was missing. Fonda volunteered to stand double watches. When the ship got to San Diego, he had a week's leave for a visit home, then headed for Naval Headquarters on Church Street in New York for officer's training. But that would leave the *Satterlee* two men short, so he volunteered to stay with the ship during its Panama Canal transit on the way to Norfolk.

After being sworn in as a lieutenant (jg) in August, he was ordered to Anacostia to make training films. But he made the case that he would be better positioned in air combat intelligence. He was transferred to the naval station in Quonset Point, Rhode Island, where he learned coding and photo interpretation, among other skills.

In the Navy, as in Hollywood, Fonda was relentlessly focused on objectives. His superior officer wrote that he "demonstrates officer-like qualities of leadership, military bearing, loyalty, judgment and intelligence." He graduated fourth in a class of forty-four, which he said, "impressed the shit out of people," although his tone indicated he wasn't one of them.

At long last, Fonda got his wish for action when he was assigned to the USS *Curtiss,* a newly commissioned seaplane tender that carried 1,195 men and officers. His task was to work as assistant air operations officer in the South Pacific. Before he left, he was given an unofficial briefing and told to bring as much liquor as he could carry, because there was none where he was going. He didn't have to be told twice; he packed fourteen bottles of Old Taylor in a parachute bag, insulated by five changes of uniform.

After New Year's 1944, he transferred to Hawaii for a two-week course in antisubmarine warfare, then was off to the Marshall Islands and the *Curtiss,* which was based at Kwajalein. "It was an awesome sight," he would remember. "The lagoon was enormous and it was filled with battleships and carriers and cruisers and destroyers. That lagoon stretched so far out I couldn't see all the ships."

At that point, Fonda had lugged his parachute bag and its precious contents for thousands of miles, but the process of getting onto the ship broke four or five of the bottles. He and his spare uniforms were both soaked with a combination of salt spray and bourbon, and his quarters quickly took on the smell of a distillery.

It wasn't long before the executive officer confronted him.

"Mister Fonda?"

"Yes, sir?"

"Where's that stink coming from?"

"What stink, sir?"

"Mister Fonda!"

A pause.

"From my laundry bag, sir."

"And where is that?"

"In my locker, sir."

"Are those the only clothes you have?"

"Yes sir, except for the ones I'm wearing."

"Mister, we can't have the ship smelling of Kentucky bourbon. It's not only against Navy regulations, it'll make the damn crew thirsty as hell. Understand?"

"I do, sir."

"Then strip to the buff and I'll send a hand for your laundry. We'll have it done right away."

"Yes, sir."

Fonda's feelings about the war and his place in it were encapsulated in a letter he wrote to his sister:

Can you barely remember Grampa Fonda swinging his Indian clubs and talk-

206

ing about the Civil War? I can, and I have been thinking it just now while I sit stupidly in front of this machine. Thinking about your children and Harriet's children and my children and when we were children and trying to recapture our childhood impressions. Grampa's war was all drummer boys and carrying messages to the General on horseback.

What am I going to tell my children? Maybe by the time Prudence has a few young ones waiting to get the word from great uncle Henry, I will have thought of something that won't make me throw up.

He wrote individual letters to his children. To Peter:

I think about working in the garden and having you working beside me — and every now and then you will say to me, "Daddy, I'm a good boy." And when I go down the hill to the stable you call out to Mackie, "Mackie, I'm going with Daddy!" So you see I think of myself as being at home when I think of you — and I forget that it must be hard for you to realize how far away I am. . . .

I am living on a big ship, and we are anchored in the harbor of an island way across the Pacific Ocean — this island was held by the Japs until a short time ago. I don't mean to give the impression that I took it away from them by myself — there were quite a few Marines that helped me.

He went on to describe his living quarters and told his son that the walls were covered with pictures of Peter and Jane and their mother. "I know there is no good in my trying to explain to you why I am away from home — war doesn't make any sense even when you are grown up — but I think that some day you will understand why I had to be in it."

He took a similar tack with Jane, thanking her for sending him a big envelope. He told her that even though he was busy, his curiosity got the best of him "and I asked everybody to stop fighting the war long enough for me to go to my room and open the envelope."

He found that his daughter had sent him a red, white, and blue hat box holding a licorice kiss, an orange kiss, some green mint candy, and a candy Easter egg. (His letter was written in October, but he wasn't about to complain about the late delivery.)

And then he opened some papers that

turned out to be drawings, one of which was of a woman standing next to an incinerator and crying because her husband had gone off to war.

Nobody would believe that I had a daughter who could draw like that — and when I told them that you could swim, too, and play the piano and went to Brentwood Town and Country School — they said "You mean Brentwood Town and Country School Hooray!" and I said yes — and we all sang two choruses and the Japs couldn't understand why we were singing and so they ran faster.

Six

The Eighth Air Force flew out of England. The work of the Eighth was divided between B-17 Flying Fortresses, and B-24s, known as the Liberator. The B-24 was the most modern plane in the American arsenal and carried a heavier bomb load and had a greater range than its sister ship. Yet the B-24 didn't inspire much affection, because function had decisively trumped form. The fuselage was square, it had a stubby nose and large twin vertical stabilizers that gave the plane an ungainly look. B-24 crews referred to it as the Banana Boat, the Flying Brick, the Pregnant Cow, and the Agony Wagon.

Preceding Jim in his journey to England and combat had been Clark Gable, who had enlisted at the age of forty-one because of what was generally believed to be a death wish — his wife, Carole Lombard, had been killed in a plane crash while selling war bonds. Gable was a gunnery officer assigned to the 351st Bomb Group, but because that unit hadn't started operations he was temporarily handed off to the 303rd Bomb Group.

Gable's first mission took place on May 4, 1943, on a flight to Antwerp. "He . . . spent quite a bit of time with us," said a staff sergeant named John Ford — not the film director. "At the officer's club one evening he was teased quite a bit and fed a bunch of Irish whiskey."

Gable left the club late, but not as late as Ford, who was walking down the road back to his quarters when he heard a voice. "Won't someone help me back to my quarters, please?" Ford looked into a ditch and saw Gable in a sodden heap. Ford helped him out of the ditch and got him back to his quarters safely. Gable flew only five missions as a gunner when MGM's rising panic caused him to be reassigned to make a training film called *Combat America*. The film didn't emerge until the war was over — undoubtedly Stewart's worst nightmare.

Stewart had landed in the middle of serious jurisdictional squabbles. There was a lot of PR about friendly relations between the Americans and the English, but the reality was quite different. Air Marshal Arthur

Harris, since February 1942 the head of the Royal Air Force Bomber Command, was regarded as an irascible egomaniac by his own peers, and he was particularly scathing about the Eighth Air Force.

Harris was convinced that a scorched-earth bombing offensive would succeed to such an extent that a land war against Germany would be irrelevant. Unfortunately, precision bombing was impossible at night, so competition for daytime bombing slots was intense. When the Eighth landed in England, it brought the Norden bombsight, which testing indicated could drop a bomb down a chimney from 25,000 feet in daylight. This, claimed the Americans, was the secret to strategic bombing that could be devastating without slaughtering civilians, not to mention American and British aviators.

As far as Harris was concerned, this was ridiculous. The British had tried daylight bombing and casualties were too high. Harris wanted the Americans to join with the British on massive night raids against city centers, but that would negate the value of the Norden bombsight. In 1942, this had been an academic debate, because the Eighth didn't have enough planes to mount anything but small raids across the English

Channel; most American planes were being sent to the Mediterranean for the invasion of North Africa. Harris's air force could mount raids encompassing a thousand bombers.

Harris was also fighting for land. The Eighth was taking East Anglia airfields away from British squadrons, which meant the British had to fly return routes that were more dangerous than routes the Americans flew. Harris wanted the East Anglia airfields for his own planes.

For his part, American General Hap Arnold thought the English were incapable of thinking in terms of global strategy; in his view, they simply chased "the next operation," whatever it happened to be.

A further complication was that a lot of people didn't think the American strategy would work. Many of those people tended to be English, such as Peter Masefield, the air correspondent for the Sunday *Times* of London. Masefield was a pilot and had flown sorties with the RAF, and he didn't believe that either the B-17 or the B-24 could do what they were supposed to do. "American heavy bombers . . . (are) not suited for bombing in Europe," he wrote. "Their bombs and bomb-loads are small, their armor and armament are not up to the standard now found necessary and their speeds are low. . . . It would be a tragedy for young American lives to be squandered through assigning either Liberators or Flying Fortresses to raids into the Reich night or day."

Masefield was reflecting more than a touch of xenophobia; while it was true that the American planes couldn't carry payloads as large as some of the British planes, they were more accurate and more rugged. He was reflecting the wounded pride of England's military and political leadership about precision daylight bombing raids: If the RAF had failed to successfully bomb Germany by day — and they had — how could the Americans succeed?

By January 1943, the Americans had worn Prime Minister Winston Churchill down, at least slightly. "Young man," he told the American Brigadier General Ira Eaker, "you have not convinced me you are right, but you have persuaded me that you should have further opportunity to prove your contention."

A more unified approach to a joint bomber offensive was decided on when President Roosevelt and General George Marshall agreed on the need for both day and night bombing of Germany. The first American raid on a German target took place in January 1943, when fifty-nine bombers attacked the port at Wilhelmshaven. Arthur Harris set as his goal for 1943 the devastation of Bremen, Kiel, Duisburg, and Wilhelmshaven.

The continual jostling and lack of any real communication led to one British observer saying that the Americans were "loud, bombastic, bragging, self-righteous." The provost marshal of the Eighth reported that a lot of the Americans had a "Limey complex" that made them indifferent to the English unless sex was involved.

All this led to the prevailing English attitude that there was nothing wrong with the Americans except that they were "oversexed, overpaid, overfed and over here." The English seemed to take serious offense at what they regarded as the American propensity for bullshit. Dirk Bogarde, at the time a second lieutenant in the British Army specializing in intelligence, thought that English impatience was a bit over the top: "Intolerance of each other bred suspicion," he wrote. "We lived together in a state of discreet discourtesy . . . a pity; because we could have done well in the future peace. Really well, not diplomatically well."

In the spring of 1943 the Eighth was still

constructing a viable organization — numerous bases for maintenance of the planes, which meant a transoceanic supply system, as well as larger airfields, solid runways, and large depots.

Losses were already considerable. From the beginning of 1942 to the early part of 1944, a crewman in the Eighth stood about a 50 percent chance of being shot down. It got worse; in 1943, as the Eighth was bulked up by delivery of new planes, an American flier had only one chance in three of surviving his allotted twenty-five missions.

But in spite of all these obstacles, the tide began to turn in the latter part of 1943, as more American planes rolled off the assembly lines, while others were reassigned from other areas. The increase in matériel mandated a corresponding increase in recruitment, as each B-17 needed a support group of thirty-eight men on the ground. By December 1943, the Eighth had 283,000 servicemen and civilians, and nearly 1,630 heavy bombers stationed in England. And that was necessary, because in October of that year the Eighth had been directed to speed up its assault on German targets marked "essential," in order to soften up the enemy for the invasion of Europe, code-named Operation Overlord and scheduled for May 1944. For the Eighth, the war was growing more intense.

The Eighth was divided into three air divisions, each consisting of three or four combat wings, which in turn were comprised of three groups of thirty-six planes each. Each combat wing had its own tactical headquarters. A bombing mission could include as many as 1,200 bombers. "Formation bombing like that was brand new," remembered Stewart in one of his exceedingly rare comments about the war. "Nobody had ever really done it before on that scale. . . . Each B-24 could carry more than two tons of bombs, and we had to fly awfully close to each other, and, at the same time, awful close to our escort planes."

The B-24 Liberator was 66 feet long and 18 feet high and had a 110 foot wing span. It carried a crew of up to eleven and had ten .50 caliber machine guns, four Pratt & Whitney 1,200 horsepower engines, and 18 gas tanks that held 2,750 gallons of fuel. The bomb load was 8,800 pounds — two tons more than the B-17 Flying Fortress.

The plane was considerably more imposing than the crew accomodations at the bases, which consisted of concrete slabs supporting corrugated half circles that housed six men, with a latrine behind the hut. Huts for officers were similar in construction but slightly larger, housing eight men. In either case, there was a small pot-bellied stove for heat and lots of blankets to ward off the chill that the stove never quite dispelled. Crews usually outfitted their huts with radios and some shelves for pictures and books.

Stewart buckled down to his job with typical focus — total effort all the time. When the wing communications officer gave a talk about radio aids, Stewart sat through it twice. When he was finally assigned his first combat mission, in the third week of December 1943, he was introduced to the London press at the Eighth Air Force Officer's Club. A woman reporter told him that he looked sunburned, at which point John Hay Whitney, who was a colonel on the public relations staff for the Eighth, rose and said, "It is my pleasure, ladies and gentlemen, to present to you Captain Stewart."

The questions were just about what he had expected, and what he had hoped to avoid. What was it like to kiss a movie star? Did autograph seekers bother him? Would he return to Hollywood after the war and make more movies?

For his first mission, Stewart led a twelve-plane formation at 27,000 feet to Kiel, Germany. A smooth bombing run, no problems, no losses. After that came a mission over Bremen, with the same results. Stewart's piloting abilities were apparent — he was "thorough, deliberate, unspectacular and conscientous."

In March, he led a run to Brunswick, when he was faced with a tough decision. He had been ordered to bomb the target visually, and if the primary target was obscured by clouds, to bomb a secondary target using radar. The weather forced him to choose the latter option, but coming in he felt he was off course. There was heavy flak about four hundred feet to his left, and Stewart had a hunch that that was where he was supposed to be. The decision came down to whether he should let his bombs go and miss his target by half a mile, or circle around and relocate his planes right into heavy flak.

Stewart quickly made an executive decision: go for the second run. Circling around took nearly eight minutes, and his plane plowed through the heavy flak to release its bombs. Damaged but intact, all the planes made it back to England.

During March, April, and May, he led bombing missions to Berlin, Oberhofen, Siracourt, and Troyes without encountering any major problems. He was one of the few who didn't, in April alone, the Eighth Air Force lost nearly four hundred bombers.

It was the mission over Troyes that won him the permanent respect of his men. The assigned target was a railroad yard, and before they got there Stewart realized they were 10 degrees off the assigned heading. He told his navigator and bombardier, but they both insisted they were on the right course. Stewart was talking to the navigator when his deputy tried to tell him he was heading for an entirely different railroad yard a few miles from Troyes. Stewart was on the intercom and didn't hear the message, so he dropped his bombs on the wrong target. Back at the base, Stewart took the fall; he and he alone was to blame for the mistake. No alibis.

There were other mishaps, but Stewart's luck held. A bombardier named Jim Myers flew with Stewart on many missions. He remembered a bombing run over Stuttgart when one of the shells from a German 88 flak gun tore through the underside of the B-24, passed through Stewart's seat, between his legs, and out the top of the plane.

"When we landed, he was blue from the cold whistling through the holes in the plane, but he hadn't received a scratch," said Myers.

The day before a mission, there would be a 4 p.m. conference of key personnel during which weather would be discussed, and which targets were likely; target folders would be checked; fighter escort planned; calculation of the number of bombs in the number of aircraft would be set; axis of attack, rendezvous points, routes in and out, altitudes, and so forth. After that there was a second briefing at the airbases of the different bombardment wings, with a briefing for commanders and crew that lasted about two and a half hours. Separate meetings were then held for pilots and copilots, navigators and bombardiers, gunners and radio operators At the end of all the meetings, watches were synchronized.

A typical mission began at 4 a.m., when a staff sergeant woke up the officers. At the briefing, an officer would pull back a curtain in front of a huge map of Europe. Colored ribbons ran from the base in England to the targets for the day. The longer the ribbon, the more dangerous the mission. At 8 a.m. the final decision to proceed or abort was made, depending on the weather. If the mission was a go, the crew picked up their parachutes and gear and were trucked to their planes. "The flight surgeon came out to the line before takeoff," one pilot reported, "and gave us some kind of amphetamine if we had flown the day before."

Getting in the air on the runways in East Anglia was always a near thing. Clouds over England were invariably thick up to 23,000 feet, so until then most planes flew on instruments. After the clouds broke up, the planes would gather in their formation. Until then, radios were tuned to the BBC, so the crews could listen to Vera Lynn singing sentimental love songs. "It somehow didn't compute to be hearing . . . love songs reminding us of girlfriends and family," said Bernard Jacobs, "and be heading into combat. It was like a bad dream."

Stewart developed a knack for laconic understatement. One pilot remembered meeting him for the first time. "Well, fellows, we are sure glad to see you guys," Stewart began. "Glad you're here with us. You know — you fellows are — uh — replacing one of our fine crews that hit a water tank on landing approach last week. You fellows will just have to be more careful, you know?" His trademark as a leader was to always remain in the control tower until the last crew returned from their mission.

On Christmas Eve 1943, Stewart briefed his crews on their mission for the day, to Bonnières, France. "The Germans have some kind of — uh — it's a new rocket machine they've cooked up. They are going to use it to hit London and a lot of other cities over here in England. We have to stop them before they go that far."

The mission entailed flying at only twelve thousand feet in order to insure maximum accuracy of the bombs. Stewart then announced that the mission was voluntary. "Anyone who doesn't want to go on a Christmas Eve mission does not have to go. You can just get up and walk out now. Nobody will hold it against you. But — I'm going. Fellas, you can count on that. I intend to go along." No one left the room. Stewart continued the briefing.

The Army Air Corps was dotted with men who would become powers in show business. The future director Robert Altman was copiloting B-24s in Borneo and the East Indies. Walter Matthau was a staff sergeant and gunner in the Eighth, and Norman Lear was a radio operator and gunner on B-17s in the 15th Air Force out of Italy. Lear was a scrounger who liberated enough bricks to serve as a floor for his crew tent, not to mention six bomb bay lights to brighten up an area that had made do with just one. He also repurposed a couple of P-51 wing tanks into fuel and water tanks, and acquired headsets tuned into Armed Forces Radio for each bunk. Overall, Lear's crew tent was the envy of the base.

Matthau flew only four missions, after which he taught instrument takeoffs. He enjoyed attending Stewart's briefings and noted how the other men were initially thrilled to see a movie star, but gradually forgot about all that because Stewart so easily wielded the authority of a born commander.

As he settled into his role, it became clear that Stewart was typical of the command structure of the Eighth, which was largely made up of men from business and professional backgrounds. There was a corresponding emphasis on process and managerial practices. According to a manual on tactics, commanders had an obligation to "work out each mission in minute detail. The struggle here is of the life and death variety."

The popular image of the Allied Air War is of pristine planes raining death down on the Nazis with an air of clinical detachment, but the reality was quite different. If the payload was hit by any one of the anti-aircraft missiles, the men would be shredded.

The vast majority of the flight crews were young: between eighteen and twenty-five years old, many between eighteen and twenty-one. Almost nothing of what they were told in training prepared them for what they would encounter in actual combat. For one thing, neither the B-17 or the B-24 had heat. Flight temperatures could descend to thirty below zero, which made a serious dent in the comfort level of the crew, despite their thermal clothing and the plug-in electric heat in their flight suits. If the wire broke — and it often did — the crew had to function in frigid cold.

That was bad enough, but there were other problems. The long flight time for missions, as much as eight or nine hours for a round trip, meant that exhaustion could set in. Adrenaline couldn't be counted on for such a long period, so amphetamine use was common.

Someone once asked Robert Altman what flying a B-24 was like. "It was cold," he said. Besides that it was loud, "like a steel foundry." Wind blew through the cracks, the gun turrets, and the bomb bays. Altman wasn't particularly scared because he was fatalistic by nature — he always believed he was going to die. It was only when the war was over that he realized he had to start taking life seriously. Altman flew nearly fifty missions, consumed with competing feelings of invulnerability and an underlying realization that death was never more than a split second away.

Stress was off the charts. In 1943, the Eighth lost 8,800 men in combat and 2,000 from noncombat accidents. Officially, the maximum number of missions was twenty-five, largely for psychiatric reasons. The reality was, as one historian wrote, "most crew on a tour of 25 or 30 operations died before they reached their total." One of the reasons for the disconnect between the English and Americans was the laissez-faire attitude the English had toward their fliers. An RAF flier named John Wooldridge flew 108 missions. After the war, when he wrote a film based on his experiences, he reduced the number because he thought — correctly — that no one would believe it possible.

Climbing into a bomber before a mission, knowing the odds, demanded either massive bravery or an unlikely degree of psychological detachment. Before the planes took off in the morning, there were always a few men who had to throw up. Some of them were officers, some of them were enlisted men; some of them were veterans, some of them were first-timers, but they were all united by the way they processed fear.

One flight engineer tallied twenty raids, the last of which involved the death of the rear gunner, whose body caught fire. The engineer grabbed an ax and hacked off the flaming parts of the gunner's body so the flames wouldn't spread. The slipstream from the hole in the fuselage blew what was left of the gunner out of the plane. The plane crash-landed and the engineer survived, but had to be permanently laid off combat duty.

Bailing out of a damaged aircraft was at least as dangerous as staying. Bodies without parachutes were regularly seen falling from burning planes, men pulling their heads to their knees in a death spin while they fell through bomber formations. Some German pilots machine-gunned American flyers floating down to earth, while others would salute and fly on. If you did make a successful parachute landing, there was a good possibility of being murdered by German civilians.

The crucial element was learning to live

with the fact that you and your crewmates could be highly skilled, do everything right, and still die. Survival was a question of preparation only up to a point. After that, luck took over. It was luck that determined whether or not a plane had a mechanical failure that made it vulnerable to enemy fighters or sent it slamming into another bomber; it was luck that determined whether or not the trajectory of a plane's flight path intersected with a random burst of flak or an antiaircraft shell.

What plagued Stewart most was not fear of death, but fear of failure — of screwing up a mission with a bad decision. "Fear is an insidious and deadly thing," he remembered. "It can warp judgment, freeze reflexes, breed mistakes. Worse, it's contagious. I knew that my own fear, if not checked, could infect my crew members. And I could feel it growing within me."

Stewart remembered his feelings before a mission over Nuremberg, thinking of "all the things I had to do, all the plans I must remember for any emergency. How could I have a clear mind if it were saturated with fear?" Some conversations took place, some didn't. The crews never talked about the odds. "We all prayed a lot," said Stewart. "I didn't pray for myself. I just prayed I wouldn't make a mistake."

The most you could hope for was a feeling of wonder at having survived one more mission, one more day. Jack Valenti, later assistant to President Lyndon Johnson and later still the head of the Motion Picture Association of America, was a bomber pilot with the Twelfth Air Force. He reminisced about the "brutality and the danger and the absolute inhumaneness of an air war. My experience was that the men, including myself, were frightened out of our minds all the time, but we did our jobs anyway. Churchill was exactly right: 'There is no greater exhilaration than to be shot at and missed.' "

When planes returned from a mission, "four finger shots of Irish or Scotch whiskey" poured into water glasses were given by the medical officer to anybody who wanted it, which was nearly everybody. Some men developed a taste for terpin hydrate — basically cough syrup with codeine. A couple of swallows would give you a high. Some crews flew two or three days in a row; some of them flew as many as a week's consecutive missions, which got you a pass for London.

On the ground, things were quieter but still resolutely uncomfortable. Everybody was cold all the time. The potbellied stoves were fueled by coke, but the stoves were too small to heat the huts. Besides that, the men were issued only enough fuel to keep the stoves lit for a few hours each day. Most of the crews would burn their ration between five and seven in the evening, which meant the forecast for the rest of the night was chilly, slowly turning frigid.

As far as Stewart was concerned, the temperatures were a close second to stress. He was always cold, especially his feet. Alex sent various gimcrack inventions meant to keep the cold at bay, among them plastic-lined gunny sacks that Jim would fill with hot water and place around his mattress.

Some of the men in the flight group had the same problem but had no plastic sacks to help relieve them of the cold. They resorted to stealing coal from a communal pile guarded by English caretakers. This was a minor problem that Stewart dealt with by indirection.

One of the men, Robbie Robinson by name, remembered that

Jimmy Stewart came into our hut one night, walked to the end of my bunk by the potbelly stove, sat down and took his shoes off and said, "Fellows, I just don't know how ya'll keep a red hot stove. It is

230

always red hot when I come in here. I've just got to get my feet warm. I can never get them warm in my hut."

Almost burning the bottom of his socks, he got them warm. Then said, "Ah! That feels so good." He put his shoes on, stood up looking at his feet and walked out, saying, "Goodnight, fellows." We all wondered if he was trying to tell us not to steal so much coal from the Limeys' coal pile.

Some time later, Stewart walked in and once again warmed himself before the same hot stove, then strolled over to a pile of cots. He lifted up a blanket, revealing a beer keg. He got a canteen, removed the cup, opened the spigot on the keg and poured a ration of beer. He sat down on a bunk, heaved a sigh, and drank the beer. "Well, this black English beer is pretty good — if you can't get anything else. Right?" He helped himself to another cup, while informing the men that a keg of beer had been stolen from the officer's club a few days before. "Ah — you guys hear anything about that?" he asked.

Stunned innocence was the order of the day. Nobody knew anything.

"I thought not."

Replacing the cup, he pulled the blanket back over the keg, tucked it in very neatly so the keg couldn't be seen, once again complimented the men on the warmth of the stove, then said he was sure they didn't have a thing to do with stealing a keg.

It was a scene from a Jimmy Stewart movie, but Stewart was one of those lucky men who didn't have a large gap between who he was and who he pretended to be while acting. "Somehow he always made me feel that he was my friend," said one of his men. "I knew when I had ten missions, Jimmy had flown five of them alongside or near me. He had a great feeling for all of us. You felt it when you were around him. Even when he was trying to give you hell for something you deserved, he got his point over without hurting you deep inside."

One Eighth Air Force crew member named Mel Schulstad said that the emotional key to survival in the Air Corps was simple: "You keep on going because the other guys are going. And if they're going, you're going. It was a fantastic thing the way we came together as a group of people. We didn't know each other from Adam's . . . ox when we came together, but by the fourth or fifth mission we were blood brothers. You would do anything to keep your crew alive and well and happy. And you'd stay with them through hell and high water.

And you did."

Those men who needed more than blood brothers, who were in danger of collapsing with a nervous breakdown — or "flak phobia" as it was called — were sent to one of seventeen rest homes the Air Corps contracted. They tended to be hotels or converted estates or manor houses, where men would stay for a week or two in a stress-free environment until their hands stopped shaking.

Stewart's own estimation of this experience was typically laconic: "Everybody's scared. You have to learn to handle it."

SEVEN

As a naval intelligence officer in the South Pacific, Henry Fonda spent the last year of the war hopscotching through islands whose names were on everybody's lips in 1944 and 1945, and which few have thought of since.

In the days after Pearl Harbor, the American war effort was reeling; the Japanese took out America's air wing in the Philippines, dismissively trounced a bunch of World War I–era American ships at the Java Sea, destroyed overmatched garrisons at Guam and Wake Island, then took Bataan and Corregidor in the Philippines.

Admiral Chester Nimitz devised a strategy he called Calculated Risk, which stated that the American Navy would go into battle with Japanese ships only if they had a good chance of inflicting more damage than they sustained. The American Navy simply didn't have the ships to cope with a war of attrition.

The tide turned with the Battle of Midway in June 1942, where the Japanese lost two cruisers, three destroyers, and four aircraft carriers, not to mention 322 planes and 3,500 men — devastating losses. (The Americans lost the carrier *Yorktown,* a destroyer, and more than a hundred planes.)

After that, the Navy began a strategy of island-hopping, with Allied forces striking at weaker Japanese installations and severing supply lines that ran to heavily fortified positions. The war in the Pacific was a series of brutal battles in the air and in unspeakable heat in the jungles.

Among other refugees from Hollywood serving in the South Pacific was the MGM star Robert Montgomery, who was commanding PT boats at Nouméa and Espiritu Santo. Montgomery's experiences would lead to his being cast in John Ford's great film *They Were Expendable.* Ford had been at Midway, photographing the battle with his 16mm camera, footage that was used in his film *The Battle of Midway.* "I have never seen a greater exhibition of courage and coolness under fire in my life," Ford remembered. "I was really amazed. I thought that some kids, one or two, would get scared, but no. The Marines with me . . . they were kids, I would say, from 18 to 22, none of them were older. They were the calmest people I have ever seen. They were popping away with rifles (bolt-action .30 caliber rifles). None of them were alarmed, I mean, a Japanese bomb would drop through and they would laugh and say, 'My God, that one was close.'

"I figured then, if these kids are American kids, I mean this war is practically won."

The Solomons were taken in February 1943, and in the Central Pacific Admiral Nimitz sliced through the Gilbert Islands and captured the Eniwetok atoll by February 1944. "The route we were carving out became the Broadway of the Pacific," Fonda remembered. "It began in San Francisco, went due west to Hawaii, then on to Kwajalein, Eniwetok, Guam, Saipan, Tinian, Iwo Jima and Tokyo."

Fonda worked feverishly, almost obsessively. One shipmate said that "our doctor has had to order him to take it easier." His only recreation was writing letters to his children in which he told charming, fanciful stories about a goldfish named Wilbur. The stories were handwritten, and illustrated with Hank's beautiful watercolor sketches of tropical fish — a preview of coming artistic attractions.

At all times, Fonda was highly conscientious. In late 1944, an air patrol sighted a Japanese sub. Fonda got the report and quickly began alerting the naval forces in the area. Climbing down a ladder, he stumbled and cut his head, but, as his commanding officer, Captain Harry Cook, reported, Fonda completed his duty and "only then did he get to sick bay for treatment."

After the *Curtiss* moved to Eniwetok, general quarters was sounded with alarming frequency. Despite that, Fonda went to battle stations only a few times. As the Pacific fleet launched campaigns against Guam, Saipan, and Iwo Jima, the *Curtiss* moved with them. The Japanese retaliated with kamikaze attacks.

In December 1944, the *Curtiss* was off Saipan when Tokyo Rose broadcast that the American actor Henry Fonda was on board one of the tenders. She promised that the Japanese would sink the ship and send Fonda and the rest of the men to the bottom of the Pacific.

In June 1945, the *Curtiss* put into Guam, and Fonda and his cabin mate went ashore for liberty. On June 21 the *Curtiss* was struck by a kamikaze off Okinawa — the final rush of the Divine Wind that the Japanese hoped would save their country. The plane hit the ship's starboard side, exploding a half-ton bomb. It took fifteen hours to get the fires under control. The sick bay, officer's mess (including Fonda's quarters), pantry, and library were destroyed, while fires almost detonated the ship's own magazines. Thirty-five men died, twenty-one were wounded.

After that, there was another kamikaze attack, this one a near-miss that was shot down and crashed only twenty-five yards from the ship. The next day, Fonda and a couple of sailors climbed into diving gear and swam down to the plane, thirty feet below the surface. The pilot and the bombardier were still strapped into the overturned plane, and Fonda remembered all his life how the heads and arms of the dead Japanese shifted slightly with the current. Fonda then recovered maps, flight plans, and other documentation.

After studying the papers, Fonda figured out that the planes were being launched from Pagan Island in the Marianas, which led to American air strikes against the island. The kamikaze attacks stopped.

At the beginning of August, Fonda and his air operations officer flew to Tinian, where they met with the crew of the *Enola Gay*. Fonda would say that he did not know precisely what the plane was carrying, but realized that it had to be something significant. Just how significant became clear when the *Enola Gay* dropped the atomic bomb on Hiroshima on August 6, 1945. Days later, Nagasaki met the same fate.

On August 15, Fonda was working in the communications hut when everybody began shouting. Japan had surrendered. Fonda didn't believe it at first, but when the hut emptied out he sat there smoking a cigarette and carefully looked over the dispatches. It was then that he realized that the war was over.

The day after the surrender was announced, Henry Fonda was awarded the Bronze Star with the following citation:

For distinguishing himself by meritorious service in connection with operations against the enemy as an assistant operations office and Air Combat Intelligence Office on the staff of Commander Forward Area Central Pacific and Commander Marianas from 12 May 1944 to 12 August 1945. He contributed materially to the planning and execution of air operations which effectively supported the Marianas, Western Carolines and Iwo Jima Campaigns, neutralized enemy installations on nearby enemy held islands and atolls, and which subsequently developed into search missions in Empire waters and strikes on the Japanese mainland. His keen intelligence, untiring energy and conscientious application to duty were in a large measure responsible for his successful contribution to the Central Pacific campaign.

When Eighth Air Force crews weren't in the air or in their huts listening to Lord Haw-Haw, they engaged in the nefarious activities common to young men in small groups. "We had a point . . . when Tibenham must have had the highest percentage of clap in the Air Force," remembered Lieutenant Howard Kreidler. "One time there was a picnic, and you'd see these guys disappearing one after another into the bushes where the hookers were. It wasn't as bad in our crews as elsewhere, but Jimmy put an end even to that by making a little speech and then marching everybody over for shots."

For recreation on his days off, Stewart and Kreidler would go into Tibenham and rent a thirty-six-foot wooden boat outfitted with a radio just in case they were called back to the base. Once, they were flying to London on a pass, but the fog got thick and Kreidler flew so low that they could see the hedges on the lawns. Finally, Stewart said, "Doc, there is absolutely nothing in London that I have to see so bad that I'm going to let you kill both of us for seeing, so let's get back." As always with Stewart at war, the tone was calm, with a lack of emotion.

Stewart went off the reservation only once, when he took a B-24 for a four-hour joy ride. It was late April 1944, the run-up to D-Day. Stewart got the plane up to about one thousand feet when he told his copilot, "My former group commander always has his nap about now. Let's go wake him up!" Stewart buzzed the base, then said, "Well, that will wake him up. Now let's get him up again."

The control tower was naturally perturbed, demanding name, rank, and serial number. "I could make those operators get out of that tower," Stewart muttered, just before he zoomed around the tower. One more dive, and the three operators could be seen scrambling down the stairs. Once he landed, Stewart tried to explain to his irate commander that "We had a chance to fly and were momentarily carried away with the exhilaration."

Years later, Stewart recalled that his acting training came in very handy during the dressing-down, as he had to portray a man who was grief-stricken at his own failings, when in fact he wasn't even slightly upset. Stewart was reprimanded, but that was all. He knew that, on some level, what he had done was necessary.

In May 1944, Stewart was awarded the Distinguished Flying Cross for a mission he had led over Germany on February 20. As the citation read, "In spite of aggressive fighter attacks and later heavy, accurate antiaircraft fire, he was able to hold the formation together and direct a bombing run over the target in such a manner that the planes following his were able to release their bombs with great accuracy. The courage, leadership and skillful airmanship displayed by Major Stewart were in a large measure responsible for the success of this mission."

By this time, the B-24s that Stewart had been flying were being supplanted by the B-29 — a giant leap forward in technology. The B-29 carried the largest bomb load of any plane and had a longer range — sixty tons of destruction that could fly for sixteen hours even when fully loaded. Not only that, the crew compartments were pressurized so they could fly in something approaching comfort, without awkward heated flying suits and oxygen masks.

St. Clair McKelway, a writer for *The New Yorker* who was working as a public information officer for the Twenty-first Bomber Command, noticed the different attitudes that the fliers had for their planes. "B-24's and B-17's seem to excite an affection, a good-humored familiarity, in fliers and mechanics. I have seen people kick B-24's and B-17's on the tail, or under the belly, and say, 'Well, you were all right today, you old bitch . . .' Ground crews . . . leave unrepaired minor bits of battle damage that give the airplane a scarred, tough look but do not interfere with flying efficiency."

By contrast, "The B-29 crews want their airplanes to look new and shiny all the time. The B-29s are silvery, without camouflage paint of any kind, and the crew laboriously smooth out tiny wrinkles on the exteriors and polish the silver skins far beyond necessity."

The pace of bombing in preparation for Operation Overlord stepped up. Missions were almost evenly divided between bombs and leaflets, the latter warning about the former. On March 22, 1944, Stewart led the wing on a bombing run over Berlin. A week later he moved to the 453rd Group stationed at Attleborough, a few miles from Tibenham. The base was called Old Buckingham, but the men called it Old Buc. Attleborough was near the North Sea between Cambridge and Norwich in East Anglia and it was cold, possibly colder than Tibenham.

Colonel Ramsey Potts, Stewart's commanding officer at the 453rd, remembered that "Jimmy Stewart was a very good B-24 pilot; he had a steady hand and a natural feel for piloting the aircraft. His greatest strength, however, was in his ability as a combat leader. Stewart led many dangerous and difficult missions . . . and, in the heat of air battle, he always maintained a calm demeanor. His pilots had absolute faith in him and were willing to follow him wherever he led."

The 453rd had recently lost their commander as well as their operations officer, and was suffering from sliding morale. Stewart became the new operations officer. He was highly regarded for his succinct but comprehensive briefings, as well as his habit of flying alongside the men, if only to insure that formations were satisfactory. His attention to detail soon began paying dividends. "Morale was unusually high," said Captain Bob Bieck, one of the lead pilots, "and much of it was due to a very down to earth Jimmy Stewart." Casualties began to decline almost immediately, and one day Stewart came out of his quarters to find his jeep had been painted with the words "Death Takes a Holiday."

When Stewart wasn't flying, he had to hang around the base, simply because if he went to town he would be mobbed. "He was so popular with his fans," said bombardier Jim Myers. "The Piccadilly Commandos [prostitutes] would have really nailed him if he had gone off the base into London."

The result was that he would have a few drinks at the officer's club at the base. After he started to relax, he'd move over to the piano and play the black keys, usually show tunes culminating in his pièce de résistance: "Ragtime Cowboy Joe." It was part of his repertoire of reliably atrocious songs (another favorite was "The Wolf of Creek Pass") that a friend had taught him when they were boys.

Stewart's crews noticed that while he talked about all sorts of things, he never talked about the movies. For that matter, Stewart was not always the easygoing guy of Hollywood lore. One of the men attached to the unit said that Stewart showed a ripping temper. He could handle the chewing out process in a blistering top-sergeant-like tirade. There was the time a first pilot, who was constantly late for briefings, came slinking in and tried to slip into an empty seat. Stewart stopped the briefing and gave the pilot a tongue lashing, pulling no punches. He was mad. The crews had never seen this side of Stewart. He laid the pilot out, sparing no words, enumerating the responsibilities of a pilot and officer — one of them being never to be late for the briefing of a mission. And, using the pointer, Major Stewart said, "You owe it to your crew, and you owe it to yourself."

He was determined to prove that he was more than an actor, more than a Hollywood star. He was determined to prove that now he could measure up as a man doing a really important job in the military crucible and not just a celluloid hero.

By June 1944, Henry Ford's Willow Run plant near Detroit was turning out a B-24 every sixty-three minutes, and the entire German transportation system was teetering from the pummeling the planes were administering day and night. Germany diverted two million workers to air defense operations, more than the entire workforce of the German aircraft industry.

Bombing runs had destroyed most of the

transportation network of France, from railroad yards to bridges and barges and roads — anything that could move hostile troops to fight the invasion. From February to June 1944, the Eighth slammed the Germans with a relentless air war. Besides doing as much damage as possible on the ground, the goal was to establish absolute air superiority by destroying the German air force, bases, and supplies. "If you see fighting aircraft over you," Eisenhower told his troops before the invasion, "they will be ours."

On June 3, Stewart was promoted to lieutenant colonel. Two days later, every briefing room in England was tense as the plans for D-Day were outlined. Stewart conducted three briefings that were typically matter-of-fact and unemotional. On the morning of D-Day, the 6th of June, warning leaflets were dropped encouraging the Normandy population to "Leave for the Fields! You Haven't a Minute to Lose!"

Beginning at 3:30 a.m., the 453rd flew four missions over Normandy. Each plane dropped fifty-two 100-pound antipersonnel bombs. Stewart flew one of the missions. At 6:28 a.m. the bombing run ceased. Two minutes later, the invasion of Normandy began.

The general air of struggle began to change after D-Day, as attrition and exhaustion finally wore down the German ability to defend their airspace. Gasworks and water networks were blown, and life for the German population at large began to spiral down.

A couple of days after D-Day, Nick Radosevich, who had learned to fly the B-24 with Stewart in Boise, completed his thirty-second mission by blowing up a bridge south of Paris. When Radosevich's plane returned to base at Old Buc, Stewart was waiting for the crew in his jeep. "This is it for you guys," he said, as he drove them to their final debriefing. "You're all done."

Stewart was still flying at the end of the year, often as flight leader. "I just can't sit here and send these fellows to death without knowing myself what I am sending them into," he told his squadron adjutant. Most of the targets were plants in occupied France and Germany that produced matériel for the war. Donald Toye, one of his pilots, wrote in a memoir that "We had faith in him. . . . That is to say, we found our targets, released our bombs with good effect and returned home safely."

The issue of safety became something of a catchword around Stewart's group, because he had developed a reputation as one of those commanders whom Providence watched out for. Steve Kirkpatrick, a navigator in Stewart's group, said that he was "a damn good commanding officer. . . . I always had a feeling that he would never ask you to do something he wouldn't do himself. Everything that man did seemed to go like clockwork."

Well, not everything. Once, Stewart's plane took a major hit to the flight deck, although he managed to bring the ship in safely. A gunner named John Robinson landed to find Stewart's plane sitting on the runway. The nose was sticking up in the air, and the fuselage at the flight deck was cracked like an egg. Stewart was staring at the damage, undoubtedly wondering just how many of his nine lives he had left. He turned to Robinson and said, "Sergeant, somebody sure could get hurt in one of those damned things."

Stewart's only other near-miss involved a Cub airplane used by staff to hop from base to base. The little plane was nicknamed Fearless Fosdick, after the stern but prodigiously incompetent detective created by cartoonist Al Capp. Jim tried to land Fearless Fosdick in a high wind and the plane flipped over on its back. He was carefully extricated by other pilots, who thought it was the funniest thing they had ever seen. No harm, no foul.

After D-Day, the role of the heavy bombers began to shift; brute domination gave way to more tactical missions. Stewart rose up the chain to become executive officer, operations officer, chief of staff, and wing commander.

Lieutenant General Jimmy Doolittle wrote in his memoirs that "If the war had gone on another month, Jimmy would have become a group commander, which was the most important job in the Air Force. . . . I have always thought him a very special individual." Stewart was promoted to colonel in March 1945, less than a year since his promotion to lieutenant colonel.

In the war's last months, Stewart spent some time in London, at the time the most dramatic, not to mention dangerous city in the free world. Ignoring the V-1 buzz bombs and V-2 rockets, men from the Eighth Army flooded the city on three-day passes, generally taking a taxi to Piccadilly Circus, then spreading out from there. In the theater there was Shakespeare, Shaw, Noel Coward, and Ivor Novello, whose operettas — *The Dancing Years, Arc de Triomphe* — were particularly popular. Stewart generally stayed at the Savoy, going to the theater and entertaining friends.

London was where Americans went for entertainment . . . and sex. Newsboys sold condoms as well as papers. In the evening, St. James's Park, near Buckingham Palace, was the preferred site for open-air sex, where people went at it after first making a feint toward modesty by spreading newspapers over themselves. Prostitutes were all over town, but especially around Piccadilly Circus. There was a little chapel near the Circus, with a sign that said, "If You're Tired of Sin, Please Come In." Someone tucked a card into the edge of the sign that read, "And If You're Not, Call Me at Mayfair 7345."

The war in Europe ended on May 7, 1945. On May 8, Stewart was awarded the Croix de Guerre by the French Air Force, which was eventually augmented by the Distinguished Flying Cross, the Air Medal, and seven battle stars. That same day he was given a commendation from Colonel Milton Arnold, commanding officer of the 2nd Combat Wing, European Theater of Operations:

You have displayed the most intense loyalty and patriotism as evidenced by your own participation on 19 important combat missions and encounters with the enemy in addition to your staff work. Your initiative, sound judgment, personality and sincere devotion to duty has contributed immeasurably to the smooth operation of this Headquarters and the morale and efficiency of the men of this entire Command.

Your keen interest and unselfish devotion to duty has been exceptional and I desire to take this opportunity to commend you for an outstanding performance of duty.

James Stewart left the Air Corps in the late summer of 1945 as a colonel in the service he had entered as a private — the highest rank attained by any Hollywood star who went to war. He had amassed more than two thousand hours of flying time in the B-24.

Between 1942 and the end of the war, the Eighth Air Force put slightly more than a hundred thousand men into air combat. Approximately 41,000 of those men were shot down. Twenty thousand of them died.

Back in Hollywood, Frances Fonda had dealt with the loneliness and exacted a bit of revenge by having an affair with a musician named Joe Wade. He was young, handsome, loved parties, and drank a great deal. Once, he shot a hole in the bedroom at Tigertail. The affair didn't end well. In 1944, when Jane Fonda was seven years old, she and her mother were walking up the driveway when Frances said, apropos of absolutely nothing, "Never marry a musician." It was the only life advice Frances ever gave her daughter.

Frances had taken Peter to see his father's 1940 movie *Chad Hanna*, a Technicolor charmer about a young man who runs away to join the circus, personified by the luscious Linda Darnell. During a scene where Hank was trapped in a lion's cage, Peter became hysterical, ran to the screen, and pounded on it in an attempt to warn his father of the danger.

Frances took Peter out of the theater, calmed him down and explained that the man on-screen wasn't his father, but a man named Chad. When Peter got home, he looked at all the family pictures and wondered how Chad had gotten into them.

Henry Fonda was officially discharged from the Navy on November 11, 1945, after receiving his Bronze Star. Fonda's naval career, the strange disassociation of fighting a bureaucratic war without ever firing a gun, would inform much of his portrait of Lieutenant Doug Roberts in *Mister Roberts,* as would his innate sense of discontent with the world.

In later years, Fonda consistently downplayed his efforts during the war. "I came home with a hangover, and that's all that mattered," he said. Fonda remained in the Naval Reserve until 1953; although he would usually roll his eyes at John Ford's ardor for the Navy, his own affection for the service was considerable. On July 4, 1957, he was living in a rented villa on the French Riviera, near Villefranche. An American cruiser was anchored in the harbor, and Fonda, having stockpiled fireworks for July 4th, decided to treat the ship to his celebration. He set off a rocket from his terrace, in the direction of the ship, and the cruiser responded immediately. Fonda replied, and so did the ship. The triumphant gunpowder conversation went on until Fonda was out of fireworks.

After his discharge, Fonda was sent to Washington to do some broadcasts for the Naval Radio Hour. "I couldn't stand it till I shed those khakis. When I was mustered out, I bought me a white shirt and a charcoal gray suit, and still sporting my crewcut from the service, I went up to New York looking for Jim Stewart."

While Hank was mopping up in Washington, Stewart had gone home back to Indiana, Pennsylvania, where Peter Stackpole did a feature on the hero's homecoming. There was a parade and photos of Stewart taking congratulatory phone calls at his father's hardware store.

There wasn't a lot of variety in Stackpole's shots, and he thought Stewart fishing at an old pond would work well. The only problem was that Stewart was not a fisherman, not at all. Wanting to accommodate Stackpole, he got some tackle out of his father's store, rounded up a friend, piled into a canoe, and went fishing. With an excess of enthusiasm and a lack of technique, he whipped up the rod, the line flew back, and the hook latched on to Stackpole's face, right under his eyebrow.

Shortly afterward, in New York for the first time in four years, Hank and Jim hooked up. Norris Houghton was also there, as was Myron McCormick. The venue was "21," where they stayed until four or five in the morning. Stewart did most of the talking. "It took so long for Stewart to tell a story," said Fonda. "Not just because he talks slowly, but he tells a story with all the embroidery that a story should be told with."

Stewart's pièce de résistance did not involve exploits in wartime London, and certainly not stories of piloting a B-24, but a recounting of his misadventure with Peter Stackpole — Stewart trying to look like he belonged in a canoe, the hook getting stuck in Stackpole's face, the rushed trip to a doctor to get the hook removed. The result was general hysteria. "We were all sliding under the table at 21," said Fonda.

Finally, after years away, Fonda came home for good. He drove to Brentwood School to surprise his kids. Peter was first out, and recognized the family car. He got in and looked at Hank, but he didn't see his father. Instead he saw the man who had been in one of his favorite movies.

"Chad!" Peter exclaimed.

Fonda would tell that story and let it stand for everything the war cost him and his family. "Isn't that enough to destroy you?" he asked.

While Fonda was reestablishing family ties, Stewart stayed in the East, where he and Johnny Swope hovered around the Hayward-Sullavan ménage. It was clear to

Swope that Stewart was still carrying a bright, flaming torch for Sullavan, who had made him godfather to her daughter, Brooke, along with Swope and music arranger Roger Edens.

"He and Johnny were at our house practically every day," said Brooke Hayward. "We had a pool and a badminton court and they would play endlessly. First they would come and swim, then they'd play badminton. We had this huge vegetable garden, acres and acres, with serious groves of oranges and limes and tangerines, and after badminton we would all work in the garden.

"Jimmy was fabulous with kids. He got down on our level. He would come and visit me in my room and cuddle and read me children's books. He loved children, or at least he loved us."

After a few weeks of this, Stewart finally decided it was time to go back to Hollywood and face his future, about which he was ambivalent. He gave the impression that the movie business held about as much interest for him as Indiana, Pennsylvania. Still, there was more promise in Hollywood than anyplace else, and there was also the matter of his MGM contract.

The two men's retrospective attitude toward the war is indicative. Fonda would talk about his war with a sense of detail and an aura of frustration that his experiences were so relentlessly inadequate compared to his expectations. When he was asked where he kept his Bronze Star, he answered, "Peter lost it." Asked if he was upset about that, he said, "No. It meant nothing to me."

Stewart talked in generalities and avoided emotional disclosure, but he came as close to revelation as he ever would when he told one reporter that World War II had been the most meaningful experience of his life.

"Greater than the movies?" the reporter asked.

"Much greater."

■ ■ ■ ■

HOME

■ ■ ■ ■

EIGHT

The war changed everything and everybody.
Even Leland Hayward.

For four years, the movie business expanded exponentially. Even Poverty Row studios such as Republic and Monogram made good profits. The demands this placed on people who sold talent were pleasant but exhausting.

"[Hayward] was forever on the phone, talking to clients or studios," observed Josh Logan. "His bride [Sullavan] began to detest her rival, the telephone. Leland made a quick decision. One day, right in the middle of a conversation, he decided to stop being an agent. He never said it was for his wife; he simply stopped taking calls. And suddenly, presto, he was a New York producer."

It was only marginally more complicated than that. Lew Wasserman was the number two man at the Music Corporation of

America, an agency founded by Jules Stein. MCA's client list consisted primarily of dance bands, which they booked across the country in exhausting but lucrative one-night stands.

Wasserman was friendly with Hayward's associate Nat Deverich, who invited him to their office. When Wasserman walked into his office, Leland was lying on a couch. His shoes were off and he wasn't wearing a tie. He didn't bother to get up.

"Hi," Leland said desultorily. "I haven't got a lot of time. My partner thinks you're a genius. Why don't you join us? We'll give you one-third of the business." Wasserman wanted to know why Hayward was being so good to him. "I hate being in this business," Leland replied. "My wife doesn't like me being in it. I'm bored with it."

Wasserman quickly offered to buy the Hayward agency for MCA. "It was done in an hour," said Wasserman. Just like that, Hayward was out of the agency business. Just like that, MCA suddenly became the largest talent agency in the world, and the most powerful agency in the movie business, all due to Hayward's client list.

Hayward promptly plunged into theatrical production. First up was *A Bell for Adano,* an adaptation of John Hersey's novel, which ran on Broadway for ten months. Then came *State of the Union* by Howard Lindsay and Russell Crouse, which ran for two years and won the Pulitzer Prize for drama. Both shows had lucrative movie sales. On the horizon were Maxwell Anderson's *Anne of the Thousand Days* with Rex Harrison and Irving Berlin's *Call Me Madam* with Ethel Merman. As always, Leland's ambition was limitless — nothing less than greatness would do: "I want to be able to do anything I want to do and spend as much as I want to. I want to knock a home run or strike out."

George Axelrod, who would write *The Seven Year Itch* for Hayward, said that he was more of an entrepreneur than a producer. Axelrod pointed out that there was never a continuing theme or specific style to a Hayward show. Rather, there was ambition, a sense of command and of ferment — a master chef expertly mixing ingredients. "He had a childlike instinct about spotting elements," said Axelrod. "An actor here, a story there . . . and the immense personal charm of a child to put it all together. If he took the trouble to want you to like him, he was irresistible."

Guiding all of Hayward's activities was a sense of intrinsic excellence; he wired Billy

Wilder and told him to read a spectacular new novel called *The Catcher in the Rye.* Not only that, he told Wilder, he thought the same author's "For Esmé — with Love and Squalor" was "the best story I have ever read in my life."

For Hayward, producing was a dream realized; for his clients, there was a sense of abandonment. Fonda and Stewart were not delighted. Fonda got the news via telegram when he was in the Pacific and remembered thinking "Who are [MCA]? And shit, we can be bandied around like baseball players?"

Late in 1945, after more than four years away at war, Jimmy Stewart came back to Hollywood. After the usual round of welcome-home parties, he sat down and tried to remember just what he had been doing in that other life that seemed so long ago. He went to MGM and screened a bunch of his old pictures, and didn't like what he saw. The ingenuousness of the young man on the screen struck him as appalling.

"I couldn't believe what I was watching," he said. "One of them, *Born to Dance,* made me want to vomit. I knew I had to toughen up."

The war had changed Stewart in ways he would never really be able to articulate, one of them being a broadening of what he knew the world to be capable of. The good part of the war for both Fonda and Stewart was that it put show business in perspective; a failed movie or three was not a life-or-death issue, not after you had spent years of your life confronting genuine life-and-death issues.

There was another pressing matter — Stewart's contract with MGM, which had, according to MGM, been suspended while he was in the service. Technically Leland was no longer Stewart's agent, but he would always act as a rabbi for his favorite clients. Leland's take on MGM's position was "The hell you say." Hayward believed that Stewart's contract had expired while he was making bombing runs over Europe. If MGM wanted Stewart back, they would have to ante up.

While public negotiations went on in Hedda Hopper's column, private negotiations proceeded more quietly. Billy Grady told Stewart that L. B. Mayer was willing to forget about the several years left on Jim's contract, and re-sign him for another seven-year deal. Mayer's best offer was $125,000 a picture, one per year, with no profit participation. (MGM didn't give actors a piece of the profits, reserving that for producers.)

Hayward thought term contracts were for dinosaurs or dopes. He had already counseled Gregory Peck to turn down a seven-year deal with MGM in order to stay independent, with the exception of a deal with David Selznick. The way to go, he told Jim, was Cary Grant's route — freelance, with profit participations. Besides, $125,000 a picture was chump change: Jim had won an Oscar, for God's sake.

While Hank and Jim were trying to figure out just where they fit in with the movies, with life, Josh Logan was picking up where he had left off. He had spent the war with Air Force Combat Intelligence, and after getting his discharge, he married Nedda Harrigan Connolly, the young widow of the character actor Walter Connolly. Josh didn't share the becalmed state that was bedeviling Fonda and Stewart; he simply went back to work in New York. His first show back was *Annie Get Your Gun,* which would be followed in due time by *South Pacific* for Hayward — which Josh also cowrote — and *The Wisteria Trees, Picnic, Fanny,* and Paddy Chayevsky's *Middle of the Night.*

Fonda and Stewart rummaged around

Los Angeles, occupying their time by attending parties, drinking, and listening to music. Finally, they decided to give a party of their own — a very special party. The telegrams went out on November 26, 1945:

HAVING RETURNED TO THE RANKS OF THE EMPLOYED WE FEEL IT'S ABOUT TIME WE DID THE SOCIAL TYPE OF THING AND WOULD LIKE YOU TO JOIN US AND A FEW OF YOUR FRIENDS AT THE CLUB ABOUT 6:30 WEDNESDAY, DECEMBER 5TH FOR A STAG EVENING. ALL HANDS WILL FEEL FREE TO GET GASSED. JIMMY STEWART AND HANK FONDA

The guest list consisted of Jules Stein, Lew Wasserman, and about forty members of the all-male contingent that constituted MCA. In fact, the party was a pretext for a convoluted practical joke that Fonda and Stewart labored over for weeks. The plans grew so complicated that they had to enlist the assistance of Billy Grady, the head of casting at MGM.

The venue was the Beverly Hills Athletic Club. Hank and Jim explained to the MCA crowd that after some convivial elbow-bending beginning at 7:30 p.m., the doors would swing open, everybody would enter the dining area, and dinner would be served.

At the appointed hour, the doors indeed swung open, but there was a distinct lack of waiters, not to mention food. Fonda and Stewart were so busy being hosts they didn't notice. Jules Stein, being a proud member of the Athletic Club, was perturbed, not to mention hungry.

After an hour or so without so much as an hors d'oeuvre, the natives were beginning to get restless. Fonda and Stewart feigned outrage, upbraided the staff, and gathered up the MCA group. As they stormed out of the club, Stein stopped to apologize to the headwaiter.

Waiting outside was a battered yellow school bus conveniently available to transport the crowd. In the back of the bus was an elderly saxophone player who began playing a song, which he repeated ad nauseam for the next hour.

Fonda remembered that the magical presence of the bus led some of the brighter agents to vague feelings of apprehension about being gulled, but not Stein. The bus was wending its way through a residential street in Beverly Hills when it was pulled over by a motorcycle cop, who was actually an actor hired by Billy Grady. The fake cop told the crowd their transportation was being impounded for violating a traffic ordinance. For the rest of his life, Fonda cherished the memory of Jules Stein leaning out of a bus window trying to talk a fake policeman out of arresting him.

The cop led the bus to an empty garage fortuitously supplied with liquor, where a man was quietly listening to a record of a society matron (Florence Foster Jenkins?) singing badly . . . played over and over.

It was at this point that the penny dropped and everybody realized that they had been had — and were in for a very long night. Stein was by now well lubricated. A musician in his youth, Stein borrowed the saxophone and began serenading the crowd to thunderous applause. After some more drinks, it was back on the bus, which took them to Romanoff's, where salad and more drinks were served. Then it was on to Chasen's, where dinner was finally served and an extremely merry time was had by all.

"It was just the most successful party they'd ever been to," remembered Fonda with a palpable sense of gratification.

Besides the intrinsic pleasure to be derived from the seamless execution of a complicated practical joke, Fonda and Stewart were also clearly investigating whether their new agents were the kind of people with whom they wanted to be in business. Although a sense of humor was never a prominent component of the MCA operation, everybody seemed to have a good time, and Fonda and Stewart stayed in the MCA fold for years.

Beyond that, the long night on the bus served definitive notice of one thing: the boys were back in town.

Stewart's house had been leased while he was off to war, and his tenant was going to be there for four months. So he moved in with the Fondas, specifically to the playhouse that Hank had built for Jane and Peter.

Once again, Fonda's predilection for cats became an issue. "There was an infinite number of cats around the place, and they made it smell horrible," said Jane Fonda. "It was a weird time when I think about it. Here was this Hollywood star living in this place that was the size of some bathrooms and that stank to high heaven. Only practice made me stop holding my nose whenever I went in there. I always liked telling people in high school that I knew Jimmy Stewart when he was living in a cat house."

Jane noticed something else: the way that Stewart's presence lifted her father's mood. "It wasn't that he cracked jokes and things, although he had a great sense of humor. What was more important was how by just being there, he could make my father brighten up, even be goofy at times."

Even though Jane was only eight years old when the war ended, she had already picked up on the particular vibe between her father and godfather: "When they were together, they relaxed and had fun, which they didn't do separately."

As Hank and Jim were trying to settle into some semblance of postwar routine, Peter and Jane grew used to the man they called "Uncle Jimmy." "I felt a tremendous bond with him from the time I was five or six," remembered Peter. "He came by the house all the time, playing Uncle Jimmy. He was a good man, and he was a funny man. Kids loved him."

Jane's earliest memory of Stewart was a visit when he came back to California on leave, probably for the Swope-McGuire wedding. "He visited our house on Tigertail. He was checking up on his godchildren for my dad."

Peter and Jane had developed a habit that upset their mother: climbing out of their bedroom windows onto the roof. They weren't the only ones. On Christmas Eve 1945, Peter heard a rustling on the roof, complete with sleigh bells. "It's Santa Claus!" he said to Jane.

When they went to the window, they saw Uncle Jimmy stomping around on the roof by the chimney while shaking sleigh bells, doing his best to replicate the sounds of Santa landing. Jane was past believing in Santa, but Stewart was going to convince Peter that the Big Elf was a living presence if it killed him. "The way Jimmy was going across the roof, it might have," said Jane.

Jane and Peter also cherished the memory of another Christmas when Jim was helping the Fondas decorate the tree. Everybody had been hitting the eggnog, none more so than Jim. He was on top of the ladder trying to put the top piece on the tree when he lost his balance and went down, taking the ladder — and the tree — with him.

In one sense, Hank and Jim resumed the relationship that had been interrupted by the war; in another sense, the foundation of the relationship had been completely altered.

"When the war was over," said Peter, "the two of them would get together quite often. I got the feeling that both of them suffered quite a bit in the war. It was clear that each of them understood what the other one had gone through, so they didn't have to talk about it. And because they were already two great men of the movies, they didn't have to talk about that either."

In this respect, as well as many others, Hank and Jim went very much with the grain of their generation of American men. "Instead of talking about it, most [American soldiers] didn't talk about it," wrote James Jones. "It was not that they didn't want to talk about it, it was that when they did, nobody understood. It was such a different way of living, and of looking at life even, that there was no common ground of communication in it."

Jane Fonda's take was similar: "Dad was a pent-up guy, but the friendship with Jimmy was as intimate as he ever got with anybody. They were both tall and skinny, both laconic and shy, both loners — it took Jimmy a long time to warm to people. And they had the same sense of humor — wry and goofy."

For Jane and Peter, nothing about their father had changed. Ostensibly, Hank's religion was Christian Science, but mainly it was Silence. He just didn't talk a lot, but the kids would be enthralled when he would occasionally reminisce about the times he and Jim had in New York, when they were poor and lived on rice, when gangsters lived down the street.

Fonda had always been aloof, but now he was remote. "I can remember long car rides where not a word would be spoken," said Jane. "I would be so nervous that my palms would be sweaty from riding in absolute silence with my own father."

Peter remembered "terrifying" silences at the dinner table; Jane was so bruised by the prevailing mood that when she printed a picture of her as a little girl with her father gazing fondly at her she captioned it, "I know he loved me when I was little."

When Peter lost Fonda's Bronze Star, his father's rage was something Peter remembered all his life, even though Fonda would always insist that the medal was meaningless. Hank's self-description was accurate: "I'm not difficult to anger. Principally, I get angry at incompetence. . . . I have no patience with people who drive me to anger. Very often I try to control myself. If it's something too close to me and involves me too much, I do blow up. A lot of people will tell you about me blowing up. Understandably, they don't like it, and probably they don't like me as a result.

"Can't help that. I don't forget quickly. I cling to my angers."

I cling to my angers . . .

But when Stewart was around, things were

274

different. They had been boys together, and now they were men together, but they maintained their boys' hobbies. Once again they began building elaborate model airplanes. "Model airplanes" does the constructions an injustice; Peter remembered the wing spans of some of these planes extending as far as eight feet, and pictures confirm their size.

"They would sit together working on these planes," said Peter, "and the only conversation would be about the airplane parts. 'You have part C-27 over there, Jim?' I was fascinated by the smells, and by their concentration. They would do this for three and four hours at a time."

Hank would mold clay to the wings for balance and ballast. When the plane was finished, the men and, occasionally, one of Stewart's girlfriends would head off to a dry lake bed to fly the planes. As the plane flew they would follow it in their woody station wagon.

"I was just a kid, and I didn't realize it at the time," said Peter, "but this was their way of dealing with the stress — of the war, of trying to figure out what their place was in the postwar movie business. They made no demands on each other. They had a secret society attuned to moments of the war that they never talked about. What happened before they were together or after was unimportant to both of them. What counted were the times they were together. Their closeness permeated the house, whichever house they were in. They were healing."

Besides the residual passion for model planes, Fonda brought something new back from the war — a passion for kites, his father's hobby, which was rediscovered in the Navy. The kites had to be large. No, they had to be very large. "My dad used a chopped-off marlin fishing rod to fly these things," said Peter. "He would say to my mother, 'We're going out to the North 40' — he always called it the North 40 — and I would launch the kites, which were bigger than I was — literally.

"Up to the moment the kite flew into the air, he was the dad he usually was — quiet, stressed. But his demeanor changed entirely as soon as the kite went airborne." The kite's freedom transformed Fonda into an exuberant man-child.

Jim remembered that the kite enthusiasm was always threatening to get out of hand because Fonda kept building them bigger and bigger. One night Stewart came back to Fonda's house around 7 p.m. to find Frances in an agitated state. "You better go out there," she told Jim. "Hank's in trouble with the kite."

"And I looked out," remembered Stewart. "It was black night, and the fishing tackle we had used for the kite was going straight up in the air and was almost off the reel, and Hank was holding this enormous kite and the wind was strong and it was almost pulling him off the ground. The kite was half as big as this room." Stewart rushed out and grabbed the tackle and the two men gradually pulled the kite out of the sky, saving Fonda from being blown back to the South Pacific.

And so the pattern was set. The war lay beneath almost everything they did, every choice they made as actors and as men, but it was not discussed. As before, Fonda could give himself only to a very select few, and in order to completely let go he would often have to be drinking.

"His way of loosening up was to get drunk," noted Jane. "My dad was almost pathologically scared of emotional display." The problem was that wives and children want — *need* — intimacy, while men are usually content with camaraderie.

Jim and Hank would occasionally play charades, and Peter remembered with some dismay that his father was "perfect at Charades. Of course." They played a lot of games in those days after the war. There was another pastime called Hide the Button, in which five ordinary objects — a penny, a matchstick, etc. — would be hidden, more or less in plain sight. A button, for instance, would be placed beneath a shot glass on a shelf. Each contestant was on the clock, and the first person to find all five objects in the shortest amount of time was the winner.

Hank also began to circle a new passion, one that would accompany and enrich him for the rest of his days: painting, which eventually became a passionate pursuit with rewards comparable to acting. "Art became one of the things he could hide behind" was the way his son put it.

Peter remembered one of his father's early works, a small porcelain plate that Fonda converted into a simulated ashtray by painting burnt matches, ashes, and stubbed-out cigarettes in tromp l'oeil style on the surface. Peter was in the living room one day when a maid grabbed the plate and swabbed it with a cloth dampened by ammonia, which smeared the painting.

When Hank came home, Peter was afraid he'd get blamed for the ruined piece, so he told his father what the maid had done. Fonda looked at his son, then looked at the plate. "With the ammonia cloth?" he asked. Peter nodded. A smile that grew into a delighted grin spread over Fonda's face. His painting was so realistic it had fooled the maid. What artist could ask for more?

There was always time for more practical jokes. One time a group gathered at Tigertail in black tie before going out for the evening. Stewart was wearing a white dinner jacket and looked quite snappy. Hank began talking about a new pen he had discovered, whose smoothness was a source of endless pleasure. Nothing would do but that Hank demonstrate the new wonder pen. As he was demonstrating how to fill it, ink squirted all over Jim's sparkling white dinner jacket.

As the group gasped in horror, Peter's first instinct was to run — once again he figured that it was somehow his fault. Hank began apologizing profusely, while Jim did a slow burn. But something magical happened: within five minutes, the ink had completely disappeared, and the white dinner jacket was again pristine. Peter realized it had been a practical joke on his father's part. Sixty-five years later, he realized that the white dinner jacket meant that Jim was in on it as well.

In that winter of 1945–1946, there were so many parties. The movie business was still thriving, although that would change soon enough. After the parties were over and the nights were quiet again, Hank and Jim would sit in the playhouse and listen to the records they brought home from their forays through the record shops of Los Angeles. "Johnny Mercer, Hoagy Carmichael and Nat King Cole used to come over and listen with us," said Hank. "Nat Cole taught Peter to play boogie-woogie on the piano."

Peter noticed that although Hank and Jim each proclaimed the other to be his best friend in word and deed, they didn't talk all that much. Rather, they took what was obviously a deep, unspoken pleasure in simply being with each other. This was possible only because they were both loners, Fonda more obviously than Stewart. But, as Burgess Meredith observed, "Jimmy is a self-contained man. He can live totally within himself."

This was emphasized over the years by Stewart's invariably uninflected interviews, in which he studiously avoided the emotional connection he specialized in as an actor. There is little revelation, about him or anybody else. But he wasn't hiding anything, wasn't covering up the hidden harbors of a secret life. He simply wasn't interested in letting the world know what was going on in his head; he was content within himself and with the silence that comes from being alone.

Fonda would talk about his war with a sense of disappointment verging on disgust, but Stewart almost never discussed the subject. His reminiscences were largely reserved for histories of the Eighth Air Force and the 453rd Bomb Group. Years later Stewart's children would knew only that their father eventually rose to the rank of brigadier general in the Air Force Reserve. For him at least, that was enough.

NINE

When he sold his agency, Leland Hayward got an MCA vice presidency, a ten-year employment contract for $100,000 a year, plus half the commissions generated by former Hayward agency clients. Those clients included Myrna Loy, Judy Garland, Gene Tierney, Dorothy McGuire, Ginger Rogers, Clifton Webb, Gregory Peck, Joseph Cotten, Fred Astaire, Gene Kelly, Boris Karloff, David Niven, Irwin Shaw, Dorothy Parker, Edna Ferber, Lillian Hellman, Ben Hecht, Dashiell Hammett, Billy Wilder, Alfred Hitchcock, Josh Logan, Henry Fonda, and James Stewart.

Besides that, Hayward was part of the MCA bonus system on all future business. In short, he was guaranteed a yearly income north of $250,000 for sitting by the pool. That his theatrical productions quickly proved successful only added to the geyser of cash.

Hank and Jim were now guided by Lew Wasserman, undoubtedly one of the most brilliant men ever to toil in the Hollywood fields, who would eventually maneuver MCA into purchasing Universal Pictures.

Jack Valenti was later recruited by Wasserman from Lyndon Johnson's White House to head the Motion Picture Association of America, and his opinion of Wasserman was succinct: "Lew was one of the smartest guys I ever met," said Valenti. "He also had a sense of prophecy — he saw TV as one of the great marketplaces for movies long before anyone else did. He had a prodigious memory; he could grasp large chunks of diverse material and could call up things faster than a computer. He never wrote a memo. And he surrounded himself with an air of mystery, which made him even more dominant."

Valenti told Wasserman that he needed to supervise all negotiations with unions and guilds, because he, Valenti, didn't have the skill or the time.

I remember at one dinner, I said to this burly union guy sitting next to me, "What's it like to negotiate with Wasserman?" And he said, "He's the toughest son of a bitch I've ever met. But he's fair. And when Lew

Wasserman shakes your hand at the end of a negotiation, you don't need twenty lawyers and a deal memo. What he told you you'll get is what you get."

And that was my experience exactly. Whenever Lew Wasserman made a promise he kept it; whenever he offered a pledge, he redeemed it. He never lied. For over fifty years he had the respect of some of the toughest union bosses in the world.

This was the man who would make James Stewart one of the richest actors in Hollywood. He could have done the same thing for Hank too, but Fonda's professional priorities were shifting.

Besides the residual effects of the war, and his professional indecision, Stewart was also in an unfinished state about his emotional life. Olivia de Havilland's instincts about Margaret Sullavan had been correct — Sullavan would call Jim, and his demeanor would immediately soften, as would his voice. "She really manipulated him, even long-distance," said Myrna Dell, one of Jim's postwar girlfriends. "I got the feeling that she'd call him whenever she was in need of a little adoration."

At Tigertail Road, Fonda again started to

grow most of the family's food. Frances Fonda would wring the neck of a chicken, and the kids learned never to make a pet of a rabbit because sooner or later the rabbit would end up in a pot.

In most respects, Fonda's culinary tastes were simple. For breakfast, he would fix himself two raw eggs and a can of hash. For the rest of his diet, he tended toward the path of least resistance — steaks and fish. If he was in the mood to cook, he did an excellent job. He could bake ham and turkey perfectly, and carve it perfectly as well.

One weekend, Stewart, John Wayne, Randolph Scott, and Ward Bond came to Tigertail Road to help Hank clear out some brush. The men piled up the overgrown grass between the corral and the barn and burned it. Peter watched his father bring out some Idaho potatoes and throw them into the fire. "He knew to the second when to take them out of the fire. Then he peeled the skins off and gave us each one of the potatoes. They were great!"

Sometimes the same group, with the addition of John Ford, would come by the house to play pitch, a cowboy variation on poker. Peter was struck by the extent to which each man was a class act, even Ward Bond, whom Hank called a "beer drunk."

Fonda had a full complement of orange and apple trees on the property, and would make all manner of juices. Ward Bond would drink a big glass of freshly squeezed orange juice and afterward let out a long gasp of "Aaaahhhhhh!" Peter thought it was a very manly thing to do, and adopted the same trait.

When Peter visited his first film set it was *Fort Apache,* starring his dad and John Wayne. He remembered the occasion all his life because Wayne personally drove him to the set in his cream-colored convertible with red leather upholstery.

When Fonda drank, which, apart from time on the *Araner,* wasn't often — Peter saw his father drunk only once in his life — it was Scotch on the rocks. Like many men of his generation, he seemed to use alcohol to settle his nerves; years later, when he had to tell his son that Margaret Sullavan's daughter Bridget had committed suicide, he sat Peter down and before he told him said, "Do you want something to drink? I really think you should have something to drink." He had never said that to his son before, so Peter knew something terrible had happened.

There is a sense that both Fonda and Stewart were biding their time, occupying their minds by trying to recapture the innocent lives they had led before the war. And waiting. Waiting for something to happen, something transformative that would launch them into the next act. But until that happened, there were movies to make.

By the time the two men were ready to go back to work, Fonda had been off the screen for three years, Stewart for four, a lifetime in a business always focused on the trending, the new. Their initial forays were erratic; Fonda clearly wanted to return to a place and a personality where he felt comfortable: John Ford.

His first movie after the war was in Ford's take on Wyatt Earp and the Gunfight at the O.K. Corral. *My Darling Clementine* was photographed with Ford's usual attentive eye for beauty and repose and it happened to be a masterpiece. The film feels as if it was directed by one of its characters — Ford's rhythm is as laconic as the dialogue. Ford was never so alert to acting subtext, to the pleasures of a physical movement. He constructed shots just to observe Fonda's walk, which film critic David Thomson described as "like a tranquil hobo used to getting no rides."

My Darling Clementine contains one of

Fonda's loveliest moments as an actor. Victor Mature's Doc Holliday is reciting from *Hamlet*. Fonda is observing Mature out of the corner of his eye with a look that doesn't seem to be acting, but rather professional interest; he seems genuinely concerned about whether or not Mature will get through the speech. As it happens, Mature does quite well.

The scene where Fonda's Wyatt Earp leans back in his chair and does a little dosey-do on a post is the ten seconds that everybody remembers about the movie — one of those little moments of actorly grace and movement that get excerpted for documentaries. It was suggested by Ford "in the moment," said Fonda, slipping into actor's lingo to talk about the director's gift for the improvisational gesture. Ford just plucked it out of the air. "As obstinate and perverse as he was, there wasn't anybody like him," said Fonda. "He was unique, as a director and as a person."

My Darling Clementine made a little money and was a critical success as well; Fonda must have felt some kind of confidence about his place in the postwar filmmaking, but then came Ford's disastrous adaptation of Graham Greene's *The Power and the Glory*, retitled *The Fugitive*. Fonda had range, but a Mexican whiskey priest wasn't in his wheelhouse. The film lost a lot of money, which Ford attempted to recoup by launching into a series of westerns, the first of which, *Fort Apache,* also featured Fonda and John Wayne.

Ford had an unnerring ability to reveal the internals of his actors, and in *Fort Apache* he had the audacity to emphasize Fonda's tightness and lack of emotional resilience. Fonda's Colonel Owen Thursday is an angry military man who feels he's been overlooked and underutilized; he gets himself and his command slaughtered for no reason other than ego. It's a brave performance in a fine film, and it made money, although not enough to make up the losses of *The Fugitive.*

Flush or broke, Ford was tough. *Fort Apache* was filmed in Monument Valley, and when they arrived on location, Ford's production manager looked at the payroll and told Wayne's and Fonda's stand-ins that they weren't making enough money; the normal rate was more than they were down for. He suggested that they go to the stars and have them ask Ford for a raise that would give them parity.

Sid Davis, Wayne's stand-in, asked Wayne about it, and the star turned pale. He was terrified of Ford and wasn't about to say or do anything that might irritate the irascible director. Wayne told Davis he'd make up the difference out of his own pocket. Charles Bidwell, Fonda's stand-in, asked Fonda if he would talk to Ford about a raise. "No dice," he said.

Bidwell had gotten to know Mary Ford through her work running the kitchen at the Hollywood Canteen during the war, so he went to see her when they got back to Hollywood. The next working day, Ford came on the set, walked past Bidwell, then stopped and turned. "You've got your raise," he said.

Fort Apache can be viewed as Ford's comparative analysis of his two favorite leading men. Wayne's Kirby York is of a piece with his other performances in Ford's films: earthy, somewhat touchy, a brawler by instinct tempered only by discipline, capable of a gentle love as well as rage. Fonda's Owen Thursday burns with a cold fire — there is strength there, but it is removed, abstracted, rather asexual, deriving from the actor's instinctive austerity.

Thursday is doomed, not so much because he loathes Apaches, but because he doesn't listen, because he arrogantly attempts to impose his version of reality on an intransigent natural world far removed from his Eastern verities. Ford heroes played by Wayne are never so vain as to attempt to bend the world to their will, preferring either an easy, mutual understanding or a proud exile — a function of Wayne's expansive spirit and underlying humor.

Fonda's stiff walk works against the flow of life around him. In *Young Mr. Lincoln, The Grapes of Wrath,* or *My Darling Clementine,* the walk translates as integrity; in *Fort Apache,* it translates as the tragic inhumanity of a martinet.

Two classics out of three attempts is a great average for any actor, but Fonda's road back was undermined by other disappointments: Otto Preminger's *Daisy Kenyon* and Anatole Litvak's terrible remake of Marcel Carné's *Le Jour se Lève,* retitled *The Long Night.*

Stewart's first film back was Frank Capra's *It's a Wonderful Life,* beloved in retrospect, but a disappointment in 1946. "I'd had no job offers," Stewart remembered. According to Stewart, he and Fonda had been malingering for seven months, and just about all they had to show for it was some model planes, some kites, and a lot of playtime with Peter and Jane. "I didn't do anything . . . except go to parties, drink cold tea and talk big," he told Louella Parsons.

Actually, Frank Capra had first contacted Stewart about the picture in October 1945, even though it didn't start shooting until April 15 of the following year, or just about seven months after Stewart got back to Hollywood.

Capra invited Stewart to a meeting, and told him the plot: "The story starts in heaven. This guy's having a hard time and decides to commit suicide. And an angel comes down and says, 'Are you gonna jump off the bridge?' The angel saves the man. The angel doesn't have his wings yet."

Capra paused. "This story doesn't tell very well, does it?"

Capra's notes of the meeting are harrowing: "Wasserman present in [Capra's partner Sam] Briskin's apartment. As I tell story, it evaporates into thin air. Tell Stewart to forget it. Wasserman dying . . ."

"I didn't know what the hell he was talking about," Stewart said "But he went on and on and it just grew on me." Capra kept going and Stewart wasn't discouraged. Finally he said, "Frank, if you want to make a movie about a fella who wants to commit suicide and an angel with no wings, I'm your boy!"

The only other actor Capra had actively

considered for the part of George Bailey was Fonda, but Stewart was his first choice because of the great films they had made before the war. Stewart signed his contract on November 5, 1945.

Actor's contracts are only occasionally interesting, but this one is different. For one thing, Stewart insisted on a clause specifying no publicity or exploitation of any kind about his war record. For another, there was the matter of profit participation.

The conventional narrative about Stewart's career asserts that he was the first Hollywood star to earn a percentage of the profits when he signed to make *Winchester '73*. But as documents in Capra's papers prove, Lew Wasserman quickly proved his worth when he negotiated 10 percent of the "Producer's Gross Receipts" of *It's a Wonderful Life* for his client. Stewart's base pay was set at $162,000. Since the picture ended up grossing approximately $4.40 million worldwide, after deducting RKO's distribution fee, Stewart's base salary, print and advertising costs, and some other minor expenses, Stewart received an additional $173,000 as his piece of the gross.

This deal was stunning in its implications for the future of Hollywood, simply because for what might well have been the first time in a movie for which the star had no production responsibilities, that star received a piece of the gross, not the net. Since net is by definition highly elastic, net percentages were as often illusion as reality. Stewart collected because the contractual definition was specific and airtight. Gross percentage meant that the star made money even if the picture failed commercially. (As of July 2, 1947, *It's a Wonderful Life* had a net loss of about $392,000.)

Like millions of other returning veterans of the war, Stewart remembered that he was emotionally exhausted and professionally unsure. "I felt when I got back to pictures that I had lost all sense of judgment," said Stewart. "I couldn't tell if I was good or bad. I mean in a given scene. Usually, you can tell what is the right thing to do when you're acting. But I couldn't. I was uncertain."

Capra couldn't help but be aware of Stewart's struggles; he had been away from Hollywood for four years himself. Jim told his director that "he thought maybe being an actor was not for decent people. That acting had become silly, unimportant next to what he'd seen [in the war]. He said he thought he'd do this picture and quit."

Stewart was beset by an overwhelming

feeling that he had forgotten how to act. "It's a skill, you know," and he seemed to have lost the knack. "I couldn't remember my lines. I couldn't remember my hat size. . . . I had to go home and study and study where before I just used to look at the script once and I knew it."

Finally, Capra asked the venerable old pro Lionel Barrymore to give Stewart a pep talk. "What Lionel did was encourage me," remembered Stewart. "I was feeling around and every once in a while he'd come up and say something." Stewart said that the most important advice Barrymore gave him was " 'not to apologize for not being in town the last four years.' He told me to just do it, not to make excuses, or feel sorry for myself. It was wonderful for me. I'll always be grateful."

For Stewart, the gradual entrapment of George Bailey might have been what his life would have been if he had never escaped from Indiana, Pennsylvania, the hardware store, and his father's expectations. As George Bailey says, "This business of nickels and dimes and spending all your life trying to figure out how to save three cents on a length of pipe . . . I'd go crazy. I want to do something big and something important."

He would never have said such a thing as

Jim Stewart, but to say it through the personality of George Bailey, to say it through his art, made the declaration of independence possible.

Some sense of Stewart's punctiliousness about money is made obvious by a check in Capra's archives. It's from Stewart to Capra and it's in the amount of seven cents. It seems that the two men had split the cost of the party for the cast and crew at the close of production. The party cost $1,799.09, and Capra had unaccountably overpaid his share by seven cents. Stewart promptly repaid the overage.

Capra's film was followed by a William Wellman film called *Magic Town,* which was a financial and critical flop. Wellman would always shrug and say simply that "Frank Capra should have directed that picture," but Robert Riskin, who wrote most of the great Capra pictures, had fallen out with the director and wanted to prove he could make magic without him.

One of the structural problems with the movie was that Stewart had no antagonist; there was no heavy, no Lionel Barrymore or Edward Arnold to personify the excesses of small-minded capitalism. Stewart didn't take the flop personally; he saw Wellman regularly at the Bel-Air Country Club for years and they would smile and joke around.

Then came *On Our Merry Way,* Stewart's first collaboration with Fonda. It's a more or less justifiably neglected omnibus picture in which their segment involves them as jazz musicians who unsuccessfully try to fix a band contest. Their segment was written by John O'Hara and co-directed by John Huston and George Stevens. Huston shot the setup scene between Burgess Meredith's reporter and the musicians, then left for another job. Stevens, who was feeling pretty shaky after the war himself, came in and shot the rest, but neither man wanted credit.

It was a catch-as-catch-can movie, shot for short money at night while Fonda was slogging away on *The Long Night* during the day. What makes it interesting is that Stevens, who had spent years photographing comedies on the Hal Roach lot before becoming a director, turned Fonda and Stewart into Laurel and Hardy.

They're a couple of endearing losers, none-too-bright and none-too-talented. Neither actor had any qualms about taking their time, but Stevens guides them to work even more methodically. Their frayed professional dignity is gradually traduced by physical indignity. Once you get the rhythm of the piece, it's irresistibly funny, with beautiful teamwork on the part of the stars and lots of sotto voce asides ("How's your embouchure?" mumbles Stewart to one aspiring trumpet player, without waiting for an answer).

"It had Jimmy Stewart and Fonda — I'm smiling already," remembered Stevens. "I wasn't worried; these people are going to be funny. . . . With ordinary actors I've tried this, and it's like playing music without an instrument, but these guys could do anything. We had a hell of a lot of fun . . . making something which was hilariously funny without a note of humor in it. It was all structural."

It's Fonda's only slapstick performance outside of *The Lady Eve,* and part of the delight is seeing two actors already accruing gravitas as they moved toward middle age clowning with such dexterity. As with Laurel and Hardy, the audience is let in on the joke, then surprised and delighted by another joke that it didn't see coming but is nonetheless logical.

Fonda approached comedy with his usual level of intensity. If he was going to play a trumpet player, then he'd learn to play the trumpet. He brought the instrument home and devised a diagram that represented which valves would be up or down depending on the musical notes. (Years later, when he was playing a musician in Alfred Hitchcock's *The Wrong Man,* he learned how to play the bass.)

As far as Fonda was concerned, playing comedy with Stewart was the culmination of their entire relationship: "It was just pure joy and laughs." *On Our Merry Way* isn't much of a picture, but it managed $1.2 million in domestic rentals, good for an independent movie in the postwar era, when the movie business went into serious contraction.

Looked at objectively, both Hank and Jim were amassing a scattershot roster of pictures after the war; they were feeling their way. Mostly, they were trying what had worked for them before the war, which would have been fine except the war had changed both the actors and the audience, who weren't terribly interested in parables of goodness anymore.

For a time their careers seemed endangered, which was by no means unusual for the great stars of the prewar years. To take only two examples, Clark Gable mostly floundered, as MGM had difficulty showcasing an older, grimmer, spiritually heavier man.

Similarly, Tyrone Power came back from a

stint in the Marines subtly altered. Initially, Darryl Zanuck was far more successful (*The Razor's Edge*) with Power than Louis B. Mayer was with Gable (*Adventure*), but Zanuck soon threw in the towel and cast Power in a succession of escapist costume pictures that avoided the question of what Power had to say to audiences in the postwar era. The deep noir experiment of *Nightmare Alley* might have been a blast of pure oxygen for Power, but it was a one-off and in any case lost $500,000.

In some respects, Fonda was the same actor after the war that he had been before. "He's the most professional actor in the business," said Charles Bidwell, his stand-in for thirty-five years. "He doesn't like any sort of tomfoolery on the set. It's strictly business with him. Although he has a fabulous sense of humor; he loves practical jokes and all those kinds of things. He's never late. Always knows his lines."

At times, Fonda's sense of humor indicated repressed rage. There was the time Hedda Hopper came to the set of one of Fonda's westerns, and he began to waltz her around in apparent good humor. Surreptitiously he took his prop gun out of the holster, put it behind Hopper's back and fired off a couple of rounds. Hopper leaped up and, as one onlooker noted, "almost messed up the stage."

Then or later, on the most basic level he was simply ill at ease with most people. He and Bidwell were being driven to their respective homes after shooting one day. Fonda was dropped off first, and he asked Bidwell if he wanted to come in.

Fonda showed Bidwell around the house on Tigertail Road, then poured him a cup of coffee. While Bidwell drank his coffee, Fonda looked out the window. There was no small talk; silence reigned. Bidwell finished his coffee, and Fonda drove him home.

Bidwell would point out Fonda's taciturnity with some amusement, but he also would speak of Fonda's honesty. One afternoon, Fonda needed to make some phone calls and borrowed a couple of dimes from Bidwell. The picture finished that night, after which Fonda left for New York. A week later, Bidwell got an envelope from Fonda with two dimes enclosed and a thank-you note.

After *On Our Merry Way* Stewart began to find his way forward with the excellent *Call Northside 777,* in which he plays a tough-minded Chicago reporter. He was making a concerted effort to alter his style, and he wasn't the only one. "I needed him for the reporter in *Call Northside 777*, but not the Capra Jimmy," said director Henry Hathaway. "I knew audiences would instinctively identify with him because of his niceness. But I was very strict — I wouldn't tolerate any of those 'ohs' and 'ahs' he'd been getting away with."

It was *Call Northside 777* that proved Stewart still had a career, that showed him the way to cope with the changing tastes of the public after a war: play it tough, play it unyielding. "That picture was the one that really got me started after the war," said Stewart.

The picture shot for two weeks at Joliet State Prison outside Chicago, and Stewart fondly remembered the question of one frustrated inmate: "Why don't you bastards get out of here?" the prisoner asked. "We want to get our privileges back. We have to stay in our cells the whole time you're shooting the damn picture. Why don't you get the hell out of here and leave us alone?" (Stewart was usually careful to censor his speech so that he sounded suitable for Hedda Hopper's column, but would occasionally slip into the argot of a man who had been in World War II.)

Call Northside 777 showed that the swoony, idealistic boy of the prewar years had been banished. In his place was a driven man in pursuit, as well as pursued. *Call Northside 777* made nearly a million dollars in profit, and its follow-ups were also highly profitable — *The Stratton Story,* about a baseball pitcher who loses a leg and keeps pitching, made a profit of $1.2 million, while a bread-and-butter western like *Carbine Williams* made $643,000 in profits.

And then came Hitchcock's *Rope,* one of those movies in which the director attempted to challenge himself through self-imposed limitations. *Rope* consisted of eight takes, each running ten minutes — an entire reel of film. In one sense, it's a marvel of technique and timing — walls would lift to allow the massive Technicolor camera to pass, furniture would slide soundlessly out of the way. The only problems were that the ten-minute takes emphasized the theatricality of the script by negating the editing function, the core strength of movies. Besides that, Stewart was miscast as a philosophy professor with a bent for Nietzsche.

Like every other actor on the picture, Stewart was nervous, since one slip in the endless dialogue and the complicated shot was ruined. Because the shots were so convoluted and only two or three takes could be made per day, Stewart had many sleepless nights, and screenwriter Arthur Laurents reported more drinking on the part of the star than he had foreseen.

"It was hard to see how the picture was going to work even while we were doing it," remembered Stewart "The noises made by the moving of the walls was a continuing problem, and we would have to do scenes over again just for sound reasons, using only microphones like in a radio play. It was pretty wearing. Nobody but Hitchcock would have tried it, but in the end it really didn't work."

It's probably best to consider *Rope* an uneasy first date that led to great things in the future. Hitchcock would experiment again with a severely limited viewpoint in *Rear Window,* but he shot and edited that film in a conventional manner, and the result was a masterpiece of both directorial technique and star performance.

Hank and Jim were both beginning to feel the need for something different, something new. Stewart scratched the itch first. In 1947, he spent the summer in New York City substituting for Frank Fay in the

Broadway production of *Harvey*. *Harvey* had become a franchise since it opened in late 1944, while Stewart hadn't acted in a play since 1935. His reviews were indicative of the general distrust New York had for actors who had abandoned New York for the movies.

But he was back the following year, again covering for Fay on his summer vacation and, quite possibly, making an extended test for the movie version that was sure to follow. (The 1948 reviews were better.) Back in Hollywood there was a fast flop called *You Gotta Stay Happy.*

Both men's immediate group of postwar pictures make it clear that, despite their emotional closeness, and similar experiences in life and war, as artists they operated from completely different intentions. Both began from the same place in that they were inside-out actors, as opposed to outside-in.

Outside-in actors (Olivier, Welles, Muni, Sellers, Day-Lewis, among others) depend on an accent, a wig, a false nose, or some other prop to give them a key to their character. Stewart and Fonda, in common with most leading men of the period, internalized the character and filtered him through their personality. Not only did they avoid dialects and extreme makeup, they might very well have felt that such things were essentially dishonest — theatrical crutches.

Beyond that, they differed in every way. Stewart's was an expansive, highly adaptive talent; he was undoubtedly the most versatile leading man of his generation, but in a familiar vein: the Good American, an innately decent man who finds himself in a difficult place. There had been actors like that before (Gary Cooper) and there would be actors like that again (Tom Hanks, although he has been careful never to play anything like *Fort Apache* or *Vertigo*).

But there hadn't been an actor like Fonda before, nor would there be again. In his sense of compression, of minimalist tightness, where emotion is communicated by a slightly emphasized syllable or the flicker of an eye, Fonda was practically Japanese. (Fonda was the only American actor who could have worked for Ozu.)

The joy in watching Fonda comes from his pointillist technique, as well as those times when his tension meets relaxation and relaxation wins — when he sees Jane Darwell for the first time in *The Grapes of Wrath* and exclaims "Ma!"; when he does his dance on the post in *Clementine*. He's a hold-and-release actor.

■ ■ ■ ■

James Stewart met Gloria Hatrick McLean at dinner with Gary and Rocky Cooper in the summer of 1948. "Rocky was always trying to get me to meet Jimmy," Gloria would say decades later. Stewart had been Gloria's favorite actor even before she knew him, because he could make her laugh and cry in the same scene.

Gloria had been briefly married to Ned McLean, son of Evalyn McLean, the owner of the Hope Diamond, and had been friends with Rocky Cooper for years. Maria Cooper Janis, Gary and Rocky's daughter, explained that "the McLean family were friends of my grandparents and my mother and father. Ned . . . traveled with my parents and myself. Gloria and Ned divorced, and Gloria was unhappy — a divorcée with twin boys.

"Gloria and my mother were cut from the same cloth, with one exception. Gloria was very happy and outgoing; she was even comfortable on TV. My mother, if you put a gun to her head, wouldn't have gone on TV. She was excruciatingly shy. Other than that, they were extremely close, almost like sisters. They would yak on the phone for hours."

Gloria was visiting Hollywood, talking things over with the Coopers, when Gary said, "Let's have dinner one night with my pal Jimmy Stewart. He's a perennial bachelor, but I think you'd get along. We'll be a foursome."

"Jimmy trusted my father's taste," said Maria Janis. "And it took."

Contrary to prior reports, the dinner was at a restaurant, not the Coopers' house, and Ronald Reagan was not there. The Coopers liked Reagan, and he would come to their dinner parties, but his habit of holding forth about politics had a tendency to clear the room. Gary Cooper would go out in the garden and smoke a cigar.

After dinner, Stewart, Gloria, and the Coopers went to Ciro's, where the Nat King Cole Trio was playing. They were dancing when Gloria noticed Jim signaling a friend not to cut in. "I pretended not to notice," she said.

Gloria was born in Larchmont in 1918, the daughter of Edgar Hatrick, who ran William Randolph Hearst's newsreel operation. She was a tall, witty brunette with green eyes — classy, tough-minded, and beautiful.

Stewart's studied withholding from serious emotional involvement began to dissipate: he had found The Girl. For one thing, he was forty-one years old, and it was time. For another, there was Gloria.

The courtship included many rounds of golf; Gloria loved any outdoor activity and was more athletic than Stewart. Golf dominated their activities until Gloria nudged things along by saying, "You know, I eat too." In Gloria's telling of the courtship, she ascribed much of Stewart's hesitance to his general tightness with a dollar, something she would always be delighted to jab him about.

Jim proposed, Gloria accepted. The night before the marriage, Lew Wasserman threw a bachelor party for Stewart at Chasen's. When Wasserman and Stewart drove up to the restaurant, Spencer Tracy, Jack Benny, and Dave Chasen were sitting on the curb. Above them, a fifty-foot sign hung across the entrance announcing "James Stewart's Final Performance Tonight." Beneath the sign were life-size cutouts of Stewart as he appeared in all of his unsuccessful movies.

Wasserman hired a British manservant dressed in livery to wipe Stewart's mouth after every drink. When they sat down to dinner, Chasen brought out an enormous serving platter. When he took the top off, two midgets with syringes squirted yellow liquid all over Stewart. It looked like urine, but fortunately wasn't. All in all, it was appropriate revenge for Stewart and Fonda's extended practical joke on Wasserman, Stein, and the MCA boys.

Jim and Gloria were married on August 9, 1949, in front of a crowd that included Spencer Tracy, Gary Cooper, Ray Milland, Jack Benny, David Niven, and Frank Morgan. (Hank was on Broadway and couldn't get away without missing performances — anathema!) Billy Grady served as Jim's best man.

Stewart had found his perfect match: Gloria was attractive, smart, a good manager, someone who understood the movie business but was not of it. "Jimmy never basically trusted anybody in the film industry," Johnny Swope said. "He never found anyone before Gloria who could separate him from his film image."

Jim and Gloria honeymooned in Hawaii, but it was a strange couple of weeks. Helen Hayes and Charles MacArthur were there trying to put their lives together after the death of their nineteen-year-old daughter, Mary, from polio. Stewart had known Hayes since the days of hobo steaks and beer in Manhattan in the 1930s, so he and Gloria took the devastated couple out to dinner, which turned into more meals, sightseeing, and a fishing trip. Much of their honeymoon was devoted to helping Hayes and her husband cope with their grief. The therapy worked in the case of Hayes, failed in the case of her husband, who proceeded to spend the next seven years drinking himself to death.

These were years when Jim made acquisitions. Besides a ready-made family, Jim also invested in a surplus P-51 Mustang, which he entered in some races that he would often win. Jim loved the Mustang, but it was too much plane for a weekend pilot, so he sold it and bought a Beechcraft Bonanza for weekend flights around Los Angeles and occasional trips home to Pennsylvania.

With a wife and two boys, Stewart had to find a bigger house. In January 1951, he bought a house formerly owned by Charles Vidor at 918 North Roxbury Drive in Beverly Hills. Despite the tony address, it was a comparatively modest Tudor structure, more like the home of a Bedford Falls banker than a movie star. Jim's architecture background meant that he knew the difference between styles, but he always referred to the house as "Mediterranean Ugly."

James Stewart would raise his children in

that house, would grow old in that house, would die in that house.

Gloria decorated the place in subtle colors — beige and green. A staircase to the second floor bedrooms rose off the entrance hall, which in turn led to the living room. Over the large fireplace was a painting of an African elephant, while off to one side was a portrait of a tiger. The blandness of the walls was broken up by brightly colored furniture — oranges and yellows. A Yamaha piano held family pictures — children, Stewart and Gloria with the Pope, and so on. Tables held a head of Jefferson and various awards and other totems of his career.

The dining room was mainly used for holidays and the occasional party. It held an oak table that could comfortably sit eight people and a French provincial bookcase that doubled as a breakfront. Most meals were taken in the breakfast room, where the family served themselves from a lazy Susan.

The library held a couple of couches with bright floral coverings and shelves full of books that were mostly Gloria's. A large niche held more photos and family stills as well as shots from a few films, but not the ones you would think of — nothing from Hitchcock movies, but shots from *The Stratton Story* and *The Glenn Miller Story.*

Most of the family time was spent in the library. The bar held a model of a B-24, his New York Film Critics Award, and a trophy from the Bendix Air Race.

The basement was a playroom/projection room, where Stewart would hesitantly thread a 16mm projector himself and show movies to the children. Upstairs, the master bedroom was shared by Jim and Gloria. They had separate baths and dressing rooms. Hank Fonda said of the house that "It's as comfortable as Jimmy, with a splash of style thrown in by Gloria."

Stewart and Gloria loved the place, and loved it even more when, a few years later, they bought the house next door and tore it down to create a garden — one of Gloria's passions. The garden caused one of the few neighborhood rifts on Roxbury. Jim and Gloria threw a lawn party to thank the neighbors for putting up with the demolition of the house next door, but Lucille Ball showed up very late, and in an obviously bad mood. The screenwriter Leonard Gershe asked her what the problem was.

"I wasn't going to come at all," she snapped. "I'm so furious with the Stewarts. When they tore that house down next door, all the rats came running over to my house and I've been with exterminators for three weeks."

Ball never said anything about the nuisance to Jim and Gloria and eventually relaxed and had a good time. The neighbors on Roxbury grew used to having Jim come to their front doors lugging a bag of vegetables from his garden. Ball would graciously accept them, at least when she was home. When she wasn't, her Chinese cook would get irate. "She no home, she no home," the cook would yell at a crestfallen Stewart. "No veg-e-table. We got veg-e-table man, come all the time!"

Jim would go back home and call Ball a few hours later. "W-w-w-aaaaal, L-l-l-l-ucy. . . ."

The marriage was happy from the beginning, because, Brooke Hayward said, "Gloria wasn't an actress. She had a good sense of humor and didn't have the hideous ego thing. That's also why Shirlee Fonda [Fonda's widow] and Hank worked out well in the end. They were both wonderful wives, and actresses are not wonderful wives. You don't want to marry an actress."

The marriage would be blessed with fraternal twin girls named Kelly and Judy, born May 7, 1951. Jim announced the occasion with a series of phone calls to his best friends: "Jim Stewart phoned your house," reported Leland Hayward's secretary. "He has twin daughters."

It was a difficult birth, and Gloria stayed in the hospital for several weeks. Her release from the hospital provided her with one of her favorite stories about her dreamy husband. Jim went to get the car to pick her up, but sometime between leaving the hospital and getting in the car, he forgot that he was supposed to get Gloria. Instead, he started driving home.

Gloria knew her man. After twenty minutes of waiting, she told the nurse that he had forgotten about her. The nurse didn't think such a thing was possible, but Gloria knew better. She told the nurse to take her and the babies upstairs. She would wait for the absentminded actor to remember what he had forgotten. On the way back home, Jim stopped at a photography studio to pick up some pictures. When the photographer asked after Gloria, Jim suddenly realized what he had done and ran for a phone. He'd be right there, he told her.

Gloria reveled in telling that story for the rest of her life. "The thing I like best about Jimmy is that special humor of his," she said. "Once we were out somewhere and I was trying to explain to someone for the umpteenth time the difference between identical and fraternal twins. Anyway, whoever it was didn't get it very well, and Jimmy, as he always does, broke the ice.

" 'Golly,' he said, 'I always thought they were nocturnal.' "

The fresh brace of twins joined Ronald and Michael McLean. The girls would have a French governess and attend the Westlake Academy. Similarly, Ron and Michael were sent to the Black-Foxe Military Institute, where so many boys of the movie colony spent time, most of them grudgingly. Michael was sent there in the second grade, Ron in the third, and each of them boarded there for part of each year through the eighth grade. The upside of the time at Black-Foxe was that the boys learned the facts of life from the other boys and were spared an embarrassed conversation with their father.

For the most part, Stewart let Gloria do most of the work with the girls, except for one occasion when he decided to be a hands-on dad. It was a birthday party when they were seven or eight, and Stewart commandeered the MCA projection room for a private screening for the girls and their friends, among whom was Sue Lloyd, Harold Lloyd's granddaughter.

The film Stewart chose to show was *Bambi.*

"About fifteen minutes into the picture Bambi's mother is killed, and very promptly there were a dozen little girls in hysterics," remembered Sue Lloyd. "It got so bad the screening had to be stopped. After that, Gloria took charge of the birthdays."

Domesticity agreed with Stewart, and his friends agreed that Gloria and a family were complete positives for his emotional balance and responsiveness. "I, too, am very glad about Stewart," Leland Hayward wrote Josh Logan, "because he seems happy and adjusted and he is getting something out of his life that he has always needed."

Life on North Roxbury was more or less that of a typically close-knit American neighborhood, except with higher per capita net worth. The two blocks that ran north off Sunset were a concentrated compendium of talent. The Stewarts were at 918, pianist and actor Oscar Levant lived across the street, and down the street from Levant were José Ferrer and Rosemary Clooney.

The Ferrers' next-door neighbors were Ira and Lenore Gershwin, and their next-door neighbor was Lucille Ball. On the other side of the Ferrers was Agnes Moorehead, and a few doors away from her was Thomas

Mitchell. Other longtime residents of the street included Eddie Cantor, Hedy Lamarr, and Pandro Berman.

It was a pleasant, low-key environment where everybody knew everybody else. Nobody bothered to lock their doors. "I never had the feeling growing up that this was a really wow, super-duper place to live," says Kelly Stewart Harcourt. "It was just our home. I remember reading an article somewhere where our house was described as a mansion, and it struck me as ridiculous."

Jim and Gloria adored another neighbor, Jack Benny — everyone did — and agreed to appear on his TV show from time to time, if for no other reason than that it seemed the neighborly thing to do. At Halloween, Lucille Ball would dress up as a witch and hand out candy at the door. If the light was on at 1021 — the Gershwins' — it meant that anyone could drop in for a drink or some poker. The worst thing anybody could remember happening was the time the Ferrers got stopped for violating the Beverly Hills curfew by walking home from Jack Benny's house without ID.

Tour buses rolled by constantly, and occasionally stopped so people could take pictures. Sometimes the braver ones would knock on doors. Jack Benny kept a supply of 8 × 10s in a hall drawer. If he happened to be home, he'd answer the door himself and greet people.

At the Stewart house, occasionally the girls would answer the door instead of the housekeeper. "Usually it would be 'Mr. Stewart is resting' or 'Mr. Stewart is away,' " Kelly Stewart Harcourt remembered. "But other times — and this happened very rarely — people were just, you know, they'd come all the way from Iowa and they were so sweet and seemed so innocent, and Judy and I would take a piece of paper and get Dad and just beg him to sign it. And if he was having a nap, I must admit a couple of times I forged his signature."

There was only one instance when things got out of hand. A group of tourists decided to have a picnic lunch on the Stewart front lawn. They put down a blanket and basket and were just getting started on their meal when an annoyed Jim turned on the sprinklers and ended the picnic.

By the time they installed the garden next door, Stewart had evolved past his early juvenile stage to become an American icon, with a capacity for anguish and rage that would have been unthinkable to the fans of the boyish prewar Stewart. The war had unlocked him as an actor.

Despite his maturation, Jim was a remarkably consistent man who was comfortable in a deep groove. (He drove a boxy Volvo for years instead of a more stylish Mercedes or Rolls simply because the Volvo offered more head room.)

Part of that groove was his continuing unwillingness to talk about his experiences in World War II. With one minor exception (*The Mountain Road*), he never starred in a World War II movie. Kelly would remember that "we grew up knowing almost nothing about those years. Dad never talked about the war. My siblings and I knew only that he had been a pilot, and that he had won some medals, but that he didn't see himself as a hero. He saw only that he had done his duty."

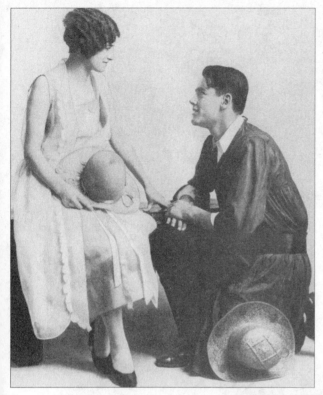

A newly stagestruck Henry Fonda at the Omaha Community Playhouse around 1927.

James Stewart as James Stewart, a young man-about-town who set ladies' hearts on fire with a motherly flame, even as he frustrated producers who tried to figure out what kind of actor he was.

In 1936, after a few months in Hollywood, Fonda was teamed with his ex-wife Margaret Sullavan in the romantic comedy *The Moon's Our Home*. The result was a brief flare-up of their infatuation, followed by a mutual agreement to stay divorced.

Two handsome young lads with their dates at the Trocadero night club one night in 1936. The ladies are Virginia Bruce and Madeleine Carroll. EVERETT COLLECTION

Fonda, the first husband of Margaret Sullavan, playing opposite Bette Davis in *Jezebel* (1938), directed by William Wyler—Sullavan's second husband. Fonda and Wyler got along just fine.

John Ford around the time he met Fonda and started converting him into one of his two primary men of the West—a slow-burning yin to John Wayne's more hot-blooded yang.

Other than a false nose, the Fox makeup department didn't have to do much to turn Fonda into a reasonable facsimile of *Young Mr. Lincoln* (1939). The rest of the portrayal came from Fonda's inner stillness and penetrating prairie rhythms.

James Stewart at his impassioned best in Frank Capra's
Mr. Smith Goes to Washington (1939).

Stewart gazing at Marlene Dietrich in *Destry Rides Again* (1939) with an unlikely but very real intensity that was replicated off-screen as well.

Stewart and Margaret Sullavan listen to Ernst Lubitsch as he modulates their performances for the exquisite *The Shop Around the Corner* (1940).

Fonda as Tom Joad, the ghost in the American darkness, with John
Carradine as Jim Casy in John Ford's *The Grapes of Wrath* (1940).
Carradine called Fonda "The most natural actor I ever saw."

Before Stewart went overseas, he visited Fonda on the set of the art western
The Ox-Bow Incident. The gray head in the foreground belongs to director
William Wellman. COURTESY LEONARD MALTIN COLLECTION

James Stewart was a decorated bomber pilot based in England during World War II. COURTESY L. TOM PERRY SPECIAL COLLECTIONS, HAROLD B. LEE LIBRARY, BRIGHAM YOUNG UNIVERSITY, PROVO, UTAH

Stewart playing the piano with great enthusiasm during a stag party given by officers of the 2nd Bomb Wing. COURTESY L. TOM PERRY SPECIAL COLLECTIONS, HAROLD B. LEE LIBRARY, BRIGHAM YOUNG UNIVERSITY, PROVO, UTAH

After leaving the Air Force at the end of World War II, Stewart hung around his father's hardware store in Indiana, Pennsylvania, for a few weeks. The burly older gent next to Stewart is his father, Alex. COURTESY L. TOM PERRY SPECIAL COLLECTIONS, HAROLD B. LEE LIBRARY, BRIGHAM YOUNG UNIVERSITY, PROVO, UTAH

Fonda and his second wife, Frances, along with Stewart and Anita Colby, attend the premiere of Alfred Hitchcock's *Spellbound* in 1945. Frances, with her head down, is to the right of Stewart.

Stewart's beleaguered George Bailey in Frank Capra's *It's a Wonderful Life* (1946). It became the public's favorite Stewart performance.

Fonda and Stewart get together for a strenuous afternoon of kite flying in 1947, shortly before Hank left Hollywood for New York. PHOTOFEST

Henry Fonda's indelible portrayal of a watchful Wyatt Earp in his first film after World War II—John Ford's classic *My Darling Clementine* (1946).

Fonda and Stewart in their hilarious shaggy-dog segment of *On Our Merry Way* (1948) with old friend Burgess Meredith, who produced the picture.

Elwood P. Dowd provided Stewart with one of his
signature roles in *Harvey* (1950).

Stewart with his wife, Gloria, his twin stepsons, Michael and Ronald,
and newborn twin girls in 1951.

James Stewart with Grace Kelly and Alfred Hitchcock on the
spectacular set of *Rear Window* (1954).

The film version of Fonda's signature stage hit *Mister Roberts* (1955)
destroyed the friendship between the actor and John Ford. Despite the fact
that nobody who made the film liked it, it was a critical and financial hit.

Stewart as Charles Lindbergh in Billy Wilder's *The Spirit of St. Louis* (1957), a good film that went far over budget and became Warner Bros.' greatest financial flop ever up to that point.

12 Angry Men (1957) was the only film Fonda produced. It provided him with one of his indelible roles as a hesitant seeker of truth.

Stewart and Kim Novak in Alfred Hitchcock's *Vertigo* (1958).
"Next to my husband, Jimmy was my favorite man," said Novak.

The Fonda acting dynasty: Fonda with
his children, Peter and Jane, circa 1960.

Stewart with George C. Scott and Eve
Arden in Otto Preminger's *Anatomy
of a Murder* (1959), which drew on the
star's total command of technique and
emotional ambivalence.

Stewart and Fonda in *Firecreek* (1968), their first film together in twenty years.

Henry Fonda and his last wife, Shirlee, who calmed many of his emotional tempests.

Fonda and Stewart in the puckish western *The Cheyenne Social Club* (1970), their last film together.

Jane Fonda's production of *On Golden Pond* (1981) gave her father an appropriate farewell to more than forty-five years of stellar movie acting, as well as an Academy Award for Best Actor. Here he is with costars Jane, Katharine Hepburn, and Doug McKeon (back to camera).

TEN

In the years after the war, whenever Fonda felt trapped he would retreat — away from wives and children, back to New York, to the theater. In 1948, he had the career-changing hit of *Mister Roberts,* co-written and directed by his old friend and occasional roommate Josh Logan. *Mister Roberts* isn't produced often anymore, but it struck a postwar nerve in the same way *The Best Years of Our Lives* did: it put the losses of the war in a universal dramatic context, with an accompanying dose of fatalism and a salting of humor.

It's the story of Lieutenant (j.g.) Doug Roberts, on board the supply ship USS *Reluctant.* Frustration is Mister Roberts's boon companion; he wants to get into combat, but the Captain won't approve his transfer. Roberts finally finagles his transfer and dies offstage in a kamikaze attack while waiting to get to the battle zone.

The story began as a short novel by Thomas Heggen and was converted into a play by Heggen and Logan, with Leland Hayward producing. When it came time for casting, Heggen told Logan, "I know it's crazy, but when I was writing Roberts, I was always thinking of Henry Fonda."

"That's a terrible idea," replied Logan. "I ought to know, because I've had the same terrible idea for a long time." Fonda had signed for a movie, but he agreed to come to a reading of the play. Afterward, Logan said, "Hank, I'm really sorry you can't play Roberts."

"Don't worry about it," he told Logan. "I'm going to play Roberts."

"What about the movie contract?" asked Logan. "You've already had costume fittings."

"They can be unfitted."

Mister Roberts began a theatrical journey that took Fonda away from Hollywood for nearly a decade. On his last night before leaving for New York, John Ford, John Wayne, Ward Bond, and stuntman Frank McGrath came to Fonda's house for a farewell session of pitch. As always, Ford brought a sack of silver dollars. The stakes were actually rather modest, but Ford liked the way the silver dollars sounded on the green felt of the table. The men played through the night, and when the game finally broke up at dawn, Fonda had only a few hours to say goodbye to his family before leaving.

The cast of *Mister Roberts* was completed with David Wayne playing Ensign Pulver, Robert Keith as Doc, and William Harrigan (Josh Logan's brother-in-law) as the Captain. Every young actor in New York tried out for the parts of sailors, Lee Marvin and Jack Lemmon among them, although neither was hired. Hank partially repaid his debt to Doe Brando back in Omaha by casting her daughter, Jocelyn, in a showy part as Nurse Ann Girard after two other actresses had washed out.

Doe Brando always yearned for a world brighter than Omaha, but never got there. She would die in 1954 after years as a hopeless alcoholic. As her son, Marlon, would tell Truman Capote, "My mother was everything to me. A whole world. I tried so hard. I used to come home from school. . . . There wouldn't be anybody home. Nothing in the icebox. Then the telephone would ring. Somebody calling from some bar. And they'd say, 'We've got a lady down here. You better come get her.' . . . She broke apart like a piece of porcelain."

Jocelyn had been part of Fonda's life since she was born; she had sat on Hank's lap when she was seven years old. When Jocelyn got measles, she gave them to Hank. And when Jocelyn was a teenager, she developed a fierce crush on Hank, as did many of her girlfriends, but only Jocelyn had a picture of him on her dresser.

"The world is only made up of six people," she reminisced. "Hank was wonderful to me, always. He's very serious about the play. He's very serious about his work, so it wasn't a whole bunch of social stuff. But he always had his eye out to see that I was OK and we would sit in his [dressing] room and talk when we had time."

Although Fonda and Logan had been pals for nearly twenty years, the actor didn't cut the director any slack in rehearsal. When Logan asked that Fonda move on a line because it would help Logan figure out the blocking, Fonda dug in his heels.

"I'm not trying to help you," he snapped at Logan. "I'm trying to play Roberts. Roberts wouldn't move a muscle on that line, Josh. This is not a Princeton Triangle Show. This is Broadway. We're going to face a New York audience."

At this point, Logan had directed more than dozen Broadway shows and was presumably aware of the venue. The two men proceeded to get into it. "Fonda has within him a small but inextinguishable flame that burns in worship of the art of the theater," Logan would write with a nearly audible sigh in his memoirs. "When he feels laxness, insincerity, dilettantism around him, Hank can fly into short-lived tantrums and his votive flame can become a holocaust."

Logan called a private meeting that night, during which he ex-postulated on the character, background, and desires of Doug Roberts. He spoke not as the director, but as the coauthor. Fonda listened quietly and finally realized that Logan wasn't trying to undermine the character or the actor playing him via slapdash staging. He thanked Logan and never questioned Logan's direction again . . . at least during the initial production.

Mister Roberts was financed by an interesting group of backers. Mrs. Sophie Seymour, Frances's mother, invested on behalf of Jane and Peter, while Jo Mielziner, John Swope, Hedda Hopper, and Billy Wilder invested on behalf of themselves. (Wilder and Leland Hayward were friends of long standing; at one point during World War II, Hayward loaned Wilder $2,500. Wilder took years to pay it back, although Hayward didn't hold it against him.)

Josh Logan was in for 3 percent of the gross for the New York run as well as 3 percent of the gross of any road companies he directed, and 10 2/3 percent of net profits. His wife, Nedda, got 6 percent of the net for "consulting," a very hefty amount for what amounted to holding Josh's hand. The percentage was undoubtedly a back-door way of pushing up Logan's royalties.

Mister Roberts opened at the Alvin Theatre on February 18, 1948. Josh Logan stood quietly in the back of the theater, while Leland Hayward sat and watched his production meet a rapturous reception, the sort of stars-in-alignment hit that happens only once in any producer's or actor's lifetime. Everyone was at the performance — Eddie Duchin, Harold Ross, Moss Hart, Mike Todd, Henry Luce, Herbert Bayard Swope — and the party afterward was even more luminous: Irene Mayer Selznick, Lew Wasserman, Myrna Loy, Edna Ferber, Charles MacArthur and Helen Hayes, Cecil Beaton, Greta Garbo. And Margaret Sullavan.

At the party, Dorothy Parker knelt at the feet of Harvey Lembeck, who was playing one of the sailors. Lembeck nearly fainted. And then the reviews came in and it became what Nedda Logan recalled as "the most electric party I've ever known . . . they all knew they had jobs for a long time."

The only discouraging word came from Lew Wasserman, who demanded that Logan cut one line: when Doc asks where Ensign Pulver had gotten fulminate of mercury, Roberts replies, "He's pretty resourceful. Where did he get the clap last year?"

Wasserman thought the line was needlessly coarse and might bring the police down on the show. Logan disagreed, but Wasserman convinced Hayward and the line was cut, except for a performance shortly after the opening, when Jim Stewart was in the audience and Logan and Fonda put the line back in just for him.

Mister Roberts won Tony Awards for Best Play, Best Director, and Fonda won for Best Actor. The show ran on Broadway for several years, after which Fonda took it on tour for another year. Leland Hayward had produced hits before, but not on this scale; he now had the considerable problem of finding alternate casts for road companies and the London company.

After heavy negotiations, Hayward hired Tyrone Power for the London company for 10 percent of the gross for a six-month contract, plus £400 weekly for expenses, plus 10 percent of the gross over £4,000.

(When the London production opened in July 1950, Hank's opening night telegram to Hayward read: "You know I won't believe a word you tell me. Love, Hank." Tyrone Power gave what Hayward thought was a surprisingly good performance, considering he had never really done much stage work, but the show proved too American for English audiences and closed at a loss after Power's contract ended early in 1951.)

Every serious actor invests himself in a part to a greater or lesser degree, but Fonda was particularly possessive of Doug Roberts, identifying strongly with his character's dissatisfaction with what was on offer from life. Because of the autobiographical elements — Fonda's and Roberts's mutual peevishness, the respect other men and cast members had for them, not to mention the tragic death Fonda avoided by not being present when the kamikaze plane smashed into his ship — the role must have been eerily satisfying to play. For Fonda, the Captain probably stood in for Darryl Zanuck and every other small-minded, dictatorial director and studio head.

The show cemented Fonda's passion for the stage, to which he would return regularly for the rest of his life. As a result, he didn't star in a movie for seven long years after the premiere of *Mister Roberts.* As a small sign of the synchronicity between actor and part, Hank even wore his own naval officer's cap onstage for the entire run of the play.

Mister Roberts became one of those shows that other actors attend in order to see the lead performance. One of the young actors in the show was Fess Parker, later to achieve renown as Disney's Davy Crockett. "Every performance, whenever I wasn't onstage, I stood in the wings, watching [Fonda] — as a student," said Parker. "I observed as far as my eye could see and my ear could hear. And every night he hit the emotional moment of discovery — the scene where he finds out the crew has gone to bat for him. He did it *every* night, night after night."

This was not an accident, not the result of lightning coming down from heaven and providentially striking Fonda at 10:30 p.m. Peter Fonda had gotten a glimpse of his father's intent when he ran lines with him. "We would sit in his office and I would read him his cue line. Sometimes he wouldn't pick up the cue, and I would repeat his cue line, and he would fly off the handle. 'I know the line, goddamnit!' What he was doing was taking a moment to think about how to get the most out of the line. *Every* line. He was a thinking actor, profoundly so."

For Fonda, playing Roberts came to encapsulate his theories about acting, about performance. It was a very simple thing, really, the sort of simple thing that can take a lifetime to accomplish — if then.

> I know what I want to achieve as an actor in whatever I do . . . and that is not to let the wheels show. There's a great deal of work that goes on in rehearsals and preparing a part — in technique, in learning a technique.
> But if that shows onstage when you're performing, then you're acting as far as I'm concerned. And if you're acting, the audience can never forget that you're acting. If you can make the audience forget you're acting and become so involved in the performance, in a play that they forget they're watching a performance — that [is] the ultimate for me.

It's possible that Fonda's identification with the character gradually eroded his allegiance to the play. Josh Logan remembered that before the national tour got to Los Angeles, he stopped off in San Francisco to check out the show and make sure it was in proper shape. He was shocked to find that the play had become bland because the comedy had been leached out of it.

"All of them were playing Henry Fonda," said Logan. "Understate, understate everything. . . . It [was] done so quietly that you couldn't hear it. . . . They seemed smug and almost pompous to me." Logan got to work and put the laughs back in, upsetting Fonda in the process.

"[Don't] you want me to bring it back to its original spirit?" asked Logan.

"No, I don't feel it's my play anymore."

"No, you son of a bitch, it's mine!"

The next day Fonda went to Leland Hayward and said, "If that goddamned Logan directs the picture, I won't play in it."

While Fonda was having the greatest theatrical success of his life, his wife and his marriage were crumbling. As he settled into the run, he took a house in Greenwich, Connecticut.

"She was a beautiful, beautiful girl," Josh Logan said of Frances, but then he pinpointed the underlying misalliance. "She really didn't talk about anything that interested Fonda. She talked about money, about investments, about clothes, about how to raise children. She had about seven subjects that she could talk about, and Fonda had 77."

Frances had found a new hobby: collecting butterflies. She would catch the insect in the Connecticut woods, then drop it into a glass jar that held a cotton ball soaked in ether. After the butterfly had stopped fluttering, she would remove the butterfly with tweezers and mount it on a white board with a long pin. She had a dozen or so of them — a swallowtail, a southern dogface, a red admiral, a clouded sulphur, and a monarch, among others.

All this was in a rented house on a big hill that that overlooked the Merritt Parkway. The house felt underpopulated, full of whispers and silences. Besides the immediate family, Frances's mother, who helped take care of Jane and Peter when their mother was indisposed, and a Japanese-American maid named Katie were also in residence.

The house in Greenwich just happened to be close by the Hayward-Sullavan house, and the Hayward kids would regularly go over to the Fondas' for lunch or dinner. Typically, Frances would not appear. "She was very difficult," said Brooke Hayward. "She was remote. She was not a charmer."

Hank was gone six nights out of seven,

doing his eight performances a week. "Fonda was . . . a stoic," said David Wayne. "His performance never varied. If anything, all our work kept improving week after week, and Hank set the example. But as far as he was personally concerned, at that time I always thought he was some poor son of a bitch who had nothing in the world except those eight performances a week."

But Fonda wasn't a natural animal of the theater; he had a way of edging away from the star's prerogatives. Logan remembered that Fonda "always wanted to face upstage. I had to use tricks to get him so the audience could see him work." But that was his way — Fonda's basic recessiveness meant that he didn't present emotions to the audience; rather, the audience was forced to search for them with the same level of intensity he brought to his acting.

Besides the siren call of the theater, there was another reason for Fonda's self-imposed exile in New York: Hollywood was tearing itself apart looking for Communists. Stewart had been a conservative Republican since birth; Fonda had always been equally liberal. Somehow or other, all this was tabled during the first years of their friendship, even when the Hollywood Anti-Nazi League formed in 1936. The league was anti-Nazi and anti-Fascist, but not anti-Communist. It successfully lobbied against the Hollywood visit of Vittorio Mussolini, the son of Il Duce, who had formed a movie company with Hal Roach, and also lobbied against the Hollywood tour of Leni Riefenstahl. The league succeeded in closing most of the industry to Riefenstahl; only Walt Disney received her at his studio.

At its peak, the Anti-Nazi League had about four thousand members, including Fonda, John Ford, Dorothy Parker, Edward G. Robinson, Paul Muni, James Cagney, Jack Warner, Bette Davis, Groucho Marx, Ben Hecht, Dick Powell, Spencer Tracy, and Lucille Ball. By 1939, in the aftermath of the Hitler-Stalin nonaggression pact, membership began to decline and the organization changed its name to the Hollywood League for Democratic Action. Its New Year's card for 1940 decried "the war to lead America to war."

After the war, when the House Un-American Activities Committee swung into action, Fonda joined with Humphrey Bogart, Lauren Bacall, John Huston, and others in forming the Committee for the First Amendment, which sent out an open letter castigating HUAC. The committee circulated a petition that said that "any investigation into the political beliefs of the individual is contrary to the basic principles of our democracy. Any attempt to curb freedom of expression and to set arbitrary standards of Americanism is in itself disloyal to both the spirit and the letter of the Constitution." Among the people who signed the petition were Fonda, Billy Wilder, Ava Gardner, Benny Goodman, Humphrey Bogart, Lauren Bacall, Ira Gershwin, Sterling Hayden, Gene Kelly, Danny Kaye, Katharine Hepburn, Myrna Loy, Gregory Peck, and Norman Corwin.

Opposing the committee was the conservative Motion Picture Alliance, whose intellectual godmother was Ayn Rand. Sam Wood and James Kevin McGuinness ran the ground operation and John Wayne served as the alliance's public face. (Although the alliance had its own list of members of varying degrees of prestige, at no time was Stewart's name ever attached to it or to any other other blacklisting activity.)

At some point in 1947 Fonda's and Stewart's differing political allegiances led to a major blowup. Stewart remembered that the argument with Fonda was "long" and "pretty heated." It ended only when they both realized that they were stomping on very thin emotional ice. They were jeopardizing their friendship, and neither man was willing to do that over politics or, for that matter, anything else. In later years, neither man would go into detail over what was said, or by whom. "If we were going to stay friends," said Fonda, "we better just stay off that subject, and we have. It's not difficult."

"They agreed to disagree, and not to talk about it anymore," remembered Jane Fonda. "I know that it was definitely about the House Un-American Activities Committee and what became known as McCarthyism. My father would occasionally mention the late 1940s, and Duke Wayne and Ward Bond, and his disappointment in them was clear. But he never talked about Jimmy that way. I never heard him say a single word against Jimmy, even though there was that political divide."

Fonda could forgive Jim for siding with reactionaries, but in later years he avoided socializing with Wayne and his group, who took a more active position. "I told Ward [Bond] off," Fonda remembered, "[and] it ended our relationship, our friendship. I didn't ever have a confrontation with Duke. . . . When anybody's as crazy as that, you can't argue with them. We were friends at least."

In the summer of 1948 Frances checked herself into the Austen Riggs Center, a high-end sanitarium in Stockbridge, Massachusetts, which had also served as temporary quarters for Margaret Sullavan and her daughter Bridget. Frances had begun to feel ugly, fat, paranoid. Her situation, she felt, was without hope.

As Frances spiraled down, Fonda retreated ever deeper within himself. He took to working on his drawing during the waits between matinee and evening performances, and his talent began to show a professional polish.

"Jane and Peter were more or less the same age as my brother and I," remembered Brooke Hayward. "And they went to school at the same place Bill and I went, the Greenwich Academy, so we were all very close friends. Fonda would come over to our house all the time, and he would drive the kids with him. He and mother remained very close."

There was much intramural discussion between the children as to just how close they were. They came to believe that Hank and Maggie were still in love and sleeping together. "I choose to believe that of course Maggie and Henry were getting it on," Peter Fonda would say. "I know they did . . . we all knew that." (There is nothing in Sullavan's correspondence from this period to back up the children's suspicions.)

Bill Hayward, Leland's son with Sullavan, was a smart, observant kid who grew up to be a smart, observant man, and his recollections of Fonda and Stewart at this stage of their lives are fascinating. "Henry Fonda," he insisted, "was the funniest man I ever knew. He had a wit about him. And he was a practical joker, big time. He was a very clever, very funny man. He could always make me laugh. *Always.* A very dry wit. He didn't keep Peter laughing long, but he kept me rolling on the floor. I thought he was great.

"He and Peter had some problems, but you know, fathers and sons are complicated. Henry had no expectations for me. If I failed, he didn't care. He dealt with me just like a kid. But with Peter he had a lot of expectations and ambitions."

Josh Logan's take was similar. Away from the work, which Fonda approached as a clinician, "the ridiculous side of Fonda . . . was fabulous. When he is not trying to be a leading man, not trying to be a general or anything like that, he can be the funniest man that ever walked the streets. He can be Harpo Marx or Groucho Marx or he can be Chaplin, he can be anything if he wants to be."

But Stewart had that same Mona Lisa quality for Bill Hayward that he did for a lot of people. "He's a really unique character to me. He was in a bunch of movies with my mother, and my father was his agent. They put him in funny roles — romantic roles, comedic roles . . . western[s] as a kind of bad guy — and it was interesting because he got away with it on some level, with that weird presentation of his. He was a funny man . . . always a regular guy to me."

Fonda was innately attuned to sparse Protestant distancing, but he didn't partake of other traits of that time and place. He didn't, for instance, trust Greenwich; it was too suburban, which to him reeked of middle-class hypocrisy. Jane first heard the word "nigger" in Greenwich, and used it shortly thereafter. Her father was driving at the time, and he stopped the car, turned around and smacked her lightly across the face. "Don't you ever, *ever* use that word again!" he ordered. It was the only time he ever hit her.

"Jane was jealous of her father," said

Brooke Hayward. "I was eleven or twelve, and so was she. Because Hank was doing *Mister Roberts,* he'd eat around five, then take the train into New York for the performance. Mrs. Fonda never appeared, but I was there, along with my sister and my brother. And Fonda. He would be sitting there at the table, and Jane would begin to misbehave. And I distinctly remember thinking, 'All she wants is more attention.' And that would be the case throughout her life."

The kids went back and forth between the two houses, but the Fondas were invited to the Haywards' for dinner only once, an invitation Frances never returned. "Something in Dad became more alive when Sullavan was around, and if *I* picked it up, Mother must have," Jane Fonda remembered.

The Hayward-Sullavan marriage broke up when Sullavan discovered that her husband was having an affair with Slim Hawks, the ex-wife of Howard Hawks, who had used her as the model for the cool, insolent women in his movies.

Brooke Hayward wrote a nonpareil account of her parents' marriage and what came after in *Haywire,* but the progression can be charted in a couple of documents.

In September 1941, Hayward sent his wife, who was on a steamship, a telegram: "Darling children wonderful and absolutely enchanting house wonderful tree wonderful pool wonderful awning wonderful you're wonderful and I love and miss you terribly." By October 1949, Sullavan was writing him snippy letters haggling over child custody arrangements, with Hayward backing away in abject confusion. Men are generally terrified of angry women, and Sullavan could go from zero to sixty in two seconds flat.

Beneath the Golden Couple facade it had never been an easy union. Although he had sold his agency, Hayward was still constantly moving between coasts, while Sullavan preferred to stay home. He loved Hollywood, while she loathed it. He was easygoing with their children, which meant she had to play the disciplinarian, refusing to let them read comic books or listen to the radio.

"Your mother is a remarkable woman," Leland told Brooke, "but she can't tolerate what she can't understand." Once the divorce was final, Leland married Slim Hawks, who settled in for a ten-year run, while Sullavan married Kenneth Wagg, an English businessman. "Ken was a very nice man," said his stepdaughter Brooke, "but he was in over his head."

Over at the Fonda house, things were equally fraught. Frances was in and out of Austen Riggs several times. With her mother becoming increasingly frail and withdrawn, Jane was drawn to Margaret Sullavan's zest and knack for games and laughter. She was particularly entranced by Sullavan's ability to walk on her hands — a trick that Fonda had taught her during their courtship and brief marriage.

With his wife unable to function, it was only a question of time until Fonda found someone else to share his glory with — someone less complicated, someone younger. Much younger. She was Susan Blanchard, the twenty-one-year-old step-daughter of Oscar Hammerstein II. It seems to have started as a fling that gradually boxed Fonda in; he said that Hammerstein braced him one day and asked, "Are you going to do right by my little girl?" For a man who was something of a moralist — assuming you can be a moralist and marry five times — there was only one possible response.

In mid-1949, Henry asked Frances for a divorce, which had the inevitable result of sinking her deeper into depression. A few days after the conversation, Frances told Jane, "If anyone tells you that your father and I are getting divorced, tell them you already know."

Right around this time, Frances asked her daughter if she'd like to see the scar from a recent kidney operation. The scar was pink and thick and ran around her waist. "I've lost all my stomach muscle," said Frances. "Doesn't that look awful?" Then Frances showed her daughter one of her breasts, which had a disfigured nipple from a botched breast implant. Jane believed that the surgeries were why her parents were getting divorced — who would want to live with someone who had been cut in half?

If Frances was looking for sympathy, she didn't get it; Jane was beyond embarrassed. Like any child, she wanted a mother who was lovely and healthy, not one who was damaged inside and out.

In January of 1950, Frances was back at Austen Riggs, but she was spiraling beyond the expertise of the Riggs staff, or of any staff. She was moved to Craig House Sanitarium in Beacon, New York. On April 14, her forty-second birthday, Frances wrote a series of notes — one to each of her children, one to her mother, one to her nurse. The latter read, "Mrs. Gray, Do not enter the bathroom, but call Dr. Bennett."

And then Frances Seymour Brokaw Fonda

slashed her throat with a razor she had smuggled into the sanitarium.

That night, Fonda went on as Doug Roberts. "We were all stunned," said Jocelyn Brando. "Billy Hammerstein, the stage manager, called us all together and told us what had happened. And that Hank wanted to go ahead with the show and not have anybody say anything about it. . . . I think Hank felt that it was good for him to go ahead and do it. . . . And we played it with love and concentration and it was a fine show. The night Frances died."

Fonda believed the children were too young to know the truth, so their grandmother told them that Frances had died of a heart attack. With a breathtaking, garbled imperviousness, Fonda remembered that "Frances had been away so long it wasn't difficult [for the children to adjust]. It wasn't as though their mother that they saw every day and greeted them at the door when they came home from school and tucked them into bed at night and everything had suddenly dropped dead." Then and later, he blocked himself off from any recriminatory guilt about his wife. "Frances was a hypochondriac. . . . Hypochondria and emotional things are not related, as far as I am concerned. I don't put them in the same category."

Sometimes he would go down the roster of catastrophes that he had survived and relegate Frances to the second tier: "I survived [Sullavan] . . . and I survived Frances' death and a lot of others. There were many. But I guess that [Sullavan] was probably the worst." And sometimes after saying these things, he would pull back. "I hear myself telling these stories, and I don't like myself, because it sounds like I'm saying that it had nothing to do with me. [But] my wife ceased being a wife." He knew he had something to do with the catastrophe, but he couldn't bring himself to accept responsibility; it was more convenient to ascribe the disaster to mental illness.

"The day after Frances committed suicide," remembered Brooke Hayward, "the headmistress at the Greenwich Academy called an assembly and told the entire school to never bring up the fact that Mrs. Fonda had committed suicide. Her children, she said, had been told she had a heart attack."

While Fonda attended to the funeral, he sent Jane to the house of her friend Diana Dunn. Jane was there for several days, but nothing was said about the death of her mother. Jane carried on as if nothing had happened. She didn't cry, and her friend was afraid for her.

"About six months later," Brooke Hayward said, "Jane and I were in an art class and we were being naughty and reading a movie magazine. In the center of the magazine there was a dictionary of all the stars. And there was a mention of Mr. and Mrs. Fonda and how she had committed suicide. I read the sentence and turned the page rapidly, and Jane reached over and turned the page back and read it again. And then she looked at me. I didn't know what to say.

"She never mentioned it again."

Jane never told her father she had learned the truth about her mother's death. She was afraid that bringing up her mother in any context would upset him.

The conspiracy of silence went deeper. "After her death, my mother's name was never mentioned in the house." said Peter Fonda. The children were never given the notes that their mother had written to them.

The production of *Mister Roberts* was a nest of psychological misfits. Josh Logan's breakdowns and ancillary issues would eventually become show business legends, and Thomas Heggen, the author of the novel and coauthor of the play, would commit suicide in

1949. ("I was never impressed with Josh Logan the man or Josh Logan the director," Tennessee Williams said. "He operated under the delusional notion that we were similar in nature, being Southern and queer and all, but I found his taste deplorable.")

When Fonda took *Mister Roberts* on its national tour, Leland Hayward kept Josh Logan apprised of events, and of their star's volatile moods. In years to come, Jane and Peter would personalize Fonda's silences and spasms of anger, but it's clear that his behavior had nothing to do with his children.

By April 1950, Fonda had developed a passionate dislike of Henry Hull, who was playing Doc. "I talked to Fonda this morning," wrote Hayward to Logan, "and he is of course pleased that Hull is out, but Hank is in one of his disagreeable moods. You know, the same old story — we should have had Hull out months ago, it has become only a duty to him to play the part to make money and not for pleasure, everybody has neglected the show, etc., etc., etc.

"You know Hank as well as I. When he has a personal problem that is troubling him, I think completely subconsciously but nevertheless effectively, he takes that problem out on everybody else in connection with everything he does."

Another Hayward letter began, "You know how mean Fonda can be." It seemed that Dick Van Patten, playing Pulver, got more laughs than usual one night. Van Patten was wondering what he had done differently, when Fonda told him, "You didn't do anything different. It's just that your [new] haircut makes people like you better."

Hank stayed with the New York production of *Mister Roberts* until late October 1950. He married Susan Blanchard in December, and they honeymooned in the Virgin Islands, where Susan lost her wedding ring. She was devastated and began to cry, whereupon Fonda blew up and began yelling that he never wanted to see her cry again.

Blanchard proved warm and nurturing to Jane and Peter; after the years of gloom and depression that surrounded their mother, Susan was the sun. She and Hank even adopted a child, a girl named Amy. The children grew to adore Susan, but as far as their father was concerned it was another misalliance. The marriage would last six years.

After *Mister Roberts,* it seemed obvious that Hayward and Fonda should do another show, and the choice was *Point of No Return,* an adaptation by Paul Osborn of a best-selling John P. Marquand novel about a man in a gray flannel suit who tries to retain his personal integrity. The investors included Fonda with $10,000, Billy Rose, Josh and Nedda Logan, Mary Martin, George Abbott, Hedda Hopper, Irwin Shaw, Billy Wilder, and Irving Berlin. The entire production cost only $200,000, and it ran for a season in New York, more or less because of Fonda's career momentum from *Mister Roberts.*

It was a troubled show, ostensibly directed by Hank Potter, Jim and Josh's old friend from Princeton, but in fact Elia Kazan quietly redirected the show in return for 5 percent of the net, which was more than Potter got. Fonda was paid $1,500 a week plus 10 percent of the weekly gross over $15,000. Most weeks he netted between $2,300 and $3,000, although his net pay went down to $1,600 a week by the summer. On tour he got a straight 10 percent of the gross.

The play was a high-toned slog, and Fonda thought it lacked the courage of its stated convictions. It was the tour that caused his disaffection to boil over. "Do we really have to finish this?" he wrote Hayward in January 1953 from Columbus, Ohio:

Why don't you . . . bring us all home? If you're not ready to call it off — at least send [general manager] Marshall [Jamison] out to see if he can do something about it.

It's embarrassing not to have a good show.

Get a load of the enclosed.

Love and kisses . . .

Enclosed were reviews from the three Columbus papers, whose opinions were summarized by the phrase "adequately enacted by Henry Fonda and company."

Hayward was disinclined to put too much credence in Fonda's black moods, and the tour successfully wound its way through the country for a season. Grudging reviews aside, Fonda always enjoyed the road. There were always good museums to explore — he particularly loved Kansas City, which featured a lot of Thomas Hart Benton's paintings — and zoos. "I'm a zoo freak," he would proclaim — another bond between him and Stewart.

ELEVEN

Beginning in 1950, Stewart reeled off a long succession of hit movies that resonated for audiences at the time and ever since: *Harvey, Broken Arrow, Winchester '73, Bend of the River, The Naked Spur, Rear Window, The Far Country, The Man from Laramie, The Man Who Knew Too Much, Vertigo, Anatomy of a Murder.* In the critical imagination, the 1950s belong to Brando, Monroe, and Dean, but none of them racked up the roster of smashes that Stewart did. He was the favorite culturally respectable movie star of middle America.

Except for *Harvey,* he avoided comedies in this period as if they were a staph infection. He made eight films with Anthony Mann, three for Alfred Hitchcock, one for Otto Preminger. He played cold, he played cynical, he played bloviating, he played manipulative, he played obstinate, he played obsessive, he played crazy, he played just about every quality an actor could play, and he was believable every time.

Winchester '73 took the tenacious Stewart of *Call Northside 777* and moved him out west. As far as Jim was concerned, it was an obvious choice. When he was asked about the difference between the gentle prewar Stewart and the man on view in *Winchester '73* and after, he would say, "I'd matured."

Winchester '73 was an add-on to Stewart's deal for *Harvey.* Everybody figured *Harvey* was going to be a commercial smash. Wasserman's recollection was that it was a two-picture deal and Universal could either pay Stewart $200,000 per picture or half of their respective profits.

Universal opted for the percentage deal because, said Wasserman, "Universal didn't have the $400,000." But to Universal's surprise *Harvey* underperformed and took a while to turn a profit, while the modestly budgeted black-and-white western overperformed and made a lot of money for both the studio and Stewart. Wasserman said that Stewart earned between $800,000 and $900,000 for his piece of *Winchester '73* alone, making him the highest-paid star in the movie business by far. The beauty part was that the money was taxed at the lower capital gains rate rather than as straight income.

Winchester '73 is a fine western with an innovative circular structure that follows the Winchester rifle through its various owners, with Stewart in constant pursuit. His character, Lin McAdam, is edgy and borderline hostile, and Anthony Mann uses more deep focus than any film since *The Best Years of Our Lives.*

Winchester '73 provided Stewart a new friend in the person of Dan Duryea, who specialized in sniveling heavies, but who in reality was the most solid of citizens. The two men bonded over a mutual love of long, rambling stories and practical jokes, and Duryea would work in three more films with Stewart. In *Thunder Bay,* Duryea's character asks Stewart if he has any entertainment skills.

"I can do a swell imitation of that tall, drawling movie star," says Stewart.

"*That* guy?" says Duryea with evident distaste. "Never mind!"

Winchester '73 was followed by *Harvey* — the only picture that would have jibed with Stewart's prewar screen character. But even there he converted Elwood P. Dowd into less of an amiable drunk and more of a willful eccentric — Elwood's speech summing up his worldview makes it clear that if it

353

weren't for his invisible friend, life might well be a burden he could do without. It also captures something else about Stewart: he acts with his entire body as well as his face and voice. He emphasizes Elwood's age and isolation by slightly stooping, his heavy worsted suit hanging loosely from his shoulders.

Stewart's deal with Universal, and the resulting cascade of money, earned him a new respect with his peers. More than forty years after *Winchester '73,* Bob Hope, a very close man with a dollar, talked about Stewart's deal with awe and not a little envy. "I didn't think that Jimmy Stewart could move that fast," Hope said. "He had that slow way of talking, but he could sure talk fast if the money was right. He could out-talk me!"

Winchester '73 also opened up a new genre for Stewart, as he became viable as an action star. The Stewart-Mann westerns (*Winchester '73, Bend of the River, The Naked Spur, The Far Country, The Man from Laramie*) are unusually homogeneous. Stewart's characters are haunted by a past trauma and he proves capable of violence every bit as extreme as his antagonists — in *Winchester '73* he takes Dan Duryea's head and slams it into the surface of a saloon bar, something audiences had wanted to do since *The Little Foxes.*

Borden Chase, the screenwriter of *Winchester '73,* said that "When the picture was given a sneak preview, there had been some titters in the audience at seeing Stewart's name in the opening titles of a western. . . . But once he smashed Duryea in the bar, there was no more snickering."

The Mann-Stewart westerns can be compactly characterized as harsh men doing harsh things in harsh places. As Terrence Rafferty noted, they bring the haunted heart of film noir to the western, to which Mann added his gift for jagged, ominous landscapes. Along with *Call Northside 777,* the westerns were the definitive emergence of the postwar Stewart, in which he integrated the emotional upheaval of his war experiences with the tenacity that audiences had grown to love before the war.

Winchester '73 also introduced Stewart to one of the great loves of his life — a horse named Pie. Half quarter horse, half Arabian, he was owned by a woman named Stevie Myers, whose father, Roy, had supplied horses for westerns since the silent days. About five or six horses were brought out for Stewart to choose for his ride in *Winchester '73.* "There were all these big, sloppy things that moseyed around," said

Stewart, "and I saw this horse peeking around the corner. I said, 'Who's that?' She said, 'That's my horse.' And I said, 'Well, could I just see him?' "

Pie did not have a great reputation — Stevie Myers felt honor-bound to tell Stewart that Pie had thrown a few people in his time — but no other horse but Pie would do.

Stewart had been partial to horses since his childhood, when he had helped tend a horse his father had kept. "My father always had a horse," he said. "What cleaning the stable did for me was rid me of any fear of horses.

"My father had taught me how to behave around horses. People will tell you that horses have mean streaks. I don't think any horse has one. But they know right away when you come up to them if you don't know what you're doing, and they don't like that."

Myers let Stewart ride the horse, and agreed to keep him off limits to every other star of westerns. "I just fell in love with the horse," said Stewart. The feeling was mutual.

He would do things that I just have never seen in a horse. We were *friends.* I swear he knew what he was doing. He was very sensitive about being a star. He knew the moment they clacked down that sound board that he was on — his ears would go straight up. He listened to everything I said to him too — I could tell by the way his ears moved.

We could go along at a full gallop, and before we got to the mark where we were supposed to come to a sudden stop, I'd just tell him. And, honestly, he'd look for the mark without looking as if he was looking for it, and then he'd stop right on it.

Stewart rode Pie in every western he made between 1950 and *The Cheyenne Social Club* in 1970. "It's such a tremendous advantage in westerns, if you can get the feeling that the horse and you are partners. It was a very important thing in the western part of my movie work. It was not only me, but a cameraman and many people would say, 'The horse is amazing.'"

Stewart's favorite story about Pie involved a night shoot for *The Far Country.* "Throughout the picture I'd had a little bell hooked onto the horn of the saddle. But the shot was: they were all in the saloon and somebody said, 'Shhh.' They heard the bell. And they cut outside . . . at Pie's feet . . .

coming along. The guys start moving out . . . and I wasn't on him. He was walking alone."

Anthony Mann explained that they wanted the horse to walk down the street, then stop in front of the saloon. How could they get him to do that? "Well," said Stewart, "I'll just tell Pie what I want him to do."

I went one time with him. I said, "Just keep going — and I won't be on you. Just keep going — now, come back faster, then; we'll do this once more." The assistant director came up and said, "How long are you going to talk to him?" And I said, "He's fine; he'll do it."

So they shot it. And he did it. Perfect.

We just became friends.

Bonding with Pie was only part of the story with Stewart when it came to animals. Gloria was devoted to Bello, her German shepherd; Jim would say that the only reason he had married Gloria was to ingratiate himself with Bello. Later, Gloria transferred her affection to golden retrievers. Stewart insisted that the family adopt the dogs in pairs, because he felt that a single dog was apt to become lonely.

"I have been told by people who know a helluva lot more about dogs than I do that they're not capable of loneliness. But I just don't believe it. I think every living creature is capable of feeling left out, and I almost look at it as a duty for one creature to look out for another."

Now in middle age, Stewart was a man who stuck with his preferences. One wife . . . one house . . . two dogs . . . one car . . . one diet. At Chasen's, where he ate twice a week for decades, he invariably ordered white food: sole, vichyssoise, and a single scoop of vanilla ice cream for dessert. He never showed much enthusiasm or interest in broadening his palate. Jim Stewart knew what he liked.

Bessie Stewart, Jim's beloved mother, died in mid-1953 of heart problems at the age of seventy-eight. Alex was devastated, but not for long; eighteen months later he married the seventy-eight-year-old aunt of one of his neighbors.

Alex's grandchildren would say that Alex remarried primarily "to irritate people," and there might have been an element of truth in that. Jim didn't care for his stepmother — he didn't mind the fact that she was lively, but he thought she drank and swore too much. Nevertheless, he was always correct and polite with her. His mother would have expected no less.

The pictures he made at Universal gave him leverage at the studio that never went away. In April 1953, Universal donated their facilities for a day so Stewart could shoot a sequence for a tribute to Josh Logan that was going to be shown on Ed Sullivan's TV show. The segment featured scenes from Logan's Broadway hits such as *Wish You Were Here, South Pacific, Mister Roberts,* and *Picnic.* Stewart's contribution was a re-creation of a Triangle Club production from 1930 in which he sang a song Logan had written called "On a Sunday Evening."

Along came Hitchcock. *Rear Window* was a tour de force for director and star, as Stewart sat in a wheelchair for 99.9 percent of the picture, continuously reacting in a stunning display of seamless technique. *Rear Window* was the first picture in a nine-film deal between Hitchcock and Paramount negotiated by Lew Wasserman. Hitchcock was to get $150,000 per picture plus 10 percent of the net profits, and ownership of five of the pictures. *Rear Window* was followed by two other films starring Stewart: *The Man Who Knew Too Much* and *Vertigo.* The two men got along beautifully, with the light-eating Stewart being mightily amused by the heavy-eating Hitchcock.

"Hitch is the champion eater of all time," Stewart said in a burst of ungracious candor. "Put a whole fish or steak in front of him and it just disappears. He's a big round canister-type vacuum cleaner. You turn away for a minute and the food is gone."

Rear Window was a hit, but it paled next to Stewart's biggest smash of this period: *The Glenn Miller Story,* with Stewart miming playing the trombone and June Allyson pining, with musical arrangements by Henry Mancini, all directed by Anthony Mann with an admirably straight face. It amassed rentals of nearly $8 million. A project that was closer to his heart was *Strategic Air Command,* which was instigated by SAC commander Curtis LeMay, who asked Beirne Lay if Hollywood was ever going to make a movie about SAC. Lay cobbled together a story about a baseball player recalled to active duty, a variation on Ted Williams being ordered back to fly missions in the Korean War.

Lay took his story to Stewart, who was now a colonel in the Air Force Reserve, and he immediately agreed to star in the picture. With LeMay's support, SAC supplied B-36s and B-47s (the first jet-powered nuclear bomber) to the production, all at taxpayer expense for the financial benefit of Paramount Pictures, which, it must be said, gorgeously photographed the hardware in VistaVision.

The film that got away, that Stewart was interested in but didn't make, was *The Seven Year Itch,* which featured a husband bothered by guilt over having an affair — the stage production — or from not having an affair — the movie version. It would have been something radically different for Stewart, but in other respects it clearly was a comfortable fit. "I'm in the boob business," he told playwright and screenwriter George Axelrod. "You wrote a pretty good boob. I can play the hell out of that boob."

The anecdote catches Stewart's canny sense of self-appraisal, his ability to see himself as the public saw him, but Billy Wilder instead cast the much cheaper Tom Ewell, who had played the part on Broadway.

Stewart's only real flop of the decade was *The Spirit of St. Louis,* a film about Lindbergh's flight to Paris produced by Leland Hayward and directed by Billy Wilder that Stewart desperately wanted to make for obvious reasons, but for which he was twenty years too old.

The production was fraught from the

beginning. For what seems to have been the only time in his career, Stewart acted like a petulant movie star. He came to *The Spirit of St. Louis* directly from the exhausting shoot of *The Man Who Knew Too Much* — Wilder wanted him available for location shooting from the cockpit as the re-creation of Lindbergh's plane flew over Ireland and France. Stewart groused that these shots could just as easily be achieved at the studio with rear projection. He hated Paris, he hated the Ritz.

"His big point," wrote Hayward to Jack Warner, "was that this is the most important picture in his whole life and it's essential to him to look as physically well as possible. . . . He says he needs two or three weeks of absolute rest. . . . He said he couldn't rest here, he hated Paris, the food made him sick, his wife had the trots."

Stewart was domestic by nature, but the problem ran deeper than that. He was forty-seven years old playing a man who had been twenty-five at the time he flew the Atlantic, and acting will get you only so far. He was worried that makeup wouldn't be able to do the job. (He was right.) Another possible problem was Wilder's allegiance to his script — he wouldn't allow an actor to change a contraction, let alone a sentence. Hayward was clearly stunned at this reversal of character: "I've known Stewart longer than anyone, and I've never seen him behave in the irrational, ridiculous, kind of crazy fashion he did in Paris."

A couple of meetings failed to alleviate Stewart's emotional bleeding and he left Paris in the middle of September 1956. When the first unit finally began shooting in mid-November, the script was unfinished, and by December they had blown past the original budget of $2 million. In February, they were ten days behind schedule. By the time they finished shooting a month later, a sixty-four-day schedule had become a 115-day schedule, a $2 million budget had become a $6 million budget, and Stewart was questioning the entire basis of the drama. Charles Lindbergh visited the set one day, and Stewart asked him at what point he had become tired.

"I never got tired," replied Lindbergh.

"That was rather disconcerting," Stewart said with understatement that verged on the British — in the absence of any mechanical problems with the plane, exhaustion was the central dramatic problem Wilder had devised for Lindbergh.

An openly alarmed Jack Warner wrote a

curt memo to Hayward about the runaway costs:

It is needless for me to tell you what I think of the picture.

The big thing is to get . . . down in continuity form what still has to be photographed, especially with Jimmy Stewart.

As I told you after Billy had left the projection room, we definitely should not go over the golf course or greenhouse once the plane gets into the air. By now the severity of the load has been completely milked and we should get right into the next hazard. Don't worry about the length of the picture — it's the quality that counts.

Again time is the important factor. It is entirely up to you fellows now to get it done as fast as you humanly can. I know you and Billy know the complete score . . . Jack.

Even after the production officially closed, Wilder kept shooting. He had never made an outdoor picture before and was nervously shooting miles of protection footage that would ultimately end up on the cutting room floor. In May, with the picture no-where near its final shape, Wilder jumped ship to prepare *Love in the Afternoon,* and the Lindbergh picture was dumped in the lap of John Sturges, who did the final retakes and editing polish.

Despite painstaking production and good direction, the result was a financial disaster — only $2.6 million in domestic rentals, the greatest flop in Warner Bros. history up to that time. Besides the problem of Stewart's age, Lindbergh was still persona non grata with the American public after his heavy flirtation with anti-Semitism and isolationism before World War II.

Wilder knew what went wrong. "I liked the book very much, and I thought it would be a change of pace. The loneliness of it, the foolhardy aspect, the danger of it appealed to me. What it taught me is that for a thing like that to come off, you have to get into character and that was a no-no. Lindbergh was a very elusive man and you couldn't get to him."

The experience wasn't a complete loss. Lindbergh wrote Stewart a thank-you note complimenting him, one pilot to another, for a brief moment when Stewart tapped "the oil gauge when you were starting the engine." Stewart and Lindbergh both knew that the oil pressure gauge on an airplane of that vintage was crucial — if the gauge didn't rise, it meant the pistons weren't being lubricated. The result would be a disaster.

Hitchcock's *Vertigo* was also a financial disappointment, returning less than $3 million in rentals to the studio, a shortfall that Hitchcock blamed on Stewart's age. Hitchcock would occasionally wonder if he should have cast another one of his favorite actors, perhaps Cary Grant, but Grant would never have played such an exposed neurotic on-screen.

Hitchcock and Stewart never worked together again, although Stewart thought they were going to. All through the writing of *North by Northwest,* Stewart kept calling Hitchcock's office to see how things were going. And all through the writing of *North by Northwest,* Hitchcock was negotiating with Cary Grant. "I knew that the picture was for Cary Grant," said screenwriter Ernest Lehman, "and so I tailored the role to suit him . . . Jimmy Stewart would have taken too long to deliver that dialogue." Which didn't mean a thing to Grant. The actor spent most of the production complaining that it wasn't a Cary Grant picture, it was a David Niven picture.

Despite what must have been some dismay at being displaced from Hitchcock's realm, it was a great period for Jim. Acting gave Stewart permission to express the extreme emotions — anxiety, outright fear — that he could not express during the war. Speaking about *Vertigo,* Stewart said that, "I myself had known a fear like that, and I'd known people paralyzed by fear. It's a very powerful thing to be engulfed almost by that kind of fear."

All of these performances are remarkable because Stewart always contrived to let us see the Jimmy Stewart that the public had grown to love before the war, his decency still visible beneath a burdensome pile of dread.

Not everybody realized what Stewart was doing, or what it cost him. With any great star with a strong personality, there's always a sense with the public — and often with critics — that they're just playing themselves. But if Stewart was playing himself in *Vertigo,* he would have been a suicide years earlier.

Kim Novak, his costar in *Vertigo,* said, "He'd go deep inside himself to prepare for an emotional scene. He was not the kind of actor, who, when the director said *'Cut,'* would be able to say 'OK,' then walk away. He'd squeeze my hand real hard and I would squeeze his hand, and we would allow each other to come down slowly, like a parachute."

For Novak, a woman who never felt comfortable in the movie business, Stewart would always be

> My all-time favorite man, next to my husband. The best, nicest person I ever worked with — so kind and endearing.
>
> What did he give me? He gave me comfort. *Security.*
>
> Hitchcock didn't talk to actors; he didn't say much to me, or to Jimmy. I got nervous and it was Jimmy that talked to me. "He hired you," he told me. "That means he believes in you. You go ahead and give your performance. You're doing fine."
>
> He was a deeply rooted man, and not in Hollywood. I always think of him like wearing a pair of morning slippers that you'd had all our life, with that comfortable feeling that made you feel like you wanted to come to work every day, wanted to be with him. How could he have been such a gentle person and have lived in Hollywood all his life?

The two would team up again for *Bell, Book and Candle,* a charming romantic comedy directed by Richard Quine. Once again, Novak felt an intense simpático with her costar. "We would sit on the set during lunch breaks and not say anything. We didn't even eat, just quietly relaxed in each other's company."

Stewart was now a master of the middle register, the place where gradations of doubt and ambivalence reside. Otto Preminger's *Anatomy of a Murder* was a critical and financial success in 1959, and the intervening years have only deepened the picture's complexities, as well as Stewart's own performance. The Method-oriented Ben Gazzara gave the impression that he came to snicker at an aging movie star and stayed to watch in rapt appreciation.

"He closeted himself, because he had a great deal of dialogue," said Gazzara. "I never even saw him taking lunch, actually. I think he did that alone, totally concentrated on this character, totally immersed in it. I watched in awe. I said, 'Holy shit, look at this. Actor's Studio, Schmactor's Studio, this guy can act.'

"How natural, how simple, what a sense of humor, tongue in cheek, how he could pause and hold it forever, hold your attention. He had all the moves. I was really awestruck. It taught me a great deal." Moreover, Gazzara was impressed by Stewart's generosity. "You never had a sense from Jimmy Stewart that he wanted to crowd you out, that he wanted his moments framed, that he wanted you to change your rhythm to help him along, which a lot of greedy actors do. He let you be yourself and work and think."

The part of the defense attorney in *Anatomy of a Murder* was endlessly long, and Stewart couldn't let his concentration lapse. Always accustomed to setting his own pace at an amble, he slowed things down even further. Between shots, he disappeared to run lines with his assistant. In front of the camera, he was letter-perfect and on-point every take.

"He does not so much plunge as slip into acting," wrote Geoffrey O'Brien years later, "and the sense of freedom he finds there is always visibly tentative. His famous stammering pauses create an anxious space in which the scene's progression is held at bay while he plays for time, defending himself against being rushed into anything."

Over dinner with Gazzara, Stewart talked about how he'd been sidetracked into acting. The crucial moment was the first time he heard audience applause at Princeton. That was it — the wave of love cascading over the footlights did its job, and another actor found his life's work.

Gazzara noticed that if you asked Stewart a question, he'd pause and think before answering, gathering his thoughts, just as if the camera was rolling. He preferred talking about other people than about himself. Hank, for instance. Jim told Gazzara that he was worried about his friend. Fonda was big on Broadway, but his movie career was in the doldrums and Stewart was unhappy about it. "He said Hank didn't pay enough attention to building up a name for himself as big as his talent, that he seemed more interested in doing little plays or, even when he did movies, doing little pictures set in New York that didn't give him the boost that he needed. Jimmy really wanted him to give Broadway a rest. He was very sincere, thought Fonda was selling himself short."

For his part, Fonda's persistent critical function would sometimes lead him to say that Jim had spent too much time in Hollywood and had gotten a little lax in his choices of collaborators.

When it came to work, Fonda was completely different from his friend. He would talk to other actors only grudgingly, and then the conversation would be kept to a bare minimum lest his focus be diverted. Stewart's good manners precluded that kind

372

of response, but on the emotional level he would have understood completely.

Stewart's friend Gary Cooper also tended toward the taciturn. On one occasion, Cooper dropped by Stewart's house and asked if he wanted to go for a drive in the Hollywood Hills. The two men were gone for three hours; when Stewart got back to the house, Gloria asked how Cooper was. "I don't know," he replied. "I didn't ask him."

"Coop didn't waste many words," Stewart would remember. "Remember once we went for a long walk. Aaaah, big bird flew overhead. Cooper pantomimed a gun and said BANG! . . . High point of the afternoon's conversation."

The Stewarts were regular attendees at the Coopers' parties, some black-tie, some not. The women loved getting dressed up. "Jimmy Galanos and Dior were the couturiers of the day," said Maria Cooper Janis. "The women liked looking elegant. But the parties were never stiff, never formal affairs. Everybody always had a great time, and things would always end up in jam sessions around the piano. Everybody would get up and sing: Judy Garland, Sinatra, Tony Martin, Gordon MacRae."

If you asked Stewart who his best friend was, he would have said Fonda. If you asked

Cooper the same question, he would have mentioned either Stewart or Pat DiCicco, Gloria Vanderbilt's first husband and, based on her testimony, a nasty piece of work.

"I don't think my mother thought Pat's friendship was a very good thing for the marriage," Maria said, "but my father loved his hunting and fishing contingent. He got as much fun talking to guys fixing the telephone line as he did talking about acting. He could talk about politics and other things with his hunting buddies more than he could with his friends in Hollywood."

Yet the Stewarts and the Coopers were very much part of each other's lives. "There were never any shake-ups in the relationship. My father and Jimmy understood each other on a deep level. I always suspected that Jimmy didn't bring his work home with him. Neither did my father. He never talked about a role, or the machinations at the studio. And they were both very private. They didn't need to build themselves up, so they didn't talk about themselves. I do think my father was more versatile than Jimmy in the sense of being socially comfortable in any situation. He was as comfortable in blue jeans as white-tie and tails. Jimmy was less international, more old-shoe."

■ ■ ■ ■

Stewart's concerns about Fonda's career choices were not entirely wrong. While Jim was making *Vertigo* and *Anatomy of a Murder,* Hank was trapped in pictures that were either second-string (*Warlock*) or worse (*The Man Who Understood Women*). But Jim had been around long enough to know that careers are strange things, with their own peculiar rhythm. They have peaks and valleys, and no matter how problematic the career of a great actor might be at any given time, he's only one part away from a comeback.

Occasionally, Stewart would offer his take on the industry at large, and it was almost always pragmatic and very much an insider's view: "After the glamour and glitter is stripped away, you've got to realize that movies are pretty much like any other business. We exist on supply and demand, too. The demand . . . is for solid, reliable performers who can get people out of the homes and into the theaters.

"People don't have the movie habit anymore. They won't go to the theater unless they're pretty sure of getting their money's worth. When they know that Duke Wayne or Gary Cooper is in the picture, they can judge from past performance that it ought to be pretty good." He might have added his own name behind that of Wayne and Cooper, but he was too modest for that.

Anatomy of a Murder occasioned one of Alex's rare admissions that his son had talent. But first he had put him through the wringer. "I understand it's dirty," he told his son, to which Jim said he thought it was pretty good. Alex wasn't convinced. "The boys down at the paper tell me it's about a rape case. Sounds pretty dirty to me. I'm not going. I'm telling all my friends not to go." But Alex did go, after which he called his son and told him that he thought it was the best picture Jim had ever made.

After *Anatomy of a Murder,* Stewart made *The FBI Story,* a paen to J. Edgar Hoover, and one of the few times he let his politics show. Director Mervyn LeRoy thought it would be fun if Jim's goddaughter Jane Fonda played his daughter in the movie, and Hank must have thought it was a good idea, because he took twenty-two-year-old Jane to Warners for a meeting. But she thought the idea was entirely too clubby, and her lack of enthusiasm communicated itself to both LeRoy and Stewart. Diane Jergens played the part.

For Stewart it was an astonishing decade, both commercially and creatively, a remarkable deepening of the screen character he had created before 1941. He was still intrinsically decent, but now that decency was buffeted by doubts that could ascend to fury . . . and madness.

Personally, Jim was the same man he had always been. Mildred Bantis, his personal secretary, wrote a letter to a friend in which she reported that "I have a very soft and pleasant job for Mr. Stewart. . . . There is certainly nothing hectic about it and he is such a fine man that it is a pleasure to work for him. I see him only once in a while because he works most of the time."

Jimmy's conservatism was not just political, it was social and industrial. When *The FBI Story* was released in 1959, he gave an interview to *Variety* that bewailed the growth of independent production. He much preferred, he said, the "classic" style of storytelling. "Hollywood's horde of independent film companies have fallen far short of their promises; that they have in most cases failed to deliver quality product. As a result, it's up to the major studios to exercise leadership. Independents are cutting corners and cheating, clipping expenses and shoe-stringing things. That's at the sacrifice of quality."

He was conveniently forgetting that he had just done *Anatomy of a Murder,* which had been made independently by Otto Preminger and had succeeded splendidly, as it deserved to. He was also forgetting that his best friend had produced and starred in *12 Angry Men* independently only two years earlier. Certainly Fonda hadn't forgotten. "I would've died and been out of work if I'd just done *Ox-Bow* and *12 Angry Men,*" Fonda said. "No box office, they're not interested. They don't send you scripts anymore. They just say you're poison."

After Jim's spectacular run in the 1950s, the 1960s would begin a slow descent — it was not an era for actors leaning into late middle age who were frequently compared to comfortable slippers. Like every other actor, Jim had to be vigilant in looking for good parts. But he wasn't sure where his next one was coming from.

By this time, each man had settled into a preferred attitude toward the other. Fonda would say that, while he had to labor and plan and sweat and stew over every moment, Stewart was one of God's naturals: "Jim is a man who became an actor in spite of himself. I remember just sitting and looking at him and studying him and wondering how in hell he got so good. You see, I'd been at it for eight or nine years, playing literally hundreds of parts of all kinds and really working at being an actor, and here was this skinny son of a gun who hadn't even tried hard for more than about a year or so, and I'd just seen him do about the most moving job I'd ever seen in the theater."

Stewart was impatient with this point of view. "The fact is that once we'd decided on the theater, those of us at Princeton and Hank and the others . . . we all worked hard and we all starved a lot."

Their different takes were a function of their very different personalities. The character actor Harry Morgan, who worked with both Hank and Jim, observed that they approached the job with totally different attitudes.

"Jimmy was Jimmy," said Morgan. "You'd think he was just another actor earning his daily bread . . . [but] Fonda lived to be an actor. He never thought about anything else. Twenty-four hours a day with Hank, it was acting — what he had just done, what he'd hope he'd do. Jimmy never gave you that feeling until he actually began acting. When you worked with Hank, you knew you had to be set to go before you ran into him. With

Jimmy, it was anything else under the sun until the director was ready to shoot. Then the monster of a performer that he is came out."

Joshua Logan had a more succinct way of expressing Fonda's devotion: "He is a priest."

Fonda carried his accumulated tension in his hands; onstage, he would often hold his thumb, middle finger, and ring finger together. It was a trait that ran in the family; Jane's tension was carried in her mouth and chin, while Peter would occasionally catch himself holding his fingers in the same manner as his father. Peter referred to the trait as a "hands-down performance," meaning a performance of physical and often emotional compression — no gesticulation. "Most actors can't get there," he would say, "but my father was always giving a hands-down performance."

As an artist, Fonda had become a creature of rare delicacy. As an old man, he would stitch complicated needlepoint patterns he designed himself — most of the needlework on the chairs and pillows of his houses was his — or make macramé baskets. And certainly there was a tenderness in much of his acting.

But even as they became adults, his children remained scared of his anger, even though every once in a while they would get a glimpse of a different Fonda. When Stewart was around, things always lightened up, and Logan usually nudged Fonda into a good time.

"Josh could remember all the lines of dialogue of every play he'd ever been in," said Bill Hayward. "And every song. He had an *amazing* memory. And he would tell these stories about working on [*Garden of Allah*] with Charles Boyer and Dietrich, and they were the best stories you ever heard."

Once, Peter Fonda was helping his father organize his home movies and was holding a film up to the light to identify the participants. "What ya got?" asked Hank.

"Josh."

"What's he doing?"

Peter mimicked a motion Josh was making, which prompted Hank to yell, "Oh my God, give it to me!" Fonda grabbed the film and out came the story: In the days of the University Players, the troupe had been on a train late at night trying to sleep while being constantly awakened by a crying baby. The next day Josh worked up a mime routine that involved Josh picking up an imaginary baby and starting to change its diaper. As he was performing the task, he looked down at the baby and flicked it with his finger. The hostility escalated and climaxed with Logan twirling the baby around his head, and finally heaving it like a football. It became a favorite party piece for Logan.

For the young — and childless — kids of the University Players who had been on that endless train ride, the bit was gloriously transgressive and hilarious. Other people figured you had to have been there. "I remember we did it one night at Katharine Cornell's," Fonda remembered. "She wasn't amused."

Johnny Swope had come back from Edward Steichen's photographic unit in World War II and quickly became a fixture at *Life* magazine. But that wasn't enough for him; for most of the 1950s he was also the executive director of the La Jolla Playhouse, where Norman Lloyd, who'd been blacklisted in the movies, directed shows for him.

The Playhouse was founded in 1947 by Dorothy McGuire, Gregory Peck, and Mel Ferrer with the goal of presenting nine plays every summer. The shows were predominantly cast with movie stars trying to keep their stage muscles supple. Rehearsals lasted six days, and there were eight performances per play, which ensured sellouts at all performances. Actors got $55 a week, a hotel room, and two meals a day. Among the actors who leaped at the opportunity were Charlton Heston, Patricia Neal, Joan Bennett, Jennifer Jones, David Niven, Olivia de Havilland, and the three founding members.

"Life with John was very exciting," said Lloyd. "I loved him, but everybody loved him. He was generous, he was thoughtful, and he was very talented. In the course of a very long life, I would have to put John at the very top of all the people I've known. He was a natural aristocrat, you see. He came by it naturally, through his family, but he didn't act like an aristocrat; he downplayed it."

Swope and Lloyd produced plays like *The Lady's Not for Burning* with Vincent Price and Marsha Hunt; Dorothy McGuire and Don Taylor in *I Am a Camera;* Lee Marvin, James Whitmore, and Teresa Wright in *The Rainmaker; Billy Budd* with Vincent Price as Captain Vere; Price again in *The Winslow Boy;* and *The Time of the Cuckoo* with Claire Trevor.

Swope would attend the dress rehearsals of the shows Lloyd was directing. About twenty minutes into the first act, Lloyd would look over to see Swope sound asleep. After the show, Swope would give Lloyd his notes, and they were invariably concise and thoughtful, delivered in what Lloyd would remember as "his enormously attractive indirect way. I always wondered how he could do that while he was asleep. I guess he dreamt them."

After each show ran its week, Lloyd and Swope would get on the train at Del Mar and go to Los Angeles to cast the next show. Lloyd would grab a newspaper so he could check the baseball box scores, while Swope would forcibly rip the paper out of his hands, telling him that he couldn't read the paper until he'd read the next play.

Dennis Hopper was a sixteen-year-old general assistant at the Playhouse. In his own telling, Hopper was primarily distinguished by his incompetence. "John Swope was elegant, quiet, intelligent, steadfast," remembered Hopper. It was Swope who got Hopper an agent and his SAG card, as well as giving him the opportunity to work with actors like Vincent Price. "These [men] . . . are the ones who gave me my first real education in art and photography," said Hopper.

When Johnny wasn't working at the Play-house or shooting for *Life,* he was helping manage his wife's career. "They had a wonderful marriage," said Norman Lloyd. "He adored her — Dorothy was his life. Well, photography was his life, but seeing that Dorothy was accommodated as a star was his other occupation. He was very assiduous in that regard. Not pretentious, not a pain, not pushy, but taking care of things in the natural course of events."

Stewart's and Swope's work kept them in and near California, but Fonda's life and work was now centered in New York. It didn't make him any more comfortable with human failings than he had been in Hollywood. There was still the need to be perfect, the inevitable falling short, and the resulting disappointment in himself, not to mention the plague of people who didn't understand his need. His wife, Susan, told her stepdaughter, Jane, "Your father is the kind of man who could stay in his art studio all day long, every day of the year. He never needed to see me. All he needed to know was that I was there."

Josh Logan had a more clinical view of Hank's third marriage. "I don't think [the marriage] ever had any joy in it, any fun in it. . . . If Fonda was shy, Susan was yellow shy. She was extra shy. I would say they were painful to have in a room when a party was given, because they'd only sit in a corner and look and watch. . . . They were both gloomy as hell, and I'll never know why exactly."

Fonda's anger wasn't limited to family. He was rehearsing *The Caine Mutiny Court-Martial* with director Charles Laughton and growing increasingly irritated. Laughton had made some cuts in the script that enlarged Lloyd Nolan's part of Captain Queeg and reduced Fonda's Barney Greenwald. To maintain equilibrium in the script, Laughton compensated by spending a great deal of time on the play's coda, when Greenwald throws a glass of wine in his own client's face as a mark of his contempt for the man's reflexive anti-authoritarianism, neatly reversing the conventional morality of the previous two hours.

This didn't placate Fonda's grievance, and when Laughton made some remark about a military detail, Fonda exploded and said, "What do you know about men, you fat, ugly faggot?"

That, at least, was the version reported by Simon Callow in his excellent biography of Laughton. The story derives from a journal kept by an actor in the company named Charles Nolte, who later became a theater professor and gay activist. But Peter Fonda says, "I doubt that story tremendously. For my father to say something like that, it would have had to be preceded by a very violent argument. He had a lot of gay friends. He didn't necessarily approve of homosexuality, but it didn't bother him — he wasn't threatened by it.

"Besides, he and Laughton discussed doing a theatrical version of Plato's *Dialogues,* and that was after *The Caine Mutiny.* I can't imagine Laughton wanting to work again with someone who had said that to him." Beyond that, Fonda was always highly laudatory in talking about Laughton, even when the conversation was off the record.

"It was a wonderful, wonderful experience for me," Fonda told his biographer.

Whatever the state of his relationship with Laughton, *The Caine Mutiny Court-Martial* had a difficult birthing. Herman Wouk had seen Laughton's production of *Don Juan in Hell* and thought it would be easy to condense his bestselling novel into a courtroom theater piece. Result: royalties.

Fonda was offered his choice of either the paranoid Queeg or Barney Greenwald. He chose Greenwald after Wouk told him he thought he was the ideal man for the part. But Wouk remembered the rehearsal period as "crisis after crisis." Laughton told Wouk that Fonda was "unmanageable" and the entire production might explode before it could get to New York. Yet, on opening night, everybody knew they had a hit. "We're going to *kill* them," Fonda declared, vibrating with excitement. This, he knew, would replace the bad taste left by *Point of No Return.*

Wouk said that Hank's sculpting of Greenwald never stopped, even after he had played the part for months. He was constitutionally incapable of phoning it in. "He could go into a scary fury at any mere facile or sketchy or phony treatment of a scene," remembered Wouk, "and he called a 'scene' an exchange of three lines. . . . He never wasted an inflection or a single motion of his body, and he never seemed to do anything for show. It was all sheer storytelling."

The part of Queeg, with his gradual breakdown under cross-examination, was the obvious show-stopper, and Wouk was concerned that the closing scene with Greenwald at the party would prove anticlimactic. "Greenwald's monologue at the banquet . . . has proven too much for nearly all the actors who have tried it. Henry managed, night after night, to make it the true dramatic climax of the evening."

Fonda told Wouk that there was no way to play the monologue technically, that it had to come out of pure emotion, as if it were actually happening, and that he could only get to that place a few times a week. "On those nights, he ended up in tears," remembered Wouk, "and the effect was explosive. But from night to night, no audience could have told the difference. It always seemed brilliant."

One of the actors playing a judge was Jim Bumgarner, who later changed his name to James Garner. He had no dialogue, just had to stay attentive. Night after night he watched the three main actors and marveled at their consistency, the high bar they set. John Hodiak had occasional off nights, but "Fonda never let down. Lloyd Nolan was the same. They both gave a solid performance night after night."

Watching them, Garner learned that stage acting is about listening, about discipline, about relentless focus — the only way to stay engaged for a long run. Watching Fonda and Nolan, Garner learned technique, concentration, and, most importantly, the meaning of the word *professional*.

As anybody who ever saw Fonda on stage realized, he had a remarkable presence and, according to Garner, "tremendous self-confidence when he was in character. . . . But he never thought he was any good. We'd have a great audience, they'd love the performance, and everyone would be happy but him. He was never satisfied, but never blamed anyone but himself."

TWELVE

Nobody ever doubted the deep friendship that existed between Fonda and Leland Hayward, but business is business and Fonda was far from first choice for the movie version of *Mister Roberts.*

Hayward had thought William Holden would make a great Roberts ever since he saw *Sunset Boulevard,* and Holden was interested in the part. Other Hayward candidates included Kirk Douglas or Montgomery Clift, the latter of whom passed because, he told Hayward, he felt Fonda's performance was definitive and he didn't think he could get anywhere near it.

In July 1953, Marlon Brando told Hayward he wanted to make the movie, and Hayward was thrilled, even though Brando would cost him $125,000 as opposed to Fonda's standard $100,000. But by March 1954, Hayward and Brando agreed to disagree, although whether that was because

Brando had changed his mind, or because of a contractual contretemps with Fox — he had walked out on Darryl Zanuck's production of *The Egyptian* days before production was due to start — is unclear.

Brando didn't try to convince Hayward to fight for him. "With your cast insurance problems and your complete ignorance of my present slug fest with the Twentieth Century not so Foxy (ha ha) I completely appreciate your position . . . Regards to Hank, should you see him."

At no time was Josh Logan slated to direct the picture, because Hayward didn't want him. On the other hand, Logan was a partner in the enterprise and no director could be hired without his consent. Hayward told Jack Warner's assistant Steve Trilling that "Logan would always do what Hayward told him to do. If Logan was ill, if necessary Hayward would go to Logan's wife . . . and obtain the permission from her." In fact, Logan was recovering from a nervous breakdown.

The casting decision was expedited in March 1954, when Hayward hired John Ford to direct, and Ford insisted on Fonda. Ford got his way, as usual. "I thought Ford was the only man to direct [*Roberts*]," Fonda remembered. "He's queer for the

Navy, he's a great man's director, he's a location director."

John Patrick (*Teahouse of the August Moon*) was hired to write the script for $65,000, and both Hayward and Ford were pleased with his first treatment, which didn't stop Ford from hiring Frank Nugent to do a rewrite. Ford also wanted Jack Lemmon for the part of Ensign Pulver, but whether he would be allowed to make the picture by Columbia, to whom he was under contract, was a matter of some doubt. Hayward asked Ford to call Harry Cohn and ask for the favor, but, he wrote, "I don't know if he will or not — you know what a strange guy Jack Ford is." Ford eventually asked Cohn for Lemmon, and got him.

In the last week of August 1954, the crew and cast gathered in Hawaii before leaving for Midway Island for locations. Jim Stewart flew over for a visit. Peter Fonda was with his father, and had a glimpse of the pressures of the movie business.

"We were all sitting in Leland's rented house. Jimmy and Dad and Leland were talking about airplanes. And they were passing around a tray, taking these things out of the tray, unwrapping the paper and popping them into their mouths. Leland, Jim, and Dad all took one. I thought it was candy or chewing gum, so I reached out and took one. Leland shook his head and said, 'No, Peter. It's not candy. It's Tums.' "

Production began on September 1, 1954, but what seemed to be a dream pairing of director, actor, and story quickly unraveled. Fonda's feeling for the show had been proprietary from the first rehearsal and his point of view conflicted with Ford's vision, which Fonda felt overemphasized comedy.

"It was too broad," Fonda said. "I just assumed that this is going to be an extension of this great play, and when I did discover that not only was the nurse now multiplied by five — because if one nurse is funny, five nurses are funnier — but there were a lot of other things done that were not of the play." He had a point; there are some scenes where the sailors are so rambunctious they seem ready to break into a rousing chorus of "There Is Nothing Like a Dame."

For his part, Ford began to feel that the grumpy recalcitrance of his star — whom he had insisted be cast — was undermining the picture, not to mention the director. The disagreement exploded one night on location at Midway, during a conference between Ford and Fonda, during which the latter outlined his objections to what Ford was doing. Ford, whose thin veneer of tolerance was always in danger of cracking under pressure, jumped up and sucker-punched his star, knocking him out of his chair. Jack Lemmon, who witnessed the aftermath of the initial punch, said that Ford was "windmilling," throwing wild punches while Fonda tried to fend him off.

When the dust settled, Ford knew he had done something that was not merely unprofessional but unforgivable. He began drinking on the set, guzzling beer by the case — one of two times in his career where he began drinking on a picture. The production managed to get through the location photography and grimly trooped back to Burbank. On October 16, Ford's gall bladder blew up and he had to have surgery. Mervyn LeRoy took over for the rest of the interiors, and in December Josh Logan came on for retakes.

With one breath, Logan would say, "Mervyn LeRoy saved the picture," and in the next he would declare that he came in and directed six weeks of retakes after LeRoy was finished, which would have meant he reshot every one of LeRoy's scenes.

Everybody involved felt squeamish about the picture. Jack Warner's (quite modest) cutting notes on the picture are addressed to Hayward and LeRoy, not Logan. John Patrick asked that his name be taken off the picture, and the Screen Writers Guild arbitration evidently agreed with him — they awarded credit to Frank Nugent and Josh Logan. On December 20, Ford wired that as far as directorial credit was concerned, he preferred "Mervyn take precedence [for the] majority [of] direction." (Ford ended up with top billing over LeRoy.)

The result was that the friendship between Fonda and Ford was over. Publicly, Fonda would always say nice things about Ford, the man who did more than anybody to create his screen character; privately he would invariably acknowledge Ford's genius, but just as often refer to him as "a son of a bitch." What made it even more frustrating to Fonda was the fact that the resulting film was a considerable financial and critical hit, and revived his claim to movie stardom after a long hiatus.

After the film of *Mister Roberts,* Hank went to Italy to play Pierre in *War and Peace* opposite Audrey Hepburn for director King Vidor. He was too old for the part, and every bit as miscast as Stewart had been in *Rope,* but got out alive in what was, on balance, an honorable effort by all hands. Then it was back to Warner's and Hitchcock, this time for *The Wrong Man,* an audacious one-off for its director, who generally preferred to type himself.

The Wrong Man is a strange, haunting picture that cuts deeper than most Hitchcock. It's a neorealist noir, based on a true story, in which Fonda plays a jazz musician named Manny Balestrero who is falsely accused of armed robbery. Manny is a complete victim, overwhelmed by circumstance, and his wife's sanity is destroyed by their ordeal. He's finally cleared, but only by accident.

Balestrero again draws on aspects of Fonda's own history, not to mention his personality. Manny more or less lives in his own head, and he's oblivious to his wife's spiraling chaos. As far as he's concerned, his two children come first, then his mother, then his wife. After he gets arrested, he becomes so focused on proving his innocence that he doesn't notice that his wife, played by Vera Miles, is collapsing until his lawyer points it out. The more Balestrero has to plead his innocence, the more his Catholic sense of guilt grows. The confidence a middle-aged, middle-class man has in foundational issues such as justice gradually dissipates. As Richard Brody noted, "innocence is merely a trick of paperwork, whereas guilt is the human condition."

When Manny is finally freed, he visits his wife in the mental institution where she asked to be sent. When he tells her that the charges have been dismissed, she flatly replies, "That's fine for you," then retreats into silence. *The Wrong Man* was a flop at the time, but audiences have slowly grown to appreciate it as one of the few Hitchcock pictures that doesn't fit into his stylistic niche.

"I think it is very fine," said Fonda decades later, "but because Hitchcock shot it almost like a documentary, without his usual flash, audiences were disappointed. I remember very clearly going down to Fort Lauderdale, where Manny was playing at a little club up the road, and meeting him with Vera Miles. Manny's wife was out of the hospital by then, but she was still shaken by the thing, and we were warned not to talk to her about it. She just sat there at the table, silently, with her hands folded in her lap."

In its portrayal of the way the irrational can intrude upon a well-ordered life, the film is deeply unsettling, with none of Hitchcock's typical flaunting of his stylistic virtuosity. It's as if he had just plowed through the ouevre of Vittorio De Sica and been temporarily seduced by grim, implacable reality. As the sole collaboration between Hitchcock and Fonda, *The Wrong Man* is a revealing window into the deepest fears of two control freaks.

By this time Fonda's marriage with Susan Blanchard was on the rocks and he was surreptitiously seeing Afdera Franchetti, a beautiful Italian butterfly he'd met while making *War and Peace*. It was awkward at first, because, as Franchetti would put it, "He was married and I was engaged." Afdera was a creature of society and parties, which must have been agony for a man without small talk of any kind. She also provoked shudders from Fonda's friends — for one thing, she called him "Hanky." The misalliance was obvious. Afdera was, as Nedda Logan observed, "an extrovert" who "talked a great deal. Constantly. Never stopped."

Fonda and Afdera married in 1957, divorced four years later. "She was a nightmare," said Brooke Hayward. "A train wreck. A complete horror." The Afdera interregnum mostly revolved around café society. In the summer of 1957 Fonda rented a villa on the French Riviera. The

Agnellis were there, the Volpis, the Kennedys. Elsa Maxwell lived next door and Aristotle Onassis hosted the Fondas on his yacht, which prominently featured a Picasso. As a matter of fact, the Fondas visited Picasso, not to mention Cocteau, Hemingway, and Chaplin. One day Greta Garbo took Jane Fonda swimming. Garbo was nude, Jane wore a swimsuit.

Jane's primary memory of the summer was her father's discomfort with his environment; he spent a great deal of the time hiding behind his camera and snapping pictures.

There are men who marry the same woman over and over, and then there are men who try every possible key that might fit their particular lock. Fonda was the latter. Nobody could quite figure out what Fonda thought he was doing, including, in retrospect, Fonda. "I hold myself in complete contempt for marrying her," he would say.

Afdera seems to have blamed herself for the failure of the marriage and looked back on Fonda with sympathy and considerable feeling. "He really was a husband. I was not a wife. He was a husband, he could have been a husband, he could have been a friend, he could have been a father. Cer-

400

tainly he was a lover. Everything. But I mean, I didn't give him a chance."

It was right about then that Fonda's self-image began to merge with the way the public thought of him: He was a man who didn't believe he was infallible — quite the contrary — but didn't think anybody else was either, and who wanted, *needed* to do the right thing. Take, for instance, juror number 8 in *Twelve Angry Men,* the only picture Fonda ever produced, and very efficiently, too. Rehearsed for two weeks, shot in three. Cost: $340,000.

It wasn't a commercial picture, but the ads tried to make it sound as if it was: "Life Is In Their Hands — Death Is On Their Minds! It **Explodes** Like 12 Sticks Of Dynamite!" Deservedly well-regarded now, it was a fast flop in 1957. Fonda never produced another picture, but late in life he would say that the film's gradual ascent to classic status had incrementally put more money in his pocket than any other movie he had made.

He had now achieved an eminence accorded to few actors. Respected by the critics for his frequent returns to the theater, held in affection by audiences for his consistently high batting average on-screen.

Toward the end of 1957, Fonda was looking to get back on Broadway with a new play. He found *Two for the Seesaw,* aptly described as "a reluctant romance between two people who are lonely but don't want to admit it." The girl is a Jew named Gittel, a dancer living in New York; the man is a WASP named Jerry, a Nebraska lawyer separated from his unstable wife. In the end, even though Jerry falls in love with Gittel, he goes back to his wife.

Producer Fred Coe and director Arthur Penn cast Anne Bancroft as Gittel, but at the time she wasn't a name, and they needed one in order to finance the show. Van Heflin turned it down, as did Eli Wallach, Don Murray, Barry Nelson, Jack Palance (they were clearly growing desperate), Robert Preston, and Jack Lemmon — twice.

Finally, Coe approached Fonda. There was a reading, after which Fonda thought his part was underwritten. Playwright William Gibson went back to work, and Fonda committed, even putting up a quarter of the budget.

When rehearsals began, so did trouble. Both Fonda and Penn wanted Jerry to be sympathetic and he wasn't. Gittel was kinetic — alive and energetic, the life force incarnate. But Jerry was distant, capable of deception, and he abandoned his mistress emotionally before he went back to his wife. Beyond that, Coe and Penn had made a cardinal error in casting a repressed man to play a repressed man. "I thought this was a play about two charming people," Fonda complained to his director.

Devin McKinney would write that Jerry is "an unattractive version" of Fonda. But John Ford had done the same thing in *Fort Apache,* and Manny Balestrero certainly contained strong elements of Fonda's own nature, and the actor hadn't minded, let alone rebelled.

In addition, Bancroft was a Method actress. "He hated the Method because the Method requires plumbing your depths," said Jane. "Dad hated process and emotions and probing. He lumped religion, psychoanalysis, and Method acting under the category of crutches."

In addition, "Dad had a real hard time with Anne Bancroft," said Jane. "She began to cry during a scene they were rehearsing, and he stormed offstage, got a mirror and came back. He held the mirror up to her face and said, 'Look, look how disgusting you look. Don't cry!' "

"We went into production," remembered Gibson,

and then Fonda found out that it was the girl's play. It wasn't his play, and he was the big star, and it was a couple of months of constant humiliation for him. He didn't take it, perhaps, with maximum grace.

It was complicated by the fact that Annie was such a talented performer and Hank wasn't. I mean, Hank had a marvelous quality on stage — everybody said "star quality" and it's true — when he got on stage . . . you looked at him. But when he said my lines, you didn't listen to him. I would write jokes for Fonda, and Annie would feed him the line and get the laugh on the feed, and Fonda would be left with limp jokes. This happened a dozen times.

Gibson was a man in the middle; not only were he and his close friend Penn not seeing the play the same way, but his wife, Margaret Brenman-Gibson, was a psychiatrist at the Austen Riggs Center in Stockbridge, where Frances Fonda had spent time before her suicide. Brenman-Gibson knew the family backstory and believed Fonda to be a virulent narcissist.

Adding to Fonda's unease was the fact that Gibson and Penn were rewriting right up till the New York premiere in January 1958. In spite of everything, the play got great reviews and settled in for a long run.

A few months later, Bancroft called in sick one night, and Lee Grant, her understudy, was called to go on two hours before curtain. But Grant had memorized only the first act, had more or less ignored her sessions with Arthur Penn, and had never run through the play with Fonda. It was a real-life replication of the classic actor's nightmare: walking on completely unprepared.

Grant rushed to the theater and began memorizing the second act on the fly. At half-hour, Fonda came in and she told him the situation. It wasn't just the second act dialogue; it was the turntables that revolved for alternate scenes depicting their respective apartments. What if she fell, or screwed up the timing of the revolves?

Fonda saw the animal panic in her eyes and summoned all of his reserves of resolution. He told her that he wouldn't abandon her; he told her they would get through it together. "I'll take you through it. Hold on," Hank told her.

"I never took my eyes off his strong, steady, blue, blue eyes," remembered Grant. "He never took his off me. He was holding me and leading me like a dancer, a doctor-dancer, and I made it to the end. He got an ovation at curtain; the audience had watched him make this happen. It was his night. Hank once told me that he was more comfortable onstage than any other place in his life. To experience that real strength and intimacy with him was a life lesson and a privilege. No other actor . . . could have done it."

Two for the Seesaw ran for several years, even though Fonda left the show as soon as his contract ended, to be replaced by Dana Andrews, who was newly and shakily sober and shadowed by his sponsor in Alcoholics Anonymous. The final insult came when Bancroft won a Tony for her performance.

Fonda didn't think the primary problem was Bancroft ("I loved her in the part and I loved her as a person") but Gibson and Penn. "They were bush league," he said in an off-the-record comment. "He [William Gibson] is not bush league anymore because he's had a few plays. . . . There was no reason for [Bancroft] to be upset. She had a beautiful part with four dimensions and I was fighting a guy with one dimension and trying to make it balance and getting no help from the author."

After that came a paycheck gig in Sidney Lumet's film *Stage Struck,* a remake of the Katharine Hepburn vehicle *Morning Glory* that was supposed to make Susan Strasberg a star but didn't. *Stage Struck* was followed by Anthony Mann's *The Tin Star.* With the exception of *Mister Roberts,* all of Fonda's pictures of this period were commercial disappointments.

He was still living in New York, still close to Maggie Sullavan. Whenever he would visit her at her home in Connecticut, they would go into the living room so nobody else could hear what they talked about. "Jane and I wanted them to get married again, but I don't think it would have worked," said Brooke Hayward. "I don't think actors can stay married to each other. The only two actors I knew who had a successful marriage were Bogie and Betty Bacall. I don't know of anybody else." (There was also Paul Newman and Joanne Woodward, but the list of successful movie star marriages is not lengthy.)

By 1959, Slim Hawks Hayward, prone to sarcasm and adultery, was spending as little time with her husband as possible. Hayward's children with Maggie Sullavan all disliked their stepmother and Slim felt she was "an underpaid nanny saddled with troubled children."

Leland was setting up the Broadway production of *Gypsy* and negotiating *The*

Sound of Music when he was asked by William Paley's wife, Babe, to take Pamela Churchill to the theater. She was the ex-wife of Winston Churchill's deeply unpleasant son Randolph, and had carved out a career as a high-end professional mistress to the likes of Edward R. Murrow, Gianni Agnelli, and Aly Khan.

The play was *A Raisin in the Sun,* not that it mattered, because Hayward and Churchill left at intermission in order to hustle back to her hotel — he reported to Bennett Cerf that Pamela could do miraculous things with ice cubes. As usual, Hayward had lined up his next wife while his present wife was still surveying alternative husbands. Hayward took Brooke to Le Pavillon to tell her of his plans.

"But you're already married," she pointed out.

"True," he said. "I've got to get a divorce." Details, details.

He went on to tell Brooke that Pamela was something special, not like most Englishwomen. "They all have bad teeth and talk through their noses; they're also all amoral, as opposed to immoral — big difference — all without exception. Don't know why that is. They all lead restricted lives until they get to be about sixteen and then they start screwing anything." He concluded his analysis by telling his daughter, "I'll tell you, this is the greatest courtesan of the twentieth century."

The news that Hayward was changing wives again electrified New York's literary and theatrical society. "Your item about Leland and Pam C. *stunned* me," wrote Truman Capote to Cecil Beaton — the two most voracious gossips of their time. "Toward the end of May, just before I came here, I saw Leland and Mrs. C. at a *tete-a-tete* — at a restaurant — and I kidded them, and said I was going to write Slim (who had already left for Europe, where Leland was supposed to join her, but never did). As a matter of fact, with my usual gaucherie, I *did* write Slim asking if she knew her husband was running around with the notorious Mrs. C. Oh dear! Are you sure it's true? Has he really left Slim? Please write me what you know."

Slim was appalled at Leland's choice of her successor. "Whatever you do, for your own protection, for your own dignity, don't marry her. You don't have to. Nobody *marries* Pam Churchill."

Leland Hayward married Pamela Churchill.

Margaret Sullavan had made her last movie in 1950, a weepy called *No Sad Songs for Me* that concerned a dying woman who picks out her husband's next wife. Since her husband was played by the invariably sullen Wendell Corey, it seemed as if she was spreading misery with more enthusiasm than was absolutely necessary. Sullavan's daughter was played by the young Natalie Wood, who remembered her as "maternal" and "very kind." But Wood was confused when Sullavan would get impatient with other actors, whom she accused of not "giving enough." In fact, they were only lowering their voices for a quiet scene, and Sullavan couldn't hear them. It was the first sign of impending deafness.

Sullavan had had some big Broadway hits — *The Voice of the Turtle, Sabrina Fair,* Terence Rattigan's *The Deep Blue Sea* — but the one that got away was undoubtedly *A Streetcar Named Desire.* Sullavan was producer Irene Selznick's preference for the part of Blanche, but Tennessee Williams wasn't impressed. "Sullavan is strictly compromise," he wrote after she read for the part. "She is the sort of actress that would get 'excellent personal notices,' but do the play no good." Williams could not see her as expressing "anything stronger than pathos" in the part, and thought she lacked fragility.

For Sullavan, Broadway was every bit as nerve-wracking as the movies. The boredom of a long run set in early for her, whereas Fonda found giving the illusion of the first night an endless challenge. As the 1950s wore on, Sullavan's own fragility became increasingly apparent. There was a nervous breakdown in 1955 over her children choosing to live with their father, and her hearing got steadily worse. In a December 1955 appearance on *What's My Line?* she had trouble hearing comments made by the celebrity panel, with moderator John Daly having to restate a number of questions.

On December 28, 1959, she opened in *Sweet Love Remember'd* by Ruth Goetz at the Shubert Theatre in Philadelphia. Leland Hayward sent his ex-wife his customary good-luck telegram: "Dear Maggie, All the best as always tonight. Leland."

Four days later, on New Year's Day 1960, Margaret Sullavan was found dead of an overdose of sleeping pills. The play wasn't working and her hearing had made it impossible for her to pick up cues. Brooke had

411

called her stepfather to wish her mother a happy new year, and he told her that Maggie had just died — her heart, he said, had given out. Pamela, Brooke's new stepmother, picked her up at the theatre where she was acting in a play, to take her home. She promptly told Brooke that her mother had committed suicide.

"How do you know it's suicide?" asked Brooke.

"Sleeping pills," Pamela replied.

"I don't believe you. I seriously doubt if it was sleeping pills."

"Yes, she did; it was sleeping pills. She was a very, very disturbed woman."

"Which was undoubtedly true," remembered Brooke, "But I didn't want her critique at the moment. I wanted her to say, 'I know you loved your mother very much.' But there was never anything cuddly about Pamela. She was reptilian."

Maggie's death devastated everyone who knew her, particularly Fonda and Hayward. The coroner officially judged her death to be accidental, but few people believed the verdict. Fonda couldn't quite bring himself to think that Sullavan had committed suicide, although he would admit that he might be guilty of "wishful thinking."

Despite her professed indifference to acting, Sullavan was careful to preserve a full record of her career, from her debut at a Cotillion ball in 1929 to the good-luck telegrams for her opening nights that attest to Fonda's attentiveness — for decades he sent her cards saying "Love and luck, Hank" before every opening.

In December 1959, Fonda opened in a new play, Robert Anderson's *Silent Night, Lonely Night,* costarring Barbara Bel Geddes. Once again, he was using his art in an attempt to understand his life. It's the story of two strangers who meet at a snowbound New England inn on Christmas Eve. His wife is in a mental institution, her husband sleeps around. The two strike sparks, make love, and leave in the morning to go back to their respective spouses.

Anderson said that Fonda "was almost desperate for a strong play with a long run," but at the same time "was not directable." The reviews were mediocre, and the play ran for only 124 performances.

One night during the run, Gary Cooper and his wife came to the show. "My father thought Fonda was a wonderful actor," said Maria Cooper Janis. "After the performance, they went backstage, and my father learned to what extent he and Fonda were polar opposites.

"When they came into Hank's dressing room, he went nuts. 'Oh my God, I didn't know you were in the audience,' he said. It turned out that he felt he'd had an off night, hadn't liked his performance. He started banging his head against the wall and hitting it with his fists. If he'd had a whip, he'd have flagellated himself. Intense emotional drama. He had to be perfect."

Jane Fonda's proximity to show business had resulted in a young woman with a tentative interest in an acting career, which became obvious when she and her father traveled to Omaha to appear in *The Country Girl* opposite Dorothy McGuire.

Jane had a small part in the production. One scene called for her to make an entrance in a distraught state, so she got the stage manager to rough her up. Her father was disturbed by what she had to do to get to the proper pitch of the character. You either had talent or you didn't, he said, and if you had talent why did you need externals like getting slapped around? As with Laurence Olivier's legendary remark to Dustin Hoffman on *Marathon Man* ("Why don't you try acting, dear boy?"), the younger generation's emphasis on emotional actuality seemed to Fonda to be a negation of the whole point of acting.

But all that became beside the point as he watched Jane act. She was, he said, "natural, unself-conscious, beautiful. And I remember watching her on stage from the wings and thinking . . . if that girl ever decides this is what she's going to do, she's going to do all right."

Maria Cooper was similarly blessed by nature, although she lacked the performing urge. One day Fonda appreciatively noted Maria's blossoming when he told her mother, "Maria's got the body, but Jane's got the face."

To Jane the remark was a clear indication that her father was "a misogynist" and "objectified women. Men were supposed to be a certain way; women were supposed to look a certain way."

A less contentious father-daughter relationship might have led to Hank's remark being accepted as a well-meant compliment from a different generation.

As with his sister, Peter Fonda also eventually went to Omaha to do theater, specifically a production of *Harvey* in which he played Elwood P. Dowd, the part Uncle Jimmy had made his own. His father came to see the show and Peter anxiously awaited the verdict.

When Hank came backstage, he didn't overwhelm Peter with enthusiasm, but he complimented him on one specific thing — Peter had played a man in late middle age without resorting to the clichés that are often present when young actors play old — no indications of stiffness in the legs, or a bad back.

That was all, but Peter understood. By his carefully calibrated appreciation, his father had given him the green light to be an actor.

In the years when Fonda's heart was in the theater and he was headquartered in New York, he and Stewart would go long periods of time without seeing each other. It didn't get in the way because they never lost their psychological connection.

"We would go a couple of years without seeing each other," said Jim, "talk on the phone every once in a while . . . but when we would see each other, it was like it was Monday and we hadn't seen each other since Saturday night."

Just as the friendship had never been endangered by separation, so neither of their careers was ever truly endangered by anything but age, although you wouldn't have known it by talking to them. Each of them shared the common actor's anxiety that every job would be their last, that the phone was about to stop ringing.

One night in the early 1960s, the two men went out to dinner and then to a theater to watch one of Stewart's pictures. Afterward, Stewart said, "Know something, Hank? I'm depressed. I don't know if I'll ever get another picture again."

"You too?" replied Fonda. "That's the way I feel."

"He was *always* worried about getting the next job," said Jane Fonda. Linda LeRoy Janklow, the daughter of Mervyn LeRoy, knew both men and said that "Jim and Hank [were] the only two actors of their caliber that I've ever known who were totally insecure. . . . The difference was that Hank was absolutely neurotic about it, while Jimmy kind of leveled off at simple anxiety."

Fonda increasingly compensated for his worry about jobs by shifting his focus to creative alternatives. As Stewart wrote in a note to Josh Logan, "I hear Fonda is in the painting business up to here."

The Stewarts were more hands-on as parents than a lot of the families in Beverly Hills. Jim's deeply ingrained sense of polite-

417

ness and correct behavior was drilled into the children more by osmosis than speeches. The environment at 918 Roxbury was actually more Midwestern than Californian.

"It wasn't a Hollywood upbringing," said stepson Michael McLean. "Movies were his job, not his life." In line with the overriding Midwestern viewpoint, strict behavioral guidelines were mandated. Tardiness was completely unacceptable, and when discipline was needed it was usually administered by Jim, who was not an absentee father.

"You didn't want to hear a knock on your bedroom door at 5 o'clock," said McLean. "Then you knew you were really in trouble. His jaw would be tight and his lips had disappeared. He didn't yell, but it was still terrible. He would say, 'I'm *really* ashamed of you,' and you just wanted to crawl away. And then Mom would say, 'Your father is *really* ashamed of you.' " There was an alternative admonition from Jim: "How could you do this to your mother?" which would be inevitably followed by Gloria saying, "How could you do this to your father?"

The only show business people at the house were Hank, Lew Wasserman, Gary and Rocky Cooper, Rosalind Russell, and producer William Frye. When Jim was asked to sign autographs, he always gracefully complied, and explained to the kids that it was part of his job.

Michael McLean's favorite story about his father and Hank involved a train set that Jim had bought for the boys and was manfully attempting to assemble on the floor of their bedroom, with a notable lack of success. Nevertheless, a man was supposed to be able to assemble a train set, so Stewart refused to give up or call for help.

Fonda appeared in the doorway and quietly observed his friend's palpable frustration for some minutes. The once and future gentleman farmer with a facility for machines must have been amused.

"Looks like you're having some trouble, Jim," Fonda said.

Stewart looked over his shoulder. "Yeah," he said, "I guess I am."

Fonda nodded, watched a little bit more, then said, "Well, I'll be seeing you," and ambled away.

Stewart didn't talk much about work, his attitude toward it, what parts he had been offered or turned down. He would sit in the armchair that no one else sat in when he was home and study his scripts while the kids watched TV, his lips moving as he committed his dialogue to memory. For particularly demanding scripts, he would retire to his bedroom to get a firm grasp on the material.

Alex Stewart visited fairly regularly. Age had not mellowed him. He struck the kids as "Ornery. No nonsense." If Alex went missing, he could generally be located at the bar of the Beverly Hills Hotel, where a crowd had gathered around the sage of Indiana, Pennsylvania, who was telling stories to an eager audience.

Alex continued to give the impression that his son's choice of career was a temporary aberration that would pass as soon as the public wised up. It was a bombastic form of passive aggression mixed with very occasional spasms of praise — pretty much their relationship in a nutshell.

When Jim had first arrived in Hollywood, Alex had been appalled to find out that not only was he not attending the local Presbyterian church, he didn't even know where it was. Alex left the house and came back a few hours later with five Presbyterian Elders in tow. Alex then informed his son that Jim was going to help them build a better church. It was another imposed obligation, one that Stewart kept.

If Jim made a picture Alex liked, Dad would pester the local theater for posters. People would come into the hardware store asking for "Jimmy Stewart's father," which mightily irritated Jimmy Stewart's father. He recruited Andy, the town drunk, to do odd jobs around the store, after which Andy would sit by the potbellied stove and snooze. When people would ask for Jimmy, Alex would say "Ssshhh! Let's not wake him, but that's him right over there."

"It was his way of telling me what he thought of 'movie actors,' " Jim would muse.

Generally, Jim's pictures would play for only three days in Indiana, Pennsylvania. Alex would attend on Saturday night after the hardware store closed. "He would call me up every once in a while to talk about it," said Jim, "and I could tell exactly when he'd fallen asleep. He'd start wandering about the plot."

When Alex visited the set of one of Jim's westerns, he watched him mount a horse, and snorted, "He climbs on that nag as if he's going to kiss it." That Alex was referring to the beloved Pie as a nag is a mark of how little he cared for his son's sensibilities.

Whatever Alex said, Jim deferred to his father, as he had all his life. He never felt that he had lived up to his father's expectations, with the exception of going off to war, which was just one reason why it was the achievement he was proudest of.

Jim's resolution never to talk about the war held firm even within the family. When Michael came home from school with an assignment to write about World War II, he figured this was his chance to get his father to open up. All Jim did was gesture to the library. "There's books on the shelf," he said. "You're welcome to use any of them." It was clear that the subject was closed. Gloria told her children their father was prone to nightmares involving the war. Loud noises upset him.

In most ways, Jim was a benign domestic figure. Besides the old Volvo to which he was maddeningly loyal, he would hold on to clothes until they grew worn. As his daughter Kelly would say, "He liked simple food and he liked food he knew. He used to order the same meal at Chasen's for a decade or so, and then switched to another meal for the next decade. He hated huge heaping portions — he had a small appetite."

Jim's meal of choice remained filet of sole in butter sauce, accompanied by some skim milk or just water. He liked his steak medium rare, and at social events would have a vodka and tonic, or white wine.

Jim and Gloria's marriage proved a success in every possible way, because the ingredients included not only love and respect, but balance. "Gloria was fantastic," said Bill Hayward, "the greatest thing since sliced toast. She was funny, great to be around, and great for him."

While Jim was down-home and informal, Gloria liked a certain style; she wore Chanel and Valentino, Ferragamo shoes and smoked Benson & Hedges cigarettes. Most importantly, Gloria's upbringing in the middle of the Hearst organization and the Eastern establishment had left her with a strong sense of self that meant she wasn't terribly impressed by the Hollywood hierarchy; she could handle people without offending them.

There was one other thing that united them, and that was humor — they consistently amused each other. Their actual differences were minor: Gloria was terrified of flying, while Jim kept his own plane. Jim was always cold, Gloria was always hot. Gloria was a backseat driver, but she came by it naturally because Jim, the man who had smoothly piloted B-24s, was a terrible driver — slow and indecisive.

And Gloria's passion for animals heightened Jim's empathy. They had golden retrievers named Judy and Kelly, which meant that whenever they called either the daughters or the dogs, the other pair would come running too. The dogs slept with them in an order that never changed: dog, Gloria, dog, Jim. The Stewarts had a getaway ranch in Nevada where the help set traps to catch coyotes, but whenever Jim was in residence he freed any coyotes that were caught.

As the kids grew older, they would occasionally ask leading questions. Judy once asked her father if he had ever fallen in love with one of his leading ladies. Jim's eyes grew moist and he paused. "Well . . . *Marlene,*" he finally said. Another time she asked him if he had ever talked with Hank about Frances's suicide.

"Ah, honey," he said, "we-we-we don't *ever* talk about that." And Judy wondered, not for the first or last time, well, what *do* you talk about?

Kelly remembered that when it was time for her and her sister to go off to college, their father called them down to the living room. They were afraid they were going to get a lecture about some mortifying subject like premarital sex. That might have been Stewart's intent, but after some hemming and hawing about nothing in particular, he finally sent them off with one admonition: "Just remember always to be nice to people."

THIRTEEN

Scanning the horizon for something, anything, Fonda latched on to television, which had recharged the professional batteries of a number of fading stars — Dick Powell and Loretta Young, among others. Fonda's show was a western called *The Deputy* that seemed to have been inspired by *The Tin Star* and began its run in 1959. Fonda was top-billed, but his participation was strictly limited. He worked ten weeks the first year, narrated all the shows, but actually carried only six episodes, while the bulk of the screen time went to the eponymous character played by Allen Case. Fonda upped his appearances to thirteen shows in the second season, but the audience smelled a lack of commitment and the series was canceled.

Jane had decided to become an actress, and worked for Josh Logan in *There Was a Little Girl,* a play about rape that her father begged her not to do. A few nights into the

Boston run, Louis Jean Heydt, who was playing Jane's father, dropped dead just before he was to make his entrance in the second act. A few nights after that, Logan collapsed with another nervous breakdown. He was gone for ten days, leaving the play in the hands of playwright Daniel Taradash.

When Logan came back to the show, Jane noticed that his wife, Nedda, was by his side at all times. Jane's hotel room was adjacent to Logan's, and at night Jane could hear Nedda singing "Rock-a-Bye Baby" to lull Josh to sleep. The play struggled through sixteen performances before closing — the sort of accumulation of disasters that would turn anybody but the most devoted performer off the theater for life. But Jane Fonda wouldn't be dissuaded.

Hank persisted as well. In 1960 he appeared in *Critic's Choice,* a comedy by Ira Levin that ran for six months and was directed by Otto Preminger — nobody's first choice for comedy. Preminger enjoyed repeating a story involving Fonda's painstaking approach to his craft. After the play had been running for some months, Fonda went to Preminger and asked for a slight change. Instead of sitting down in a scene, would Preminger mind if he stayed on his feet?

"Imagine a man so professional!" said Preminger.

In 1962 Fonda starred in *A Gift of Time,* a play written and directed by Garson Kanin that costarred Olivia de Havilland. The story involved a man dying of cancer, and the difficulties presented by the subject matter were made even more awkward when de Havilland developed a major crush on Fonda, one that had possibly had its beginning twenty-three years earlier during her relationship with Jimmy Stewart.

She made her intentions clear at every opportunity, but Fonda had just been sprung from his marriage to Afdera and seemed at long last to have learned an invaluable lesson about frying pans and fires. He kept his distance. *A Gift of Time* ran for less than three months. "Garson can write like a fucking angel," Fonda said in retrospect, "and he can't direct for shit."

Cumulatively, the pictures Stewart made in the 1950s deepened his persona. As David Thomson wrote, in this decade he was "a troubled, querulous or lonely personality." What is remarkable is that the audience actually liked this ornery obsessive who was driven by needs he couldn't articulate, only demonstrate. His screen character had always had clarity — he was a straight shooter, an honest crusader for virtue. But the cracks that had been introduced in *It's a Wonderful Life* widened in a way that coincided with the subterranean undercurrents of a widely misunderstood era where instability was thinly papered over by official pieties.

If his acting reached a higher plateau, the pressures that motivated him were still apparent. In July 1958, Leland Hayward sent him a play to consider. Stewart's response was swift and unyielding: "The play is absolutely fascinating," he wrote Hayward, "but I do not think it is for me, and besides Alex Stewart would never stand for it."

It's possible he was kidding — Alex hadn't thrown up any roadblocks over *Vertigo,* or if he had, Jim had ignored him — but it's more likely that the script involved something that Alex would have considered inappropriate for his fifty-one-year-old son and thereby devalue the family franchise.

By now, Stewart's technique was so assured that people began to take him for granted as an actor, and he would grow a little rueful about the prevailing impression that he was just being Jimmy Stewart, just being natural. "There is nothing less natural in the world," he would grumble, "than to stand out there in front of dozens of people on a sound stage with all those lights and big cameras and equipment surrounding you and to carry on a scene with somebody as though you're completely alone."

Just as he was loyal to Hank, Stewart was also loyal to Lew Wasserman. In 1962, the Justice Department brought antitrust charges against MCA. When the lawsuit was announced, Stewart came to Wasserman's office and put his checkbook on the desk. "Take as much as you want," he said. To the end of his life, Wasserman remained moved by such a demonstration of loyalty in a business not noted for such things, and from a man who placed a high value on a dollar.

That same year, Stewart and Fonda both appeared in the Cinerama spectacular *How the West Was Won,* but they didn't have any scenes together. The picture was made economically, with all the stars accepting the same modest salaries in order to maximize the profits, a portion of which were to go to St. John's Hospital in Santa Monica, where Stewart was a trustee. Stewart's segment was directed by Henry Hathaway, who was up to his old tricks. Stewart was shooting a love scene with Carroll Baker when an assistant director noticed a snake slithering around a tree the actors were leaning against. The assistant yelled "Cut," and Hathaway went crazy.

"This is my picture!" Hathaway screamed. "I make those decisions! How do you know I didn't put the snake there deliberately?"

In the early 1960s, Stewart was still eager for risk. There were three pictures for John Ford, one great (*The Man Who Shot Liberty Valance*), two substandard (*Two Rode Together, Cheyenne Autumn*). Stewart had been friendly with Duke Wayne for years — their politics were closely aligned — so it was only a matter of time until he was recruited by Ford.

Most of Jim's favorite directors worked through enthusiasm: Capra and Lubitsch both maintained lively, upbeat sets, where the level of creative excitement was palpable and shared by the actors and crew. But John Ford worked through level intent. In many respects, he resembled Fonda — a Ford set could be tense, with everybody trying to avoid being singled out for Ford's withering sarcasm.

Harry Carey Jr. noticed that Ford wasn't as comfortable with Stewart as he was with Wayne or even Fonda. "They had a flippant kind of relationship, lots of humor between them, but I had a feeling that Jimmy made him edgy, had something that Jack knew he could never quite control the way, say, he ran roughshod over Wayne for so long. Maybe it was just Jimmy's talent and Jack's awareness that he had the real stuff in front of him."

"I always had great respect for John Ford," Stewart would say in retrospect.

He hated the human voice. He hated words. And I'd been on the set with him — three or four of us — Duke Wayne and three or four others — and we were doing a scene. And right in the middle of the scene he'd say, "Cut!" He said, "Everybody's talking too much." He said, "You fellas: do you have the same script I do? I . . . I don't . . . All this stuff isn't in my script." (Which was of course ridiculous, because he *wrote* the script.) "But you're talkin' too much. Now come over here and we'll sit down and go over this." And he'd say, "Now say the lines." And we would. And he'd say, "Well, that stinks." He'd wipe that out. And he'd say, "Now do it," And he'd say, "That's fine."

He was the visual type. I remember: he said it very specifically in everything — and he believed it with all his heart. He said, "If you can't tell your story up on the screen, if you can't tell the story visually, without depending on the spoken word, you aren't using the medium correctly." And I pretty much agree with him.

Ford would be the last of four great directors to apply a different spin to the Stewart persona. Capra's Stewart had been a small-town juvenile who becomes more of a man as the film progresses by finding the strength that lies deep inside. Anthony Mann's Stewart took the Capra character out west and added anger to the stubbornness. Alfred Hitchcock showed the pathology of a man who refuses to alter his course even when common sense — not to mention survival — indicates he should back down. And Ford returned him to the West as a man who is quietly cooperative with the corruption endemic to human society.

After the films with Ford came a series of mediocre domestic comedies (*Take Her, She's Mine; Dear Brigitte*) and undistinguished westerns directed by Andrew McLaglen: *Shenandoah, Bandolero, The Rare Breed. Shenandoah,* a story of a tough, patriarchal Virginian during the Civil War, was a fluke hit, probably because it served as family-friendly counter-programming amidst the tumult of Vietnam. It amassed a surprising $7.8 million in domestic rentals — Stewart's last big hit. The inevitable follow-ups were financial failures; *The Rare Breed* did only $1.9 million in rentals.

As they were for the entire nation, the 1960s were a time of transition for Stewart, unpleasantly so. In 1961, his father died at the age of eighty-nine. Jim had some offers to buy the hardware store, but, as he put it, "I could not endure the thought of another man's standing in the middle of Dad's life." He decided to close the business permanently.

"After it was all over and I was alone, I went to the hardware store and let myself in, with a key I hadn't touched for thirty years. The interior smelled of metal, leather, oil and fertilizer, the odors of my childhood. I sat at his scarred oak desk and idly pulled open the middle drawer. It held a clutter of pencils and paper clips and bolts and paint samples. Something glinted dully among them. I picked up the funeral train penny with the flattened Indian face and the burst grain. I had lost mine, so now I took his. Then I left the store, locking the door behind me." The merchandise was sold off and the store remained vacant until 1969, when it was torn down.

Nineteen sixty-one was also the year that

Gary Cooper died. He had been in failing health since April of the previous year, when he was operated on for prostate cancer. Five weeks later, he went under the knife again for a malignant bowel obstruction. The cancer had spread. In the fall of 1960 he struggled through his last picture, *The Naked Edge,* coping with declining energy and a loss of concentration. In December, the disease was found in his lungs and bones. Within the Hollywood community, word got around.

On April 17, 1961, Stewart accepted an honorary Oscar for Cooper. "I am very honored to accept this award tonight for Gary Cooper," he began. "I'm sorry he's not here to accept it, but I know he's sitting by the television set tonight, and Coop, I want you to know I'll get it to you right away. With it goes all the friendship and affection and the admiration and deep respect of all of us. We're very, very proud of you, Coop. All of us are tremendously proud." As he got to the end of his speech, Stewart faltered and began to cry.

Cooper and his wife and daughter were watching the ceremony. He was on pain medication but attentive and coherent. Typically, he was self-contained about Stewart's emotional display, although his daughter

Maria thought he was quietly moved. The news of Cooper's terminal illness hadn't leaked out to the world at large, but now the death watch began. He died less than a month later.

Of Stewart's films of this period, only two were worth the trouble: Robert Aldrich's *The Flight of the Phoenix,* seriously under-rated at the time, and McLaglen's *Fool's Parade,* a weird piece of rural Gothic by Davis Grubb (*Night of the Hunter*), which typically combined poetry and unhinged violence.

The Flight of the Phoenix was the last time Dan Duryea worked with Stewart, and the two men once again engaged in practical jokes. One running gag involved them competing with each other to see who could say "Good Morning!" first. Stewart would call Duryea on the phone earlier and earlier, peaking at four in the morning, while Duryea bribed the crew to announce the greeting to Stewart over a loudspeaker. When the film opened in London, Duryea arrived for the premiere to find a huge sign proclaiming "GOOD MORNING DAN!"

But even the good pictures were commercial disappointments, and several of them were outright flops. *Fool's Parade* had the signal embarrassment of being retitled

Dynamite Man from Glory Jail for its English release. Stewart was still loved — he would always be loved — but it was clear that the public didn't want to pay to see his movies anymore, and it was increasingly apparent that he seemed to lack the energy or desire to figure out a way to sustain his stardom through a fifth decade.

The sense of diminishment was amplified when the Air Force nudged him into retirement in 1968. He went, but unwillingly, and he never really accepted it. "It was the first time I became conscious of growing old," he would say in a burst of candor. "I moped around for a while and then I went out to Burbank Airport and bought myself a little Super-Cub. I keep it spotless, shined like a silver dollar, and I go out and fly it every Saturday afternoon, for three, four hours, after golf. It reminds me of when I was a kid actor, out here in the '30s and I had a little fabric-covered plane, and I used to fly back to see my folks in Indiana, Pennsylvania, navigating by following the railroad tracks. It's funny that the Air Force should think I'm too old."

Perhaps the disaffection began on the set of *Shenandoah*. The locations were in Eugene, Oregon, and one day Stewart was shooting a highly dramatic scene on a bridge where his character confronts a soldier who has killed his son. James Best, who had acted in several films with Stewart, wasn't working that day and had elected to go fly-fishing in the river below the bridge. Best hooked a trout, which began splashing around and made so much noise he was worried it would spoil the shot. After the scene on the bridge was completed, Stewart walked down the embankment to Best.

"What the hell are you doing?" he asked Best.

"Fishin'," said the actor.

"Why is it that I'm up there on the bridge working in the hot sun and you're down here fishing?"

"Well, Mr. Stewart, when I get as famous and rich as you are, I'll go up on the bridge."

What gradually took the place of acting was never going to be fishing, but, rather, travel — specifically, travel to Africa. It had begun with a safari with a couple of friends in 1962, and it became an almost yearly ritual, complete with home movies and thousands of stills. "We hunted for one year, then gave it up," Stewart said. "You get a respect for the animals." So Jim and Gloria took camera safaris, which were eventually collected in bound albums of photographs of lions and wildebeests and other varieties of four- and two-legged creatures from China, India, Africa, and Vietnam.

Africa stimulated Kelly Stewart's interest in anthropology, so Gloria gave her copies of Robert Ardrey's *The Territorial Imperative* and Konrad Lorenz's *On Aggression,* which eventually led to Stanford, a PhD, and a career working with anthropologist Richard Leakey and in academia. Both Jim and Gloria were thrilled by Kelly's career choice; in 1981 they went to Rwanda to visit Kelly, her husband, and the gorillas they were studying while Dian Fossey was visiting America. Jim and Gloria crawled through bamboo on their stomachs and got as close as five meters from the gorillas.

Other than his service in World War II, Stewart had never really taken much time away from Hollywood. But Africa awakened him to the idea of an alternative to show business — a big world out there that wasn't called Beverly Hills, as well as food that wasn't served at Chasen's.

Africa also provided the material for one of Jim and Gloria's primary comedy routines. Both agreed that the twin girls fell hard for a bushbaby on one of the early safaris and wanted it as a pet. After that their stories diverged. Jim's version involved smuggling the animal onto an airplane inside his shirt. When Stewart fell asleep, the bushbaby escaped, and Jim had to get down on his hands and knees and forage through first class trying to find the animal without waking up anybody.

Gloria's version was less romantic. After informing the listener that "not one word, not a single word of [Jim's version] is true," she simply said that the animal was shipped back to America through channels, was quarantined for a time, then tested and found okay, after which the Stewarts picked it up and brought it home. "Jimmy did not sneak that animal onto the plane."

While Jim increasingly spent the 1960s and 1970s traveling, Hank mostly spent the 1960s playing a series of authority figures undergoing varying degrees of psychological stress: *Advise & Consent*, *Fail-Safe*, *The Best Man*, *Madigan*, *The Boston Strangler*. Although most of these parts relied on his aura of integrity, Fonda's work was never less than solid, and sometimes it was moving. Sidney Lumet directed *Fail-Safe*, a stark but silly movie about an accidental nuclear strike on Moscow, which leads the president of the United States (Fonda) to nuke New York to prevent a nuclear holocaust. Lumet said that Fonda "would speak very little. He would listen a great deal. . . . I might not have done *Fail-Safe* if he hadn't been available. The premise was false, melodramatic, but Fonda brought truth."

Personally, Fonda's inability to cope with someone else's need still existed. In 1966, he made a time-passer entitled *A Big Hand for the Little Lady* opposite Joanne Woodward. Far down the cast list was Mae Clarke — at one time a star (the 1931 version of *Waterloo Bridge, The Public Enemy*) now eking out a living in bit parts. Clarke had long admired Fonda and when she spotted him sitting alone in his chair, she went over to plead her case.

"Mr. Fonda, my name is Mae Clarke, and I've been in the business a long time. I hesitate to say this, because I know it sounds so funny, but I can't let the opportunity go. I so admire your taste in what you do, I wonder if I could interest you in remembering me for some of the things you will be doing that I could be even a little part of? When I say a little part, I mean a little, effective part, but I'm not holding out for any money at all."

Now, there are various ways of dealing with someone asking for help. Fonda could have heard her out, said that of course he remembered her, thought she was a wonderful actress, and would do his best to find a bit or two for her in his films. Or, he could have graciously begged off, saying he understood her problem, but he had enough trouble finding decent work for himself.

Instead, Henry Fonda got up and walked away without saying a word.

That was Fonda, and he was no different with people he needed than with people he didn't need. His agent at this time was a woman named Stevie Phillips, who enjoyed working with him because he was one of her few clients eager for theater work. When a script came in that Fonda thought was worth doing, he would tell her the money he wanted — it was never outrageous. Phillips would make the deal and Fonda would go to work.

Once in a while, Fonda and Stevie Phillips would meet for lunch at Sardi's. He was, as Phillips recalled, "mostly silent and mysterious," though he always picked up the check. He didn't seem to mind — Stevie was a good agent. Professional courtesy and all that.

In 1965, he starred in *Generation,* a mild comedy directed by Gene Saks that ran for three hundred performances. The reviews were respectful, but among his co-workers there was the first sign of a generational divide. Richard Jordan, later to achieve a measure of success in films such as *The Friends of Eddie Coyle,* played Fonda's son-in-law, and told a friend that he detested the man. He was like a metronome, Jordan said, and didn't really listen. No matter what happened, no matter what an actor threw at him, Fonda didn't respond in kind but rather as he had planned to from the beginning. What you got was what Fonda wanted to give you, no more and no less.

Jordan was a Method actor who believed in learning his lines but also in finding original places to go with those lines. He was a good actor but might have been even better if he had been a little less intelligent — he tended to overthink. What Jordan saw as a lack of elasticity contrasted strongly with the respect that Method actors like Ben Gazzara had for Stewart's looser, more musical approach.

Leland Hayward was producing *That Was the Week That Was,* a satirical TV show done live every week. He hired his old friend Hank for an episode, paying him $10,000 with first-class air fare for a few days' work. Other actors, like Art Carney ($5,000) or Bill Cosby ($2,000) got much less.

It was a show that lived on cultural currency, but Leland was no longer current, not at all. "Hayward seemed lost," said Stuart Woods, later a bestselling novelist, at the time shadowing rehearsals for a story for *TV Guide.* "It wasn't really his kind of show at all, but he was trying to reinvent himself. The problem was that the writing felt like 1953."

Watching rehearsals for the pilot, Hayward knew he was in trouble. He put in an emergency call to Mike Nichols and asked if he and Elaine May had anything they might be able to offer. As a matter of fact, said Nichols, they had just worked up a new skit about a man buying a funeral for a close friend.

It was a typically brilliant, quietly scathing Nichols and May routine. May played a grief counselor eager to make as much money as possible. After outlining the cost of the deluxe service, complete with mahogany coffin and polished brass fittings, a sticker-shocked Nichols meekly inquired if there might be anything less expensive.

"Yes," said May. "Knobby plywood."

Woods looked out at the audience and saw Henry Fonda sitting in the first row, his lean body draped over the railing, convulsed with laughter.

Even though he was pushing sixty, Fonda looked a good ten years younger than his actual age. He had maintained his weight for thirty years, and, except for a receding hairline, he seemed to be preserved in amber. People asked him about his secret. Yoga? Exercise? Macrobiotics? The answer was good genes. "I don't do any exercise," he said, "only because I'm not good at it and I dislike attempting anything I can't be good at. The only kind of exercise I really like is when I'm in New York and I walk up Madison Avenue looking at the art galleries."

And there was something else, something that always puts a spring in a middle-aged man's step. Hank had fallen in love again, and this time would be the last time. Shirlee Adams was born in Aurora, Illinois, and spent time in an orphanage after her parents divorced. She became a stewardess for American Airlines and was modeling when she met Fonda in 1962. She was vivacious and optimistic by nature, a can-do woman in search of a home. She found one.

Shirlee had been dating the racing driver Stirling Moss, but that went by the wayside when she met Fonda. She was immediately smitten. "He was so young and handsome. Young acting. He could even stand on his head!" She loved nearly everything about him, even the fact that he was grumpy in the morning. He was a great cook, loved antiquing, and she respected his refusal to assert a star's prerogatives — when he went to the movies he insisted on standing in line and buying a ticket along with everybody else. "He was smart and he was funny. Yes, he was moody to a certain degree. But he was a good man!"

Hank and Shirlee were together for several years, but she hadn't given any thought to marriage because Fonda was so obviously embarrassed about his previous four attempts. He was doing *Generation* in New York when he told her, "I want you to be with me." She said she had no interest in being kept, and he countered with an offer — he had owned a five-story townhouse at 151 East 74th Street for years, and he offered her the top floor. She could come and go as she pleased, said Fonda. So she moved into Hank's house, met and enjoyed his friends.

One day she bought him a Turnbull & Asser necktie at Bonwits. That night he asked about her day. Then he blurted out, "Do you want to get married?"

"Marry who?"

"Marry *me.*"

"Well, OK. Yes."

"When?"

"Any Friday."

And that was that. They married in 1965, and this one took, partly because Shirlee wrapped herself around Fonda and his life without barricading him. His friends became her friends and she encouraged him without seeming to. "I wouldn't let him mope around," she remembered.

He started to do more needlepoint, even bringing the pieces onto film sets because, unlike painting, needlepoint could be put down and picked up at will. And there was one other thing, something that might have served as some kind of private comfort: Shirlee called him "Fonda," just as Maggie Sullavan had all those years ago.

"Hank loved Shirlee deeply," said Edwin Sherin, who directed Fonda in two plays. "They were the sort of couple who took a deep pleasure just being in each other's company. They were lucky to have found each other."

Hank decided that it was time to move back to Los Angeles. He bought a house and several acres on top of Bel-Air's Chalon Road for $330,000, and spent the rest of his life there. The house is a generous 9,400 feet of Spanish hacienda, with plenty of room for painting and needlepoint.

Now that Hank was back in Los Angeles, the friendship with Jim moved into higher gear because of proximity; once again they began to see each other regularly, often with John Swope in tow.

The return to the West Coast was accompanied by a return of his passion for working a piece of land. Jane would say that "He just loved being alone in nature." He kept a coop full of chickens for fertilizer, and began keeping bees for the honey.

The bees were an accident. There was an infestation in some beams in the Bel-Air house, so he called a beekeeper to get them out. After the job was done, Fonda followed the beekeeper out to his truck to pay him. There was a hive in the back of the truck and when Fonda examined it with curiosity, the beekeeper gave it to him, along with an eight-page pamphlet about beekeeping. It was a new enthusiasm for a new aspect of the natural world. He was stung numerous times, but it didn't faze him. "They won't bother you if you don't bother them," he said — a way of being he could understand.

Soon he was subscribing to the *American Bee Journal* and personally bottling "Hank's Honey" as gifts for family and friends. In spare moments he began helping out Stewart with the vegetable garden adjacent to the Roxbury house. On his own spread Fonda planted corn and zucchini, lettuce and string beans, and delivered the surplus to Jim down in Beverly Hills. There were apple trees he doted on, "apples so tart," he boasted, "they make your eyes pucker."

It was at this time that he came into the fullness of a life devoted to more than acting. "Fonda had spent his life bouncing off things that didn't bounce back," said Mark Swope. "If you're in a play or a movie, the words are set; you're interpreting the writer's or director's ideas and phrases. But with painting and needlepoint, he was creating something that was entirely his. It must have been a delight for him. The chickens, the bees, same thing."

The normally taciturn Fonda turned gabby when the subject of bees or organic gardening arose, as it tended to when he was around. "I grow anything that is possible to grow in Southern California. Three kinds of beets, four kinds of tomatoes, winter squash, summer squash, zucchini, limas, strawberries, eggplants, peaches, persimmons, pomegranates, lemons, limes, avocadoes, mandarin oranges, corn, radishes.

"There is little to compare with planting a seed and nursing it along and watching it develop into a beautiful vegetable. And I am a shameless proselytizer."

Of all of his hobbies, it was painting that Hank loved the most. He had started with pastels, graduated to oils, and then plunged into demanding watercolors. Occasionally, he would do drawings or caricatures; Shirlee always treasured a Christmas card he drew for her one year.

Fonda was enraptured by detail work because he needed something in which he could lose himself. His work in oils was even more realistic than his work in watercolor. What he lacked in imagination — "I can't paint what I don't see," he said — he gained in attention to physical detail. The paintings grew in skill and technique; Norton Simon bought a painting Hank called *Ripening,* two tomatoes sitting on a flaking windowsill in the sun.

There's something of Andrew Wyeth in Hank's work, although he's more reportorial than Wyeth. But the focus, the specificity he always brought to his acting, is there in his painting as well, as is the sense of appreciation for all things under the sun. In his painting, in his farming, in his acting, Fonda's secret was the pure soul of the true artist.

The affinity with Wyeth led to a meeting

arranged by Shirlee. Hank grilled the artist about dry-brush watercolors and Wyeth explained the technique. Fonda took to them immediately — all the necessary equipment could be contained inside a small box without lugging around oil paints and canvas.

Shirlee watched . . . and learned. "I just loved the man," she said. "I wasn't caught up in his fame; I was caught up in *him*. I was his soulmate. His friends became my friends. Burgess Meredith was so funny, and I adored Johnny Swope. Josh Logan was fun, but he was into being guided by his wife."

And Jim? "They were much alike. They were quiet and shy. They didn't like to talk about themselves. And they were both gentlemen — decent, honest human beings. You could read their soul."

Of course there were differences as well. Besides the matter of their politics, there was religion — Jim remained devout, while Fonda thought any talk of God was absurd. If Hank and Shirlee went out it was with Jim and Gloria, or John and Dorothy Swope, or James and Lois Garner. At parties, they almost never mingled. Jim would pull out his accordion or play the piano, while Fonda walked around the house examining the books and paintings. In both cases, it was a way of avoiding small talk.

Shirlee grew to understand Fonda's remoteness, his carefully maintained isolation, as a function of insecurity. "He thought he was a failure. He was terribly sensitive and his marriages embarrassed him terribly, the mistakes he'd made embarrassed him. He wouldn't even look at his own movies."

Of course he wouldn't: the act of creation is inevitably different from the honed perfection artists imagine. Intellectually, Fonda knew that creation is organic, that it alters and shifts in the process of doing it, and can never equal the pristine construct in your head. But emotionally Hank saw the differences as failures and so avoided them.

"Duke Wayne was like that too," said Stewart. "Duke said he always saw something he didn't like about his performance and then he'd get discouraged and grouch around the house. But I've never really felt like that. Of course, I like some of my pictures more than others. But I always tried, and if the script wasn't too good, well, then, I just tried a little bit harder. I hope, though, not so hard that it shows."

For Fonda, it was about the planning and the doing, never the remembering. When he had to memorize a script, he would close himself up in his office; it took him only a few days to learn the script of *Clarence Darrow,* the only one-man show he attempted. His method was grinding simplicity: He learned the first line, then the second line, then repeated both lines aloud, and so forth to the bottom of the page. At that point, he would record the page onto tape from memory, then check it against the script. If it was perfect, he moved on to page two.

There were times when he became the character. When he played Chester Nimitz in *Midway,* he had his salt-and-pepper hair dyed white and ended up looking a good deal like Nimitz. Shirlee told him she didn't like him with white hair. He shot her one of his laser looks and she never criticized his makeup choices again.

Among the younger generation of actors, Fonda favored Brando, and he loved James Garner personally and professionally. He liked to drink Jack Daniel's on the rocks, and he still loved jazz — he and Dave Brubeck had become close friends. If he wasn't working in a play in New York, on Friday nights he'd head out to the jazz clubs.

It's not unusual for artists to admire other artists who possess qualities they don't have, so perhaps Fonda responded to the freedom of jazz, the way the improvisations spin complex loops but manage to stay in loose touch with the melody. "It was *so* out of character," said Peter Fonda. "I think jazz was his improvisation. Of course, Uncle Jimmy loved it too."

Like Jim, Hank loved animals. Stewart favored larger breeds, but when Fonda did *Ash Wednesday* with Elizabeth Taylor, she gave him a shih tzu, which eventually led to several more as well as a Yorkie and a Lhasa apso.

Jane and Peter were now grabbing their share of renown in the family. Peter made *The Wild Angels* and *Easy Rider* and became a face of the counterculture, while Jane won her first Oscar for *Klute,* worked for Jean-Luc Godard, and became the La Pasionaria of the anti–Vietnam War movement. Publicly, Hank reacted to her activism with steely affection — he wouldn't allow Jane to be criticized within his hearing — but privately he seethed about her involvement in what seemed to him to be the far left.

"I married Dennis Hopper and moved back to Los Angeles," recalled Brooke Hayward. "Dennis and I were close to one of father and mother's oldest friends, David Selznick and his wife, Jennifer Jones. They had extraordinary dinners of thirty or forty people. Fonda would always be there with Shirlee, and he was always terribly kind to us. We got on very well.

"But he and Jane got into a long and difficult period — her Black Panther period.

"I remember saying to him during Vietnam, 'Hank, how is Jane?' "

"Who's Jane?"

"Your daughter."

"What daughter?" said Fonda.

His true attitude was nowhere near as curt. Shirlee said that "When Jane went to [North] Vietnam, I saw my husband cry." Yet he recognized that the strength of character that led Jane to follow her own path whatever the cost, not to mention the fierce nature of her talent, made her a true Fonda — his very own girl.

On those occasions when Hank and Jane did get together, things often ended in an argument. There was the Angela Davis matter, when Jane asserted that the young black professor at UCLA shouldn't have been fired just because she was a Communist. Hank disagreed, loudly and vehemently. "Then," remembered Jane, "he pointed his finger at me and said, 'If I ever find out you're a Communist, Jane, I'll be the first person to turn you in.' " Jane yelled that she wasn't a Communist, then ran from the room in tears. There were periods of time when they weren't speaking. With all this, he would say, "I don't think I was ever ready to disown my daughter in any way."

In April 1967, Fonda went on a USO tour of Vietnam. He thought the war was a tragic blunder, but his own experiences in the far reaches of the Pacific had made him realize that visits could be crucial for soldiers' morale. Men at arms had to be supported. Properly worried about his inability to make small talk, he took along a Polaroid camera and canvas bags full of film, correctly reasoning that shooting pictures of the boys to send back home would smooth out his own shyness.

While Fonda's and Stewart's careers continued, Leland Hayward was in the midst of a torturous third act. For years he had been plagued with insomnia, which meant he rarely went to bed before 3 a.m. To buy sleep he would take Seconal — barbiturates, to which he became addicted and which he would amass in six-month supplies. He wrote his doctor for capsules of Seconal, Carbonal, Tuinal, and Nembutal ("lots of these — they work the best" he wrote). He also wanted "some red seconal rockets and any new ones you've got that are great."

After producing *The Sound of Music* in 1959, Hayward had nothing but flops. The dire roster began with 1962's *Mr. President*, starring Robert Ryan and Nanette Fabray, with a score by Irving Berlin, a book by Lindsay and Crouse, and direction by Josh Logan. It had the ingredients as well as the aura of a can't-miss hit. It missed. After a disastrous opening in Washington, D.C., it limped into New York to dire reviews. The $3 million advance saw it through 265 performances, but it was regarded as an embarrassment. Irving Berlin never wrote another show, nor did Lindsay and Crouse.

After that came the failure of *That Was the Week That Was.* By September 1964, a column in the New York *Daily News* asked the rhetorical question, "Whatever became of Leland Hayward?" Nineteen sixty-five saw Leland co-produce *Hot September* with David Merrick, only to have the play close out of town. In 1967, he had a small stroke and began to have difficulty getting around. He developed pancreatitis and would often be awakened by a blast of pain that could be alleviated only by a self-administered shot of morphine. He had to stop drinking and smoking and adhere to a strict diet. All of this was anathema to Hayward, who now looked fifteen years older than he actually was.

In 1969 he produced something called *The Mother Lover,* which closed on opening night. There was no money coming in, so Leland and Pamela were living off capital. The result was that he had to sell his apartment at 1020 Fifth Avenue. In 1970, Leland's son, Bill, was flush from producing *Easy Rider* and he loaned his father the money to produce *The Trial of the Catonsville Nine.*

Jane Fonda would say that her father had been much harder on Peter than on her — "Peter was gentle and poetic, not a jock." Her father had given her more of a pass because she was a girl. But the relationship between father and son was evolving into something far less spiky than the one between father and daughter.

Before it was released Peter showed his father *Easy Rider,* which he starred in, co-produced, and co-wrote. It was a rough cut, but the music score was in place, not that the older Fonda liked it. "Why not tell the audience where the characters are going?" he asked Peter when the lights went up.

"Why not settle back and take the ride with the characters, Dad?" replied Peter.

Peter pointed out that the destination became clear as the movie went on. "That's awful thin, son," grumbled Fonda. Then he started in about how he hated the music, and at that point Peter began to laugh. This was one divide he wasn't going to be able to bridge. "He was a jazz guy," said Peter. "He just didn't like rock and roll."

This generational gap was more or less replicated in the Stewart house, as Jim's conservatism clashed with the liberalism of his stepson Michael and daughter Kelly. Stewart and Michael often retreated to silence during the dinner hour, an uneasy compromise over a perpetual argument neither could win.

Friendship became a refuge from mutual difficulties with children. John Swope and Dorothy McGuire began hosting wine tastings at their house, which had been built in 1928 by the silent star Corinne Griffith. The house's best feature was a beautiful terrace overlooking the Los Angeles Country Club. All the participants would blindfold themselves to ensure perfect objectivity despite the reputation — or lack of reputation — of the winery. The Swopes also made a habit of accompanying Jim and Gloria to the annual Zoo Ball — they were all supporters of the Los Angeles Zoo.

The atmosphere between the couples was relaxed and convivial. They were all comfortable with their success, and McGuire was the same kind of actor as Fonda and Stewart — the foundation of their craft was to learn their lines, period. Their characterization, their way of responding to the other actor, was all based on the text. Dorothy McGuire would complain about how younger actors didn't adhere to that discipline; she had done a TV show and as per her usual routine had learned the script. On the set she was dismayed when other actors couldn't look her in the eye because they were looking over her shoulder at cue cards.

Like many children, Mark Swope didn't quite understand the prevailing adult dynamic. How could they studiously avoid the subject of politics in such an intensely political time? Stewart was conservative, and John Swope was liberal, although not to Fonda's extent. "How much could you talk about Stewart's garden or Fonda's chickens?" Mark wondered.

Politics aside, it was a more relaxed time in Hollywood. Julie Andrews lived next door to the Swopes, and Randolph Scott was at the end of the block. There were no security patrols and very few gates. Beverly Hills was still the land of huge green lawns open to the street. But after Sharon Tate was murdered in 1969, eight-foot walls began to go up, with large iron gates the only point of access.

"I was always playing on the front lawn," remembered Mark Swope. "People would come driving by holding their maps to the stars' homes. I remember one car actually stopped and the people asked me if this was Dorothy McGuire's house. I said 'Yes,' and invited them to come in. My mother was very gracious and shook their hands and signed autographs. After they left she told me to never do that again."

Hank's capaciousness as an actor, not to mention his ambition, had a way of leaping out when least expected. For the first time since *On Our Merry Way,* he and Jim worked together in a western called *Firecreek,* in which Fonda played the main heavy. Unfortunately, it was a rigorously one-dimensional western made by some refugees from *Gunsmoke* who were so oblivious to possibilities they couldn't be bothered to write a scene between their two stars. Despite the advertising ("There was nothing between them and the rape of the town but a $2 a month farmer sheriff with a badge carved out of tin by his kids") it was, to say the least, undistinguished, with results that matched its aspirations — it barely returned a million dollars to Warner Bros.

It had been twenty years since they had worked together, but Stewart was once again dumbstruck by Fonda's capacities. "Fonda could read a scene, maybe five pages, read it again, and know it perfectly," said Stewart. "His reactions to things happening in a scene [were] part of the genius of the man." For his part, Fonda was just glad to be working with his pal, and he found that he liked playing a heavy, the nastier the better. "I tried to kill Jim Stewart and you can't get worse than that," he said with palpable satisfaction.

Sometimes the law of unintended consequences works in a positive direction. *Firecreek* wasn't much, but Sergio Leone saw the picture and it gave him the idea of hiring Fonda to play the villain in the aptly titled *Once Upon a Time in the West* — the culmination of his infatuation with the most venerable of American film genres.

The script that went out to Fonda was a literal translation of the Italian original and read as stilted. Fonda wasn't thrilled, but he called Eli Wallach to ask about Leone. "Pay no attention to the script," said Wallach, who had made *The Good, the Bad and the*

Ugly for Leone. "Just go. You'll fall in love with Sergio. You'll have a marvelous time. Believe me!"

Fonda did as he was told, but before he got to Rome he grew a thick mustache and outfitted himself with brown contact lenses — a disguise to play an utterly unredeemable murderer. Leone was alarmed, but at first said nothing. "Each day I suggested that he remove one of the elements which were masking him. First the thick black eyebrows. Then the moustache. Finally, where his eyes were concerned, I said that his contact lenses made his 'look' vacant." Interestingly, Fonda didn't mount a loud defense, just listened "without appearing to agree," as Leone put it.

It was during the massacre sequence, in which Fonda's character and his cohorts slaughter a family in cold blood, that the revelation came. Leone explained that the camera would swing around Fonda's head and into a close-up that captured his cold blue eyes. "Now I understand," Fonda told Leone. The face that had embodied tortured conscience for more than thirty years was now going to indicate a rigid sociopath, with Leone doubling down on Ford's *Fort Apache*.

The director had his reasons. "The vice

presidents of the companies I have had dealings with have all had baby blue eyes and honest faces and what sons of bitches they turned out to be! Besides, Fonda is no saint himself. He has had five wives."

That Fonda accepted this reversal of a screen character that had verged on the righteous with such alacrity speaks to a lack of ego that had eluded him in other circumstances. Although he played the part without a trace of a wink, it probably appealed to his sense of humor. Jane would say that the performance in *Once Upon a Time in the West* "was one of the few times I was surprised by him."

For the rest of the shoot, Fonda was docile, asking Leone about all sorts of irrelevant details that weren't irrelevant to Fonda — should he pick up a glass with his right hand or his left hand? Leone realized that Fonda was psychologically pointillist; he trusted behavioral and scripted specifics more than emotional response. The men discussed painting, and Leone realized that Fonda's meticulous brush technique was an extension of his artistic personality.

Although *Once Upon a Time in the West* was a major hit in Europe, it was a fast flop in America, earning only $1 million. "It didn't pull a dime," was Fonda's succinct judgment. Fonda felt that all his trouble had gone for naught, although over the years the film has probably been seen by far more people than any of his later films, including *On Golden Pond.*

Leone and Fonda reunited again for *My Name Is Nobody,* an amusing deconstruction of John Ford's dictum about printing the legend. Tonino Valerii got the official credit, but "Sergio really directed that one, too," Fonda told Bill Kelley. "It's credited to somebody else because there was some problem with the producers or something, but it's Sergio's film. He directed the entire thing."

After Leone, things got grim again: *The Serpent, There Was a Crooked Man . . . , Ash Wednesday, The Red Pony, Midway, Tentacles, Rollercoaster, The Swarm, Fedora, Meteor.* Ten years of stiffs, with Fonda renting out his name to add a thin veneer to threadbare projects. *Midway* was a commercial hit, but the rest were failures barely worth a glance, let alone a download.

But there was always the stage. In November 1969, Fonda was back on Broadway in *Our Town.* Thornton Wilder came to see a preview and thought Fonda was perfection as the stage manager, but the production as a whole was too sentimental. "We've got to get back to what we had when Jed [Harris] did the play," Wilder told Martha Scott. "And that was without sweetness."

Martha Scott didn't have the nerve to tell him that Fonda had absolutely forbidden the presence of Jed Harris in any form whatever, because he believed that Harris had treated Margaret Sullavan abominably. "He was one of a small group of people who felt that Jed had something to do with Margaret Sullavan's suicide," said Martha Scott.

There wasn't much to act in the movies, so Hank worked at improving his art. He did a TV movie with Leonard Nimoy and challenged himself with improving his draftsmanship. Whenever he wasn't in front of the camera, he drew screws, over and over again, working on perfecting the spiral lines. "I was fascinated with the care and the precision of the drawings," said Nimoy.

When he wasn't working on his hobbies, he busied himself with his friends, especially James Garner. The two men often vacationed with their wives, and Garner considered Fonda a mentor. They had a fair amount in common in that they didn't like to talk much about acting — they just did it. "He was a cultivated man," recalled Garner, "an intellectual, and a craftsman. And a gentleman."

Garner admired Fonda completely and even paid him the compliment of homage. In *Support Your Local Sheriff!*, Garner leans back in a chair with his feet against a post and does Fonda's little dance from *My Darling Clementine.*

When Hank saw the movie, he asked Garner, "Why don't you imitate somebody good?"

The huge successes of Jane and Peter had put the spotlight on the family in a way that made Hank uncomfortable. He was noticeably crabby when asked about his approach to acting compared to that of his children. "I'm very bad at trying to put it into words," he would say.

I don't consciously think of anything. My daughter, who is a Method actress, says to me, "Dad, you're a Method actor and don't know it." [Lee] Strasberg has said that to me. Now this may be true. I don't know because I don't know what the Method is. . . . Everybody's got his method, small case, and maybe that's what the Method is, whatever your method is. . . .

If I have a goal with each part, with each scene, it's "Don't be Discovered," don't get caught acting. Now that's sometimes hard to understand because obviously I am acting. But don't get caught at it . . . be so real that they can forget you're an actor.

I've had people say, "I was in back of two people walking up the aisle the other night at your play and they said, 'But he wasn't acting, that wasn't acting at all.' " That's fine. I don't care whether they put me down with it. That's success as far as I'm concerned.

Fonda had disliked working in TV and hadn't made a secret of his feelings. "Aversion wouldn't be the word," he said in 1966. "I won't do another [TV series]. I can't conceive of my ever being so poverty-struck that I would need to, that I would have to."

Never say never. In 1971 he tried again, a half-hour sitcom called *The Smith Family*, in which he played an amiable police detective. The producer was Don Fedderson, who had deposited millions of dollars in Fred MacMurray's bank account with the anodyne but successful *My Three Sons.* The beauty part was that MacMurray worked only eight weeks a year, during which all his scenes for the year's episodes would be shot, leaving the proletarian supporting actors to labor without their star for the rest of the production schedule.

It sounded good to Fonda, but *The Smith Family* lasted only thirty-nine episodes during its season and a half. The domestic scenes were supplemented by a canned laugh track, and the cop scenes lacked any semblance of tension.

The actor playing Fonda's son was the young Ron Howard, and Fonda warmed up to the ambitious boy. "He said it was important to take creative risks," remembered Howard. "And if you didn't feel like you're putting your career on the line every couple of years, you're probably not challenging yourself and doing your profession justice. I took that to heart. . . . He gave me my first film theory books. He was actually the first adult figure in my life to say, 'Don't be afraid of chasing that dream.' "

Not everything was idealism squared. "He had a lot of cagey film actor tricks of the trade: how to do a dinner table scene and not be sick at the end of the day." (Don't swallow — have a garbage can at your feet and spit the food out after every take.) Howard was in awe of Fonda's professionalism and attention to technical details — how he made sure a cigarette was the same length in succeeding takes as it had been in the first, how the water in a glass had to be maintained at the same level.

Occasionally he'd pass on an actor's trick learned in the movie trenches. "Don't ever take a pause at the beginning of a line because they'll always cut it out," he told Howard. "If you want to take a pause, lurch into a line, then take your pause and then they can't cut it!"

Fonda even did some TV commercials, lending his face and voice to GAF film and cameras. "The business of an actor is exposure," he told one reporter, "and I have no qualms about doing commercials. In fact, I think a good commercial is much better for an actor than a bad movie. In addition to that, the money is, as my children would say, out of sight."

It probably wasn't an accident that Stewart tried TV at the same time, and not just once but twice. The first was a half-hour sitcom in 1971–72 called *The Jimmy Stewart Show,* which lasted an embarrassing twenty-four episodes. If it seemed inappropriate, Stewart tried to justify it. "I'm an actor and I've got to work at my craft. I always admired Henry Fonda and George C. Scott for taking any kind of acting job just to keep busy. . . . There are less and less movie parts — let's face it — because of my age."

The show was being produced by Hal

Kanter, who was stunned one day when Stewart refused to play a scene with a black actor as a policeman who lectured Stewart's character. Kanter's version of Stewart's objection was "Blacks are bossing white people all over the country, and now we're going to have the same damn thing on prime time television? No way!" Kanter had to recast the part with a white actor, and came to believe that Stewart had some attitudes that harked back to the nineteenth century, attitudes that he might have inherited from his father.

Peter Fonda doubts the story, and says that his father could tolerate Stewart's Republicanism, but "Dad would never have abided a racist. It was perhaps the best thing I learned from him." Kelly Stewart Harcourt says that "There were not a lot of black people in Dad's life, but he was not a racist."

A year later Stewart was back with a ninety-minute show about a canny West Virginia lawyer called *Hawkins,* a riff on his character in *Anatomy of a Murder. Hawkins* turned out to be the unsuccessful predecessor of the successful *Matlock* — a lawyer people take for granted until he clobbers them in court. It was shot at MGM, which couldn't help but bring the old days rushing back. Perhaps that was why Jim kept insisting that Maggie Sullavan would have been great in an episode. Given the vagaries of show business, he may well have been right. *Hawkins* ran for a measly eight episodes. Fonda's and Stewart's TV series were threadbare vehicles for actors who were too big for the formats — or for television. Was there no one to write a good part for these men?

There were only two (marginal) bright spots for Fonda in this period: an adaptation of Ken Kesey's novel *Sometimes a Great Notion,* playing a tough father to Paul Newman's son. Newman directed and was amused by Fonda's no-sweat attack: "What struck me was how easy he made it seem. He had his character at his fingertips, came in prepared, added and subtracted a little bit — and tried to quit early. . . . He projected the truth in everything he did."

Shortly after that, Stewart received a script from James Lee Barrett, who had written *Bandolero!* for him. It was called *The Cheyenne Social Club,* and Barrett thought it would make a good vehicle for Hank and Jim. Stewart liked the script and he liked the idea of once again working with Fonda even more. But they were both pros and weren't about to cede a lot of screen time to the other. "Fonda called me up and said, 'I'm not going to do this script. You do all the talking. All I do is follow you around.' So I called [Barrett]. 'Fonda says he doesn't talk very much.' Jim said, 'Give me two days and I'll have it corrected.'

"In two days he sent me down the script. I didn't look, I just sent it along to Hank. Hank called up and said, 'Well, that's more like it. Fine. When do we start?' "

Fonda's suggestion had led Barrett to create a running gag involving Fonda talking incessantly, with Stewart forced to listen in silent fury. For anyone who knew Fonda's tendency toward dour silence, the reversal on his actual character was hilarious. "It was rambling," remembered Stewart, "just rambling. Which made the character, [and] gave me wonderful things to play off. But it was Fonda that recognized it."

All this fine-tuning became irrelevant on June 8, 1969, when Jim's stepson Ronald was killed in action with the Marines in Vietnam. When she learned that her son was dead, Gloria collapsed.

Stewart was not a man given to anger, but Ron's death led to one of the few explosions of his life. On the day of Ron's funeral service, the church organist didn't show up and the service was conducted without music. The organist came by the house to apologize, but made the mistake of saying, "Who has a funeral at 11 in the morning?"

Stewart set his jaw and his lips disappeared. "He picked her up and he *removed* her from the house," said Michael McLean. Gloria adamantly refused to attend church for the rest of her life, but Stewart maintained his Sunday attendance. "He was sorry that faith didn't become important to any of us like it was for him," says his daughter Kelly. "I think he felt it was a failure on his part that we didn't become religious."

After Ron was buried, Jim fell into a deep depression. *The Cheyenne Social Club* was a few weeks away from beginning production, and Stewart considered quitting, but that might have scrubbed the project, as there were no other actors of equivalent stature available to replace him on such short notice. Thinking that work might help, he decided to go ahead with the movie.

When Stewart got to the location outside Santa Fe, he and Fonda took long walks, trying to hold on to a sense of normalcy, even though everything had changed. Costar Shirley Jones said that there were tears. Jim would be up all night, and appear in the morning haggard and exhausted. The inexplicable choice as director was Gene Kelly, who tried to work around Stewart as much as possible; once or twice he canceled shooting for the day.

On those days when Stewart could work, the emotional disparity between him and his friend was immediately apparent. "Jim was a natural and always ready to help his fellow actors," remembered Shirley Jones. "Working with Henry Fonda, however, wasn't as much of a picnic. He was so remote, so cold, so unlike Jimmy, that it was hard for me to believe that they were best friends."

Fonda made it clear that he didn't want to communicate with anyone else on the movie other than Jimmy or — maybe — Gene Kelly. Whenever Jones met him in makeup, Fonda would be sitting ramrod straight. She would say, "Hi, Hank, how are you?" He would just look away. "I never got to know who he was as a human being, which was probably his intention, and just the way he liked it."

People always imagine that actors are just like they are on the screen. Some are. Some aren't but can fake it, and some aren't and can't fake it. Fonda couldn't fake it. "I don't really like myself," he would say. "Never have. People mix me up with the characters I play. I'm not a great guy like Doug Roberts. I'd like to be but I'm not."

Conversely, said Jones, Stewart was "great to work with. He wasn't acting; he was talking to you. I forgot my lines during a bedroom scene, and Jimmy said, 'W-w-waal, just say whatever comes into your head and I'll work with it.' "

Stewart's and Fonda's working processes were an extension of their friendship, with an assured comic rhythm. Stewart described it as "natural . . . it's a fishing around for a color and humor to inject into the character, no matter whether it's a tiny little scene, no matter whether it's one line or two lines."

The Cheyenne Social Club is an amiable comic western about two cowpokes, one of whom inherits a whorehouse. The inheritor (Stewart) is morally outraged, while his friend (Fonda) endeavors to sample the wares as extensively as possible. Gene Kelly seems to be channeling Burt Kennedy's shambling westerns. Shirley Jones said that Kelly was "maybe a little intimidated. If they [Hank and Jim] wanted to do something, he let them do it."

Things were bad for Stewart, and they were about to get worse. The location was south of Santa Fe, near a town called Ceril-

475

los. Once again Stewart had asked for Pie for his horse. But Pie was over twenty years old, and the location was seven thousand feet above sea level. The people transporting Pie to New Mexico had to stop along the way and get the horse medical attention. "He couldn't work up there," said Stewart. "The altitude was too much for him and I used a double horse."

Hank never liked horses, mostly because he didn't trust them. What if they spooked? What if they stepped into a gopher hole and got you both killed? "I hate horses," he once groused. "The only way you'll get me on the treacherous beasts is to pay me." He didn't quite get Jim's relationship with Pie, but the two men had long since learned to tolerate each other's irrational enthusiasms.

On Jim's good and bad days alike, Fonda slipped into overdrive to buck up his friend. He would pull up a chair and start reminiscing about the Martin bomber they had built in New York, the misadventures at the Madison Square Hotel, the kites they flew after the war. Sometimes Jim would respond with his versions of the same events; other times he would just sit and listen to Hank.

"Jim tried hard not to spread his grief through the company," said Fonda. "He and I avoided discussing [Vietnam] before the

476

tragedy. Now, I did everything I could to take his mind off it."

Every day after lunch, Stewart would get a carrot or a piece of watermelon from the craft services table and walk a couple of blocks to Pie's corral. The horse was laboring but stable and always glad to see his friend. As Fonda was staying faithful to his friend, so Stewart was returning the favor to Pie.

Watching this daily ritual, Hank finally realized what Pie meant to Jim. "His boy was gone and I couldn't do anything about that, but now seeing the expression on Jim's face when he reached for something to take to his horse . . ." Fonda had an idea.

He did what only he could have done. On mornings or afternoons when he wasn't working, Hank would go out to the corral and work on detailed sketches of Pie — his head, his body, his legs. Then came sketches of the barn, a carriage, a gate. When they returned to California, Hank set to work, painting a watercolor portrait of Jim's favorite horse. After a week he brought Pie's picture over to Jim, beautifully framed. "I hope you like it," said Hank tentatively.

The portrait may be Fonda's finest moment as an artist. The horse is captured standing sideways but with his head turned, looking alertly at the viewer. His left rear hoof is endearingly crossed in front of his right, suggesting his amusing character, and Fonda captures that appraising look that particularly intelligent animals can have.

The picture became the most valuable thing Hank ever gave Jim, perhaps the most valuable thing he ever gave anybody — a pure expression of love. Jim kept it framed, with a light over it, as long as he lived. "Pie," he would say, gazing at it. "I'll never forget Pie. And Fonda."

When Pie died, Stewart tried to put into words the mutual devotion he and the horse had for each other. "I really missed him. I called Stevie [Myers], who had told me that he died. I told Stevie, 'Now don't send him down to the city and have them chop him up and make dog food out of him.' " Jim sent a crew out and had Pie buried on some land he owned in Saugus. A marker is set over the grave:

PIE
1947–1974.

As with his own experience in war, Stewart reserved his deepest emotions for himself. In his only extensive remarks about Ron McLean, he said that

You learn not to look at something like this as a tragedy. Here was a 25 year old man who was serving his country. He was a good boy. He went to college. He wasn't a good student, but still he graduated because we wanted him to — not because we pushed him, mind you, but because he had faith in our judgment.

And when the war came along and he got drafted, he could have gone into any branch of the service or had any job he wanted. But instead he chose the infantry. And when he got on the field of battle with the enemy, he conducted himself in a gallant way. Now what is the tragedy in that?

I'm proud of my boy. I'm proud of him. I don't think Ronald died in vain. I believe in the cause that he died for. The war has been a trial and a tremendously difficult thing for the nation. But if there is a tragedy about it, it is the national tragedy that there has been so much sacrifice without a unified nation behind the cause. . . . Everybody says that the war wasn't even declared. Well, I don't think wars will be declared anymore.

He was a good Marine. I think of him all the time.

After *The Cheyenne Social Club* finished

production, Stewart returned to a house grown quiet. Before Ron's death, Jim had sponsored Peter Fonda and Bill Hayward for membership in the Motion Picture Academy. When they were made members, they went over to Jim's house to thank him and found him in bed, drunk. Hank had never indicated to his son that Jim had a drinking problem, so Peter dismissed the event as a temporary response to devastating loss.

Work being a viable cure for depression, Stewart looked around and found something familiar, something comfortable. He retreated to Elwood P. Dowd and a Broadway revival of *Harvey* opposite Helen Hayes. He was nervous — he hadn't been on stage in more than twenty years. "It's a pretty hard thing to get back into," he said. "Especially the voice projection."

The Stewarts stayed at the Waldorf Towers during the show, and a color photo of Ron and his mother that Jim had taken was prominently displayed on the mantel. It had been only eight months since Ron's death, and it was still weighing heavily on him. He gave an interview to *The New York Times* in which he spent most of the time fretting over the public's attitude toward the military. "These are patriotic kids, patriotic

Americans!" he said as he paged through a photo album filled with Polaroids he had taken of soldiers.

All you have to do is go to Vietnam to see that the kids are still patriotic today. . . .

The whole attitude toward the military concerns me very much. There are forces today — and where they come from I don't know, probably both from within and without — that are trying to soil the image of the military. This is a very dangerous thing. I spent 27 years in the military and it meant a great deal to me in life. I know the principles and standards I learned made me a better civilian. It's disturbing to see these forces try to discredit the military and send it back into isolation like it was after World War I.

The subject of the Fondas came up, probably because of Jane's antiwar activities. Whatever Jim thought privately, he would never criticize his goddaughter, because that might have wounded Hank. "Our views have never interfered with our friendship — *ever.* We just don't talk about certain things. I can't remember ever having an argument with him."

The revival of *Harvey* got excellent reviews

481

and was a sellout for its limited six-week run. "You've got to convince the audience that this big rabbit is your friend, and that the whole idea is wonderful," he said. "Elwood can't be a screwball or an imbecile. You have to convince the audience that, if they had [giant] rabbits of their own, it would be kind of nice!"

Josh Logan wrote Jim an unabashed fan letter: "I have seldom seen a better piece of acting in all my life. And also, I do see the huge improvement you have made in your interpretation of the part from your salad days. In fact, you are so real, so touching, so believable, so funny, so gracious and so gentle that I have a feeling that ninety per cent of the audience takes you for granted and figures they have been hypnotized — and therefore give you no credit for the fabulous technique I know you are using to put across this part. The thing about it is that [opposed to Helen Hayes] it doesn't show! Nobody can see the wheels turn."

At about the same time as Jim was doing *Harvey*, *The Cheyenne Social Club* was released, another one of the good-humored, interminable comedy westerns that were being manufactured at a time when the genre had fallen into the hands of second- and third-stringers. Mainly, it offers a chance to enjoy Hank and Jim's obvious rapport. As with *On Our Merry Way,* there is a tendency toward the dry, and there are some amusing lines about Stewart's character's compulsive Republicanism that must have tickled them both.

The film seems to have eked out a small profit, but both men knew that it was not the kind of movie that was likely to set the world on fire. They resumed their habit of worrying about the next job. Or, rather, Hank did; Jim was becoming less interested in the next job than in what might take the place of the next job.

"Jimmy is lazier," said Nedda Logan. "He hasn't the ambition that Hank has. I think Hank wants to die with his boots on. . . . He's a workaholic like Josh is."

FOURTEEN

In 1971 Leland Hayward died of gastric hemorrhages and another stroke. As he lay in the hospital for the final few days of his life, he consistently addressed his wife, Pamela, as "Maggie." Bill Hayward was sitting with his father and to pass the time he asked who were the most beautiful women Leland had ever seen. "Garbo," Leland said, "and Kate Hepburn. Slim. Maggie."

When he got word that Leland was dying, Stewart hurriedly flew to New York to see him before it was too late. "I was there, but I left the room while they talked," said Brooke Hayward. "Afterward, I asked Jimmy what they talked about. And Jimmy looked into the far distance and said, 'We talked . . . we talked about *flying.*'"

For the funeral, Pamela Churchill Hayward rearranged her husband's octagonal workroom into a private chapel. Leland's coffin was almost invisible beneath a thick blanket of bright carnations. Baskets of flowers were arranged around the floor. Pamela covered the walls with blow-ups of Hayward's primary hobby — photographs of flowers in full bloom. Above the coffin hung a huge enlargement of one of Leland's photographs of stars in the night sky. In the center of the picture was a brilliant North Star, while around it were concentric circles of light formed by the stars as they had revolved during the long exposure.

"The picture looked like a photograph of infinity," remembered Joshua Logan. "I thought for a moment that Leland had planned it that way."

Before his death in 1973, John Ford had a flurry of long overdue public attention — a CBS documentary, Peter Bogdanovich's *Directed by John Ford,* and the first American Film Institute Life Achievement Award. Stewart appeared at all of these occasions, and, surprisingly, Fonda did too. Ford and Fonda hadn't seen each other since Ford's last day on *Mister Roberts,* although Ford never slagged Fonda on those private occasions when his name came up.

For the CBS special, entitled *The American West of John Ford,* the show's director staged an on-camera reunion. Fonda was narrating a segment while standing outside the Century Plaza Hotel in Century City, overlooking what had once been the back lot of 20th Century-Fox. Ford drove up, and Fonda embraced him. Ford said all the right things, but he hadn't returned the embrace and was slightly formal toward a man who had been an intimate friend for nearly twenty years before their rupture. As Ford's grandson Dan observed, "Elephants never forget. Neither did Ford."

Fonda was able to hold two opposing thoughts in his head at the same time. On the one hand, Ford was an alcoholic with a mean streak. On the other, he was a great artist. "How can you say anybody's better than Ford?" Fonda would say. "He was a perverse Irish son of a bitch. But he was also a genius . . . and he knew where to put the camera."

Stewart's feelings about Ford were far less conflicted. When Ford died in August of 1973, Stewart attended the funeral, then fell into another depression. Finally he said, "What am I supposed to do? All my friends are dying and I haven't really made any new ones in thirty years."

Technically, it wasn't true, but spiritually it was. Dave Chasen had died a year after Hayward, and Billy Grady, the best man at

Jim's wedding, died the same year as Ford. In 1974, it was Jack Benny, his neighbor on Roxbury. These were people who couldn't be replaced.

Among the living, Josh Logan had had huge successes in the 1940s and 1950s, but the 1960s and 1970s were hard for him and in more ways than one. His career went into a spiral as his plays (*Miss Moffat*) and films (*Ensign Pulver, Camelot, Paint Your Wagon*) all failed.

And then Johnny Swope became ill with prostate cancer. A life that had once been full of people who could be called on whenever Stewart felt like seeing them now had glaring vacancies that left him increasingly isolated.

Work remained problematic. In 1972, Stewart and Fonda agreed to star in a Peter Bogdanovich film called *Streets of Laredo* as two-thirds of the names over the title. The third was John Wayne, who cruised by the project for a year or so but ultimately backed away, leaving it high and dry — without Wayne, Stewart and Fonda were insufficient ballast for an expensive western. Undeterred, co-screenwriter Larry McMurtry would rewrite the project and turn it into his novel *Lonesome Dove*.

Other actors knew how special these two

men were and wondered about the blindness of American producers. Ralph Richardson and John Gielgud were doing David Storey's lean play *Home,* about men and their pride. Richardson thought the play would work just fine with a tiny rewrite for American actors. "Why not Henry Fonda and Jimmy Stewart?" he suggested.

In 1976, Stewart gave an uncharacteristically sour interview that was a litany of misery. The subject of Vietnam came up and he went on a tirade about draft evaders. "I hate them! I absolutely hate them! Right or wrong, their country was at war and their country asked them to serve and they refused and ran away. Cowards, that's what they were. . . .

"The biggest mistake was that our country was involved in a war we were not truly committed to win. If you fight, you fight to win, or else you don't fight."

He talked about Ron and about a floating anxiety that had begun to plague him. "I don't know why but I seem to worry about everything now. For example, next month I have to go to Dayton, Ohio, to enshrine John Glenn in the Aviation Hall of Fame, and I worry: will I do an adequate job?"

He confessed to the same feelings of inadequacy regarding acting with John

Wayne in *The Shootist.* "I worry before I do a scene in a movie. . . . Would I be convincing? And I worry so much when I'm in a play that I can't even eat before I go on. And by the time the play is finished, it's too late to eat, so we just get some peanut butter and jelly sandwiches. . . . I don't remember worrying so much when I was young."

Which brought him to what was really bothering him: Age. "I'm 68 years old and I feel every goddamn day of it. I don't feel young. I feel old. And I'm resigned to it. I'm not fighting it. People get old and that's all there is to it. I've had an unbelievably wonderful life and I don't want to spoil it now by becoming bitter because life can't go on as it has for these last 68 years. So I face the fact: I'm conscious of my getting old and I'm resigned to it and I suspect I probably am not going to live very long."

When he was asked about his biggest failure, he said that he wished he had been more of a reader. Most of the books in the house belonged to Gloria. "She reads everything. I read nothing . . . I don't really consider myself a learned man."

On the larger issues, he believed his biggest failure was his inability to get his wife and children to go to church. "I'm not kidding. This has been very painful to me. I feel this has been one of my most important responsibilities and I feel I've failed in this on all counts."

Fonda was undoubtedly prey to some of the same doubts, and the reality that there was less time to address perceived failures. Unlike Stewart, he was still working, still earning respect. But while Fonda worked, Stewart began to vanish into a premature old age that mystified Fonda. "He's acting like he's 75 years old," he told his son. "I get the feeling time has run out on me," Stewart said. He listed a roster of films that he'd seen which had left him feeling out of touch with the world. "Saw *The Graduate*. Loved it. Saw *Blow-Up*. Yes — I — Ahhh — a well-made thing. Saw *Easy Rider*. Didn't like it much. Not well-made."

The house on Roxbury had grown very quiet since Ron's death. "We found ourselves sitting around Beverly Hills having conversations with our . . . dogs," Stewart grumbled. "Hollywood is a little quiet and depressing right now. It's another one of our disaster times."

In the 1970s, Stewart made only four movies, and only one of them was at all worthy of him: as the doctor who tells John Wayne he's dying in *The Shootist*. As it happens, Stewart looks much more frail than his patient, and his hearing had deteriorated to such an extent that he had trouble picking up his cues. He rallied and summoned the old power and command, and Wayne matched him moment for moment. For a few minutes, it's a twilight of the gods.

For Fonda, the 1970s were a time of a wary rapprochement with his daughter. In 1972, he lent Jane $40,000 to buy a house in Studio City. She insisted on signing a note, and repaid the loan within a year. Hank also attended her 1973 wedding to Tom Hayden, whom Hank rather liked, partly because Hayden was a fisherman like him, partly because he admired Hayden's ability to deliver an impressive speech without notes. Perhaps it was the loss of so many close friends that nudged Fonda to strengthen his ties with his daughter, so long as it didn't involve displays of emotion. In line with that, he would become what Jane called "a good grandfather and an even better uncle to my niece."

But Fonda's son thought his father was slightly awkward with Peter's children; the difference, he thought, was attributable to the fact that Jane would usually bring her children over to her father's house, where he was more relaxed than he was at his children's homes.

The calendar said that Hank was getting old, but he hadn't slowed up much, if at all. He referred to himself as an agnostic, told anybody who asked that his favorite novel was John O'Hara's *Appointment in Samarra* — he had always wanted to star in a movie version, but nobody could ever devise a good script. His favorite movie of all time was *La Dolce Vita.* He continued to have the classic actor's anxiety dream about going onstage without knowing the play, let alone the lines, but he also had dreams specific to him. In particular, there was a recurring Walter Mitty–ish dream in which he danced like Ray Bolger. "It's my favorite dream," he would say.

In so many ways, his character as a man was consonant with his values as an actor. "I won't have a gun in the house. I don't believe in guns. I don't shoot guns. I don't hunt. I'm against hunting. I'm against killing." He made movies for the money, but the theater remained his passion: "Maybe one ejaculation is better than another, but they're all pretty great. And every night in the theater for me is like that."

As always, Hank and Jim had agreed to disagree about the comparative value of movies. "Unlike Stewart . . . who felt that the stable system of the studios was healthy, I did not. I didn't agree with him then and I don't agree with him today. . . . Stewart is a different man. He doesn't feel the same way I do. He is a movie actor. He from the beginning felt that movies were the ultimate."

When Fonda told his son about a patch of insomnia he was going through, Peter suggested he try marijuana. Fonda hadn't used it since that long-ago day when smoking dope had led to him ask Margaret Sullavan to take a midnight swim. Nevertheless, he once again took the plunge. The response was a kaleidoscope of colors that had the same effect as the insomnia. "I was perfectly relaxed and enjoying it, but I wasn't sleeping."

People observed Hank's perceptible mellowing and ascribed it entirely to Shirlee's influence. "His whole life opened like a rose coming out from a little tiny tight bud," Nedda Logan said. "She gave him confidence and . . . he's now loquacious. And the whole personality came and he's absolutely adorable. And I feel like saying, 'Where were you all those years?' "

Fonda agreed: "I am better with Shirlee than I have ever been before."

■ ■ ■ ■

In 1972, Stewart transferred his performance in *Harvey* to television opposite Helen Hayes as his sister, and three years after that, he would do the play again, this time in London. The English critics didn't think much of the play but applauded the star, as did audiences. On opening night, Stewart got six curtain calls. Providentially, Fonda was also in London, so the two had a reunion. Jim had brought his accordion to Europe, and serenaded his pal in Hyde Park.

By this time, the two men had spoken often enough of their friendship that the public was clued in. *The New York Times* ran a piece that focused more on their disparities than their bonds. Fonda was characterized as a liberal firebrand, Stewart as the model American who went out of his way to be polite. Fonda was amused by equivalent simplicities ascribed to two very complex men, but Stewart was actively bothered. Jim was not without male vanity and was annoyed by his apple-pie image, even as he tended to emphasize it. Anyone who knew him was aware of the fact that he had cut a swath through Hollywood that Errol Flynn might have envied — not that he got any credit for it.

"It makes me sound pretty dull, doesn't it?" he asked Fonda after reading the *Times* story. Fonda started to reply with a glint in his eye, when Stewart short-circuited the response. "Don't say it."

If Stewart was perceived as something of a mossback, he had nobody to blame but himself: "There are too many pictures based on violence and sex," he complained, and he was just getting warmed up. "I think there's going to be censorship if they don't improve. One of the last pictures I saw was *Easy Rider.* I admired Jack Nicholson in it, but didn't care for the movie itself. It was an indictment of a part of this country and that didn't sit very well with me.

"I don't think there's any question that the Communists are behind a great deal of unrest in the U.S. In addition, I feel they are still a potential danger in show business."

The only statement Fonda would have agreed with was Stewart's take on acting: "I've always felt that the way to learn to act is to act. You can read about acting, and you can think about it. You can go to a witch doctor, or try to discover a secret process. You can go into a corner and talk to yourself for four hours. But in the long run, you must act."

The revivals of *Harvey* provided Stewart with a psychological charge that the movies hadn't given him in a long time. Either he or Josh Logan came up with the idea of reviving Paul Osborn's play *On Borrowed Time,* which had been Logan's first Broadway hit back in 1938. Logan's own career was in the doldrums and he undoubtedly saw it as a surefire commercial and critical success.

It was a solid idea — the story of a crafty old grandfather who literally chases death up a tree had worked as both a play and movie. Logan shipped Stewart a copy of the script accompanied by a dose of salesmanship (". . . might be one of the crowning glories of your life . . .").

Nothing happened immediately, but Logan kept after him, especially after a revival of Osborn's *Morning's at Seven* became a Broadway hit in 1980. He broached the idea to producers, who were immediately enthusiastic. "I love this play like you love *Harvey,*" he wrote Stewart. "To me, both plays have a universal appeal — an old man who defies death for the love of his little grandson, and the other a man who has found an everlasting way of never being lonesome."

In a later letter, Logan made some casting

suggestions for the part of Mr. Brink, i.e., Death, whom he believed should be played as a traveling salesman, full of charm. His number one choice was Burt Reynolds, followed by Charlton Heston ("whom I do not admire as an actor in romantic roles but is a perfect square"). Other options were Donald Sutherland, Jon Voight, Kris Kristofferson ("not a good actor, but a good type"), Harrison Ford, George Grizzard, Robert Preston, Richard Basehart, or James Garner.

Flush with the creative mood, Logan then made the suggestion that the role could even be played by a black actor: Ossie Davis, Lou Gossett, or Geoffrey Holder. Or a European: Max von Sydow, Marcello Mastroianni, Louis Jourdan.

Robert Preston would have been ideal — Death as a malevolent Harold Hill! — and Logan outlined a plan where they could do the play in three- or four-month spurts so as not to tire Stewart out, make millions of dollars, then perhaps do a TV production.

But it was not to be, either because Stewart couldn't summon the energy or Gloria didn't think it was a good idea. From the tone of Logan's correspondence, where he's always paying rather strenuous compliments to Gloria, he was obviously cognizant of her importance in deciding what Jim would or would not do. (*On Borrowed Time* would be revived by director-star George C. Scott and Teresa Wright in 1991. Scott made the daring choice of casting Nathan Lane as Death, and stayed mostly sober throughout the successful run.)

Logan was disgruntled by Stewart's lack of interest, especially when compared to Fonda's continuing appetite for work. "[Hank] is probably my closest friend. I would count on him more than almost anyone else in the world. Maybe Stewart, but I think Fonda has more strength than Stewart. . . . Stewart's gotten a little passive."

In 1980, Stewart was awarded the American Film Institute's Life Achievement Award. "I guess you could say that up to tonight they have honored brilliance, daring, and abundance of talent," he said, "and that brings us down to where we are. Now the American Film Institute in all of its wisdom has added a new name and a new category: James Stewart, a remarkably fortunate fellow."

The MC for the evening was, of course, Fonda, who reminisced about their days in New York and undoubtedly irritated Stewart by reiterating his version of Stewart's professional luck. "I'd worn out my shoe leather for five years, but Stewart never went out and looked for a job, parts just kept happening for him. I'd go back to his dressing room and look at him and wonder when and where and how in the hell did he get to be so good."

In accepting the award, Stewart said, "This has been a wonderful evening that is about to go downhill as I fumble for the right words. I know it's late, and I promised myself I'd talk fast. The problem is, I don't know how to talk fast."

While Stewart had *Harvey,* the one-man show *Clarence Darrow* provided Fonda with his last stage triumph. A one-man show is an intimidating gauntlet for any actor, let alone a sixty-nine-year-old one, but Hank rose to the challenge. Both in New York and on tour he was strong, word-perfect, with an astounding focus and an eye-line that never wavered — when he addressed someone in the vacant witness stand, you could see the man sitting there.

It was an exhausting show to do, and after a few weeks of performances in New York, Fonda collapsed in his dressing room and was taken to Lenox Hill Hospital, where doctors diagnosed "total exhaustion." A week later, a pacemaker was implanted — the beginning of the primary health problem of his later years.

When the show came to Los Angeles, Hank's peers were awed. "Hank my Love," wrote Barbara Stanwyck.

> Friday evening I had my yearly lesson in acting — from you! It was a lovely and rewarding lesson — as always. I am, as always, so proud of you. Years ago you promised me a photograph and now, please, may I have it? . . .
>
> Love, Barbara

Clarence Darrow reminded everyone of Fonda's drive, his devotion to his craft, and his professional honesty. "You don't stumble into this," said Stewart. "You don't just have a natural aptitude for this. This takes knowledge, concentration, absolute determination and the ability to see one's self in the mirror and to hear in one's self saying the line and knowing that it's correct and the right way to do [it]. . . . He not only makes a convincing cowboy, but it's a *complete* cowboy. . . . He plays in a western and can go from that to Clarence Darrow and never miss a step. When you take sort of an overall of the acting profession, this is quite a thing.

"[His] number one pleasure is going to be tonight when he faces that audience down in the theater. He looks forward to it every day."

And his pleasure of fifty years ago?

"I would say uncertain forms of the same thing. Because as I said, when I knew him fifty years ago this is what he was going to do. And while the rest of us were sort of fishing around and saying 'This is fun. . . .' I didn't know what I was going to do. He knew *exactly* what he was going to do."

While Fonda was being Fonda, Stewart was playing the exhausted General Stern-wood in Michael Winner's coarse remake of *The Big Sleep,* in *Airport '77,* and then in *The Magic of Lassie,* a belated, unsuccessful attempt to recapture the simplicity of the MGM dog stories of thirty-five years earlier. After more than forty years of work, Stewart's creeping loss of energy had become all too obvious.

When the Vietnam Memorial in Washington, D.C., was completed, Stewart and his daughter Judy felt duty-bound to visit. As he approached the wall, Judy saw her father's shoulders began to bow. By the time he got to the slab where Ron's name was inscribed, he was hunched over from pain. "I began to cry like I've never cried since," Judy remembered. Jim reached out and ran his fingers over his son's name.

In 1978, Peter Fonda was preparing to direct *Wanda Nevada,* a picaresque story about Peter's character winning Brooke Shields in a poker game, after which they go prospecting around the Grand Canyon. Peter offered his father the part of a grizzled old prospector. It was only a one-day job, but Hank wasn't about to lower his standards for anybody. He hated the beard the makeup man devised for him; "he thought it looked phony," remembered his son. The beard was supposed to be tobacco-stained, so Peter gave him some licorice to take the place of tobacco. Hank shook his head and pulled out a pack of Red Man he had brought along. The script said chewing tobacco, so by God he would use chewing tobacco. "I've always wished Uncle Jimmy could have seen it," said Peter. "He would have laughed."

After Hank got back home from the shoot, he waited a week or two, then wrote Peter a letter: "I felt so badly about the phony make-up, I wanted you to know that I fully understand if you [can't] use the scene." He blamed himself, saying he should have had his own makeup man construct the beard weeks before the shoot. And then he wrote this: "I want you to know how proud I am of you — your whole company so seriously worships and adores you. It's a beautiful thing to see, and I haven't seen it so often in 43 years that it doesn't impress me.

"And you're a very good director. I'd admire to be in your stock company, Sir. Don't you give up on me."

Peter treasured the letter, could recite it from memory almost forty years later, and came to tears every time. It was his father's open appreciation of his boy's talent, the father's willingness to be of service to the son, his acknowledgment of Peter's accomplishments. "This is the most amazing boy," Fonda said of Peter.

That same year, Fonda visited the house where he was born, which had been moved to the Stuhr Museum of the Prairie Pioneer, just outside Omaha. He walked through each of the rooms, looking carefully at the furniture, the walls, the floors. Details. When he got to the room in which he had been born, he looked at the brass bed for several minutes. Then he said, "That's enough," and walked out the door.

As with Stewart, as with Josh Logan, Hank's bond with the other University Play-

503

ers never lessened. Hank and Bart Quigley, a young actor in the group, always kept in touch, even after Quigley gave up show business and became a successful orthopedic surgeon in Boston with a specialty in athletes: the Boston Red Sox, various football players, as well as ballet dancers. If Hank was in Boston with a show, they'd get together, and Bart would always come down to New York for a drink with his friend.

Life has a way of closing circles, and that became apparent when Hank starred in *First Monday in October* opposite Jane Alexander — Bart's daughter. The play was written by Jerome Lawrence and Robert E. Lee, who had previously written *Auntie Mame* and *Inherit the Wind,* among others, but this time their script — about an elderly liberal justice on the Supreme Court who jousts with a younger conservative female justice — was overly schematic. No matter. It was Henry Fonda and Jane Alexander, and the director was Edwin Sherin, Alexander's husband, who had previously directed *The Great White Hope.*

"At first, I was intimidated by him," remembered Alexander. "He was so taciturn. Once I had to drive him somewhere and he never said a word the entire time we were together. I began to shake from nerves.

And yet Ed, my husband, had no problems with him at all. He loved direction, loved whatever Ed said. The word for Hank was *aura.* It extended out about seven feet in all directions."

As with Stewart, Fonda was having trouble with his hearing, which made it hard for him to pick up cues. Sherin had to speak to him about it. Fonda left the theater and came back two hours later outfitted with a hearing aid.

Despite his problems with age, Alexander said, "His instincts were always spot-on. I remember when I spoke at Hank's Kennedy Center honors, I said that 'He does not act. He *is.* There is no sense of him putting on an act.' That was the way he felt to the audience and the way he felt to another actor onstage."

Sherin observed what he called Fonda's "compact with the audience." He was, realized Sherin, scrupulous. "He had a particular genius. He would learn as much as he could about the circumstances of the character, and then he would internalize the character within himself. It was fascinating to watch.

"He was so far ahead of the crowd at the Actors Studio. He was always in search of the deepest truth, and to do that he needed environment, he needed knowledge. It was peculiar — he didn't like Method actors, but he was a consummate Method actor."

Fonda and Sherin never butted heads because "my methodology as a director is never concerned with an actor agreeing or disagreeing with me. That clarifies itself through what works or what doesn't. It's not about theory, it's about does it work or not? *Is it practical?* He adhered to that as well. Not all actors are like that. Burt Lancaster and I disagreed about something once, and he almost threw me out a second floor window, and he could have done it — he was so fucking strong! He went for my throat."

Contrary to what Richard Jordan believed, Sherin said that Fonda never locked in a performance. "He wasn't mechanical. He was smarter than that. If you lock your performance you stop learning about what you're doing. Hank was more adventurous than that."

Fonda never became gabby with Alexander, although he could go on about his bees. "I knew he was fond of me, because he said I reminded him of young Maggie Sullavan. He called me 'My other Jane.' And he gave me one of his paintings, of geraniums. After we did *First Monday* he would travel to see me in other plays.

"I think a lot of it was because I was Bart's kid — the network among the University Players was so very strong all their lives. My father learned to sail on John Swope's boat. I remember the first time I met Jimmy Stewart, he looked down at me and said, 'So you're Bart's daughter . . .' "

Besides their shared love for Alexander's father, Fonda and she connected about Nebraska — Plains reserve and the strength that lay beneath. She had heard stories from other actors, mostly revolving around what a bastard Fonda used to be, but she found him almost mellow. "He was so happy being married to Shirlee. She was the caretaker so that he could focus on the project at hand. She gave him a sense of security he had never had before."

The experience of acting with Fonda was a source of amazement to Alexander even forty years later. When they toured with the show, Fonda made a habit of walking down to the stage apron while the set was being installed and looking over the house. He would note which seats had bad sight lines and point them out to the house manager. "Don't sell those seats," he would order. "I won't go on unless those seats are empty."

"Without question, he was the most professional actor I've ever worked with," said Alexander. "I've never loved an actor on-stage like I loved Hank. He was so *present* — those blue eyes. I never saw him break the fourth wall, he never went up on his lines. If something went wrong during a performance, he'd shuffle some papers and stall for time. He never phoned it in. His passion for the theater was so strong; he had no truck with actors who would complain about eight performances a week or the monotony of long runs.

"It's interesting: as a person, Jimmy Stewart wasn't afraid of emotion, while Hank was, but Hank was highly emotional while he was acting; if he was moved, you'd know it, because you could see his eyes fill with tears."

One night during the Broadway run of the play, Eli Wallach and his wife, Anne Jackson, were in attendance. Fonda's heart troubles had made the papers, so when Fonda's character fainted, Jackson grabbed her husband and asked, "Is this real?"

It wasn't, but Wallach knew that no response would have pleased Fonda more.

As his health problems increased, Hank began the round of awards that signal the approaching end of an artist's life. An

American Film Institute Life Achievement Award, a Lifetime Achievement Award from the Los Angeles Drama Critics, an honorary Oscar from the Academy at the Fifty-third Academy Awards, recognition from the Kennedy Center. It was all pleasant enough, and Hank was especially pleased by the Kennedy Center honors, which concluded with the Naval Academy Chorus serenading him with "Red River Valley" and "Anchors Aweigh." After that, each chorus member said, "Thank you, Mr. Roberts," and saluted Fonda. Fonda saluted right back and began to cry.

The man who had once cherished grudges now began to let things go; he told Shirlee that he forgave Jane and Peter for the things they had said and done that had outraged him. "They were just acting out," he said.

On tour in Chicago with *First Monday in October* in April 1979, Fonda was suddenly beset with pain in his left hip, severe enough that he had trouble walking. After biopsies and X-rays, it was determined that prostate cancer had metastasized to the hip. The tour was cut short and he returned to California for treatment.

So there it was, at long last — not just a shot across the bow, but an entire cannonade. Prostate cancer is usually slow-growing, but the fact that it had spread was ominous.

And then there was Johnny Swope. He had been a vigorous, athletic man all his life, especially when it came to tennis, but he had been in and out with prostate cancer for a couple of years. In the first week of May 1979, Hank called Norman Lloyd. Johnny was home from the hospital and receiving visitors, Hank said. The implication was clear — it was time to say goodbye.

"John was in his living room, sitting on a sort of half-sofa," remembered Lloyd. "Audrey Hepburn and Henry Fonda were there. Fonda was sitting on the floor, looking up at John. And he was studying John *so* intently, really taking him in, as if he was trying to absorb everything he could of his old friend before he went away. It was a silent moment, nothing overt happened, there were no tearful speeches. But the intensity with which Fonda looked at John was very moving. If you had known nothing of their history, you could have understood how much Fonda loved him simply by how he was looking at him."

John Swope was seventy years old when he died on May 11, 1979. Hank and Jim were on the boat when Johnny's ashes were poured into the ocean three miles off the

California coast. In that moment, Mark Swope felt a sense of renewal, but Hank and Jim were both somber. For them, there was only loss, but they both wanted to be there. Watching John's ashes settle and disappear was the final act of devotion they could extend to their friend.

It is doubtful that Fonda told his friends of his own diagnosis; a man who had never discussed his wife's suicide and other catastrophes was unlikely to suddenly lunge toward the confessional. Besides that, there were professional considerations — if word got out that he had cancer, getting acting jobs would be difficult, if not impossible.

And nothing mattered more to Henry Fonda than his work.

By this time, Stewart was semiretired, so he had plenty of time to attend to his gardening. As with Fonda's bees and organic gardening, raising vegetables had a basic clarity that appealed to Stewart.

Unfortunately, gardening didn't fill all of Stewart's needs the way Fonda's hobbies did for him. "I used to have a house full of children and animals," he noted glumly. "When I go home today, there's one old dog. An old, old dog. I sit and stare at him, and he sits and stares at me."

Despite his cancer, Fonda attended to his farming duties with such concentration that his small patch of Bel-Air produced nearly as much as a full-time farmer would. The Stewarts grew accustomed to a weekly ring of the doorbell. Jim would open the door, and Fonda would be standing there.

"Jim," he'd say as he handed over some honey.

"Hank," Jim would say as he handed over some vegetables.

The door would close, and each of them went back to his crops. Stewart's kids, observing this impassive ritual that resembled nothing so much as the sheepdogs in Chuck Jones cartoons, grew to believe that it was Jim's and Hank's way of remembering each other's names.

Besides gardening, Stewart continued to fill time with travel. He had tried to talk a friend of his daughters' out of going into show business; so he was thrilled by Kelly's decision to become an anthropologist. "He loved Africa because it was empty and full of animals," she remembered. "And he hated India because it was teeming with people."

"Jimmy got old when he was still fairly young," said Robert Wagner. "He didn't try to fight it or pretend, you know? And he got

512

even more dependent on Gloria. He'd walk into a room and say, 'Wh-wh-wh-where do we sit, Gloria?' And Gloria would lead him over to the table. He might have been seventy when I started noticing this — an old seventy."

FIFTEEN

Hank and Shirlee spent very few nights apart. She traveled with him to locations and would decorate hotel rooms with pillows and paintings so that the hotel rooms resembled home as much as possible. He could still withdraw into long silences, but that didn't bother her because she knew it had nothing to do with any shortcomings on her part. It wasn't personal. "Fonda is a loner," she said, "but he doesn't like to be alone."

Fonda was an attentive husband, regularly leaving loving notes for Shirlee:

> My one and only Love — You have survived Ten years of me — Please strike for Twenty!
>
> Fonda

Fonda didn't just act tough — he *was* tough, as proven by a sprightly note he left for Shirlee one day:

> Darling — You've got your wish — I'm in the hospital — I'm taking a cab because there's nobody home. I'm at Cedars-Sinai where Dr. Fields is going to replace my pacesetter [sic]. Mine isn't working. He's doing it tonight and I may be home tomorrow.
>
> Love, Your Husband

There was a P.S. The cab company had been backed up and couldn't get there for a half hour, so Fonda drove himself to the hospital.

Any residual crustiness could usually be overcome by the presence of a camera. When some documentary filmmakers arrived at the house for an interview, they went over their questions with Fonda before the cameras were turned on.

"I really don't have anything to say about that," he responded about the first question, a motif that was repeated with each succeeding question. "No, I don't have any thoughts about that."

Flop sweat broke out on the filmmakers' foreheads — why had he agreed to the interview if he wasn't going to say anything? But they pushed ahead and began shooting.

Lo and behold, the indifferent old man transformed into an energetic actor-laddie full of anecdotes. The interview went swimmingly.

Once in a while, Fonda would mull over roads not taken, parts he wished he'd played. He would have loved to have played Atticus Finch in *To Kill a Mockingbird* and he never got over his agent rejecting the play of *Who's Afraid of Virginia Woolf?* without passing the script by him first. "I've had a good deal of satisfaction," he would say, "but I wouldn't say I am satisfied with my work because that sounds too smug and I don't think I'm smug."

Stewart never explained why he turned down *To Kill a Mockingbird,*" said Kelly, "but I think he was sorry he did. I believe he viewed it as a mistake. Mom certainly did. She would say, 'Your father would have been so much better in that part [than Gregory Peck].'" Producer William Frye, a friend of Stewart's, believed that the reason Stewart shied away was the overt racial politics of the story. He also turned down parts in other films, such as *Network,* because of the roaring profanity that was required.

In spite of his increasingly fragile physical condition, Fonda continued to look for good plays. In February 1981, he opened in

Stamford, Connecticut, in *Showdown at the Adobe Motel,* again under the direction of Ed Sherin.

"Shirlee was angry with me for even offering it to him," remembered Sherin. "She knew he wasn't up to it physically. She was right and I was wrong. It cost him a lot to do it, but he had a sublime loyalty to his friends. He had to be wheeled off and on the stage, and it wasn't fair to him."

It was the sort of play that needed stellar actors to get by, so Fonda's presence made a difference. The reviews were good ("There's plenty for Mr. Fonda to do and he does it beautifully," wrote Frank Rich in *The New York Times*). He went through each performance stooped over and leaning heavily on a cane, and nobody was sure if it was a function of the character or the actor.

In fact, it was the latter. By the last night of the play, a doctor told Shirlee, "You better get him home, or he's going to die right here onstage." Which, all in all, would have been fine with Fonda.

A month or so later, he was scheduled to attend the opening night of an exhibition of his paintings. He was using a walker, but didn't want to appear with it in public. Shirlee suggested a wheelchair — FDR had appeared that way, she noted. "Well, Henry

517

Fonda won't," he retorted.

Ernest Thompson's play *On Golden Pond* met with immediate success when it was first performed in 1979. It was a showcase for two geriatric actors, and there are always more of those than there are parts for them to play. Josh Logan told Stewart that he was bidding for the screen rights, and wanted Jim to star in the film. But Jim was uncomfortable with the part, mostly because he thought that the character Norman Thayer treated his daughter atrociously.

Logan was outbid by Jane Fonda, and the casting of Hank became a fait accompli. Stewart was philosophical, saying, "This goes to show what can happen when you not only have a bright goddaughter, but a bright goddaughter who's also a producer."

If Jim was going to lose a part, losing it to Hank took some, if not all, of the sting out of it. "I don't think there was ever any sense of competition between my father and Jimmy," Jane would say. "It had to be imposed by outsiders even for the appearance. . . . Frankly, given the personalities involved, I don't think they'd even have admitted it to themselves if there was any kind of jealousy between them."

Everyone's first choice for the part of

Norman's wife was Kate Hepburn; if she had turned it down, the part would have been offered to Barbara Stanwyck. The production of the film would be uneasy because of the tension between father and daughter — one shy of expressing emotion unless he was acting, the other a Vesuvius of emotion.

Even preproduction had its family issues. Jane initially offered the directing job to Fred Zinnemann, who had done a fine job on *Julia,* which was a success for Jane. Peter Fonda knew Zinnemann and asked the director to let him know if he was going to turn the picture down. Ultimately, Zinnemann passed, at which point Peter sent a registered letter to his sister asking to be considered for the job. He had, after all, directed *The Hired Hand,* an excellent film, and knew just a little bit about buried family psychodynamics.

He never received a reply. The director's job went to Mark Rydell.

The production was emotionally intense from the moment shooting began. During a scene in which Jane observed Fonda and Hepburn playing Parcheesi, she asked the cameraman to throw more light on her father's face so she could see his eyes.

Just before it was time to shoot, she asked

him, "Is it OK, Dad? Can you see my eyes?"

"I don't need to see your eyes," he said. "I'm not that kind of actor."

Jane was devastated, not merely by his refusal to need any other actor, even if it was his daughter, but by his put-down of the woman who had bought the property for the express purpose of giving him the star part.

Later, during the climactic confrontation scene on the dock, Rydell did the wide-angle master, then shot Hank's close-up. While the camera was being moved for Jane's close-up, she realized she had gone dry and couldn't get to the same place emotionally that she had gotten for the previous angles.

With the finely turned antennae actors have for crisis, Hepburn sensed something was wrong, and came up to Jane.

"How are you?"

"I'm in trouble. I've gone dry. Please don't tell Dad."

Jane didn't know what to do. Stalling for time, she told Mark Rydell that she would turn her back to the camera and turn to face it only when she was ready to start the scene. As she stood there, trying to summon her emotions, she saw Hepburn, crouching in the bushes, looking at her intently and raising clenched fists, as if to say, "Do it! You can do it!"

"With her energy," remembered Jane Fonda, "she literally *gave* me the scene, gave it to me with her fists, her eyes, and her generosity, and I will never ever forget it." The odd thing was that Jane didn't think Hepburn particularly liked her; Fonda had a husband, children, dogs, and Hepburn didn't believe actresses should have any of those things — they got in the way of the work.

That night, the two Fondas were having dinner and Jane told her father what had happened on the set that day. She asked him if he'd ever dried up.

"Nope."

"Never? Not once in your whole career?"

"Nope."

Both Hepburn and Jane were awed by Hank's control. "He wouldn't do anything that was unrehearsed," said Jane. "He was a very careful actor; he acted the same way he painted — precisely. He didn't vary much from take to take. The performance he gave in the master was exactly the performance he gave in the two-shots."

Hepburn never solved the Fonda problem either. "Henry Fonda was the hardest nut I ever tried to crack. But I didn't know any more about him after we had made the picture than I did at the beginning. Cold. Cold. Cold." That was the personal. When it came to the professional, Hepburn said, "He moved me deeply. What he expressed in a scene was the absolute truth."

Hank got through the picture, although soon after it wrapped his health began to deteriorate rapidly. But he finally got an Academy Award, partial atonement for being overlooked for *The Grapes of Wrath, The Lady Eve, My Darling Clementine, The Wrong Man,* for all the times he had impeccably portrayed men wrestling with their duty and implacable fate.

He watched the Oscar ceremony from home, where he was now in a wheelchair, too weak to go anywhere but a doctor's office. He had gotten quieter as the award day approached. "You could see he was concerned," said Shirlee. He wanted to win, but didn't want to give in to the need. When his name was announced, "he burst into tears," said Shirlee. "He was so emotional. His face got very red and I was greatly concerned about him. But I realized that was only part of his excitement."

Jane accepted on his behalf. When she came to the house to give him his statue he admitted that he wasn't all that surprised he won. "It was in the wind," he said. And then he told a reporter that no, he didn't think he would ever act again. As for Jane, the film would remain an agonizing representation of the gulf between a father and his daughter. "I can't watch *On Golden Pond,*" she would say when she was older than her father had been when he made the picture.

As Fonda's health waned, so did his energy, but he was still determined to be as useful as possible. On good days before the Oscar ceremony he would take a box out to the garden to sit on while he did some planting. More than anything else, he had come to the realization that professionally he had lived his life under a lucky star.

"I just feel so lucky to go way back when Doe Brando picked me or called my mother. What would have happened if I hadn't taken that call, or if Doe hadn't thought of me, I don't know. It never would have occurred to me to be an actor, ever."

A few weeks later, getting out to the garden was impossible. Walking had declined to a few steps. Iron will had powered him through life, but he could not will himself to energy, even if he limited himself to the most modest goals. "I just want to be able to walk to the Dover Delicatessen," he told Shirlee about a place near their New York townhouse.

He tried to occupy himself by painting. Apples seemed like a promising subject — if they were good enough for Cézanne, they could be good enough for Fonda. Shirlee would go out to the trees and pick fruit as he instructed her. "They've got to have character," he said. "No polish." But he had trouble getting the colors right and grew discouraged.

Jim visited every day. Some days Fonda spent in his wheelchair, some days he couldn't get out of bed. Shirlee had a cot near his bed and helped turn him regularly to avoid bedsores. He was usually awake, but he was also remote, as if part of him had already taken leave. Jane would visit, cooking a pork roast accompanied by tart pears from a tree at her ranch that he loved.

One time she arrived and found her father asleep. Along with everything else, he now had gout. She began to rub his feet and kept at it for twenty minutes. When she finally got up to leave, he said, "Don't stop." He had been awake the entire time.

Another time Shirlee had to go shopping and Jane came over so her father wouldn't be alone. She found him sitting with a lap rug over his knees, looking out the window into his vegetable garden. Jane sat at his feet and told him that she loved him, that she knew he had done his best to be a good father and that she was sorry for anything she had done that had hurt him. She would always make sure to be there for Shirlee.

Hank didn't say anything, but he began to cry. Jane knew he didn't want her to see him like that, so she quietly left the room. He was still sobbing when his wife returned.

Early in the morning of August 12, 1982, Jane got a phone call from Shirlee: Get to the hospital and get there quickly. By the time she got to Cedars-Sinai, it was too late. At 7:55 that morning, Henry Fonda had sat up in bed and opened his eyes. Then he sighed, perhaps in relief, perhaps in satisfaction, and fell back on the bed. He was seventy-seven years old.

The family returned to the house, where Hank's friends slowly began to arrive: Jim, Eva Marie Saint, Mel Ferrer, Dorothy McGuire, James Garner, Lucille Ball, Barbara Stanwyck. Jim told a reporter, "I've just lost my best friend," and said nothing else.

After the reporters got their quotes and left, Hank's women went inside the house. Hank's makeup man arrived and told Jane that she had never been far from her father's thoughts. He *worried* about her. "You can't imagine how much he talked about you," he said.

While everybody else moved quietly through the house and kept up a low hum of conversation, Jim Stewart sat quietly in the library. "He just sat there in this big armchair, absolutely not moving an inch and saying nothing," remembered Jane.

Nobody wanted to look at him, but it was like trying to pretend there wasn't this gorilla in the room smoking a big cigar. He must have stayed like that a good half-hour, maybe an hour, just staring off somewhere.

Then suddenly he lowered his head very slowly over his lap and brought it back up at the same time that he raised his arms out as far as they could go and said, "It was by far the biggest kite we ever flew."

Those were exactly his first words after all his quiet and from there, right in the middle of this thing he'd obviously been thinking about, he went into this monologue about how he and my father had flown these kites after the war . . . going into all the details of what they looked like and how hard some of them had pulled.

The tears were running down my face, and I know I wasn't the only one. Then after about five minutes of talking about nothing except these kites, he fell back into the same silence and same position he'd been in before he started talking. I think it may have been the only thing he said the entire time he was there. But it was enough.

Hank's will instructed that his body be cremated and disposed of "without ceremony of any kind." He left $200,000 to his adopted daughter Amy, with the remainder of the estate going to Shirlee. He inserted a sentence stating that his omission of Jane and Peter from the will was solely because they were both financially independent, unlike Shirlee and Amy. It was "not in any sense a measure of my deep affection for them."

Hank's autobiography, a collaboration with the playwright and biographer Howard Teichmann, had been published a few months before he died. The fascinating and often salty transcripts on which the book was based came to one thousand pages. Strangely, the book itself was oddly bland, denatured, as if someone had lost his nerve. Nevertheless, the book sold well.

Shortly after Fonda's book came out, Stewart agreed to write his autobiography with a writer from *Reader's Digest*. When word spread at the *Digest* offices in Pleasantville, New York, the writer's editor asked him, "Just who are you working for, me or Jimmy Stewart?" Since a gig at *Reader's Digest* was widely regarded as the cushiest in the publishing world, the writer dropped the project. An offended Stewart refused to consider picking it up with anyone else. And so he avoided putting his experiences of flying into print, images that James Salter had described as "clouds . . . dense and towering, their edges struck with light; epic clouds, the last of the sun streaming through . . . the imperishability of it, the brilliance."

But then Jim didn't have to write about it. He'd seen it; he'd done it.

A year after Hank's death, Stewart went back to Indiana, Pennsylvania, for a seventy-fifth birthday celebration. The city had erected a bronze statue of him on the town square, and Jim and Gloria stayed with old friend Hall Blair and his wife. Stewart was at his puckish best. "We're right on schedule," he observed at the beginning of his speech, "Wal . . . I'll . . . uh . . . fix . . .

that." For Hall Blair, Jim was unchanged. "As a kid, he'd always fumble over his words," Blair said. "He'd ask, 'You gonna change that fossip?' I'd say, 'it's faucet,' and he'd say, 'Right, fossip.'"

Indifferent to acting offers, sliding into old age, Jim began making occasional appearances on *The Tonight Show,* where the normally frosty Johnny Carson melted in his presence. Duke Wayne had died in 1979, so now Stewart was America's de facto grandfather — not energetic but placid, not temperamental or dangerous, as Wayne had been, but invariably amusing, a little doddering, occasionally a bit risqué. He would recite poems he had written about a beloved dog, and that led to a book contract for a volume called *Jimmy Stewart and His Poems,* which became a bestseller. The best thing you could say was that Stewart didn't take himself or his poems at all seriously.

"I know I'm forgetful," he said, "I know I have a stubborn streak. I think I have a sort of a mild straitlaced attitude about me. I approve very highly of discipline. An actor needs discipline. You hear so much about the old movie moguls and the impersonal factories where there was no freedom. MGM was a wonderful place where decisions were made in my behalf by my superiors. What's wrong with that?"

In 1983, Universal reissued a batch of Hitchcock films that had been out of sight for decades, including *Rope, Rear Window, The Man Who Knew Too Much,* and *Vertigo.* Jim's ability to play all manner of warped obsessives without alienating the audience occasioned a rapid and upward reassessment of his career. He did some dutiful press interviews, if for no other reason than his profit participation in the films. He wasn't at all sure about the trends of modern acting.

"So many actors nowadays let everything show. If they worked hard on it they want to make sure that everyone knows it. That's not acting. It's showing off. Acting should never show. It hurts the character, and making the character come alive is the actor's only business.

"I was very lucky not to be typecast. John Wayne was terrific, but he was always bigger than his roles. Hank and I were never bigger than our roles. We never thought we were either."

In between safaris in Africa — there would be twenty-three in all — it was now Jim's turn to begin the round-robin of eminent elderly actors, accepting awards at tributes and retrospectives. At one showing of *Mr.*

Smith Goes to Washington, Gregory Peck looked over at Stewart during the show-stopping filibuster scene. Jim was watching himself with a cold eye — impassive, analytical, judging himself as a professional. "His face didn't tell me whether he liked or didn't like what he saw," said Peck. "After it was over, they gave him a standing ovation. He remained cool throughout it all. He really wasn't caught up in it."

In 1986, Stewart agreed to participate in a retrospective tribute for PBS, the Public Broadcasting System. When he walked into a meeting with the film's producers, they were shocked. "The frail old man with wispy gray hair was somewhat bent over, looking tired and lacking in energy," remembered David Heeley, the director. "He smiled and shook hands but all I could think was that we had made a big mistake. . . . I had grave doubts that this person could carry a ninety minute special."

But on the first day of filming, "The frail old man had completely vanished. In his place was James Stewart, the movie star. He stood straight and tall and there was now a vigor to his step. . . . He looked ten years younger than he had two months before." Some of it was makeup, some of it was the toupee, but most of it was a burst of energy provoked by a camera.

The interview provided a few bon mots. He remembered how Ted Healy, a comic at MGM, had once told him, "Never treat your audience as customers. Always treat them as partners."

"I've never stopped believing that's true," he said.

His sole comment about his service during World War II was the fact that he hadn't enlisted, he'd been drafted. "It's the only lottery I ever won." And when he was asked to describe a bombing mission, he simply said, "No."

His resolution was not surprising to anyone who knew him. Hal Kanter, who had produced Stewart's 1971 sitcom, said that Stewart was mostly quiet, gentle, and a pleasure to work with.

But don't fuck with him. He knows exactly what he's doing, has strong opinions and can dig in his heels when he wants to. Remember, he's remained a staunch Republican in a town where most of his friends are Democrats. He's been a star in Hollywood, where divorce is rampant, but he's been married to the same woman for almost forty years, with never a breath of scandal. And most importantly, never forget that he served in World War II and was the lead pilot in over two dozen bombing missions. [Actually nineteen.]

Something got him through that war; something made him choose to stay in the Air Force Reserves for years, finally retiring as a Brigadier General; something made him support the Vietnam War even though one of his stepsons was killed in it; something makes him stand by what he believes in no matter what. There's a toughness, a stick-to-your-guns kind of courage and strength underneath that genuine niceness. People sometimes think because he's that nice, he's easy to manipulate. Believe me, the best advice I can give you is don't mess with him.

Occasionally, he and Gloria would host a small dinner party. After dinner, Jim would bring out the accordion or head to the piano, causing Gloria to roll her eyes in mock horror. The music would be one of the old vaudeville perennials for which he had an inexplicable enthusiasm: "Ragtime Cowboy Joe" or "Dear Ruth (I'm Telling You the Truth)."

There were attendant frailties of age to go along with his hearing loss, which had become severe. He had a pacemaker, a bad back, minor skin cancers. His generally wan appearance and lack of vigor gave the impression that he was, if not actively ill, unwell.

Accompanying that was the generally uncommunicative mood brought on by his deafness — it was easier to let Gloria do the talking for him, and eventually it was easier to let her do the thinking as well. By the same token, it was easier to turn down work than to go through what had become the drudgery of costume tests, learning lines, etc. His deafness isolated him, but it also gave him a convenient hook on which to hang a general disinclination. "It wasn't depression, exactly. It was more like he just felt he'd done enough," said his daughter Kelly.

Jim had enlisted Robert Wagner to serve as a trustee at St. John's Hospital in Santa Monica — one of the longtime charitable interests of the Stewarts. Jim thought Wagner would be a suitable substitute for him. Around the same time, Wagner was moving into production, and sent Jim a script about a homeless man who gets involved with a private school. In the process, the school avoids disaster and the homeless man gets cleaned up.

To Wagner's shock, Stewart not only

didn't like the script, he was angry that Wagner had even suggested it to him. "He turned on me," remembered Wagner. " 'How could you ever think I'd want to do a story like that?' he asked me. I realized that he had a very specific idea of the way he wished to be presented, and a bum wasn't it."

Stewart and Gloria had attended reunions of the 453rd Bomb Group in America, and in 1983 they traveled to Norwich, England, for a reunion. They traveled down to Old Buc, where they planted a tree in commemoration of comrades who had died.

He made something called *Afrika Monogatari* for a Japanese director because it involved another trip to Africa, made a not-bad HBO movie with Bette Davis called *Right of Way,* and voiced a quavery old sheriff in a feature-length cartoon called *An American Tail: Fievel Goes West.* The cartoon marked an ignominious exit for a fearless movie star with the greatest range of them all.

After forty years, Jim and Gloria had settled into the easy back-and-forth of an old married couple who could make cracks about each other without offending. She would joke about his hemming and hawing speech.

535

"It didn't take that long to invent the wheel," she would say. He would retaliate by mentioning her fondness for facelifts.

If Gloria wanted to do something, Jim would generally go along. A lot of the things she wanted to do were simply because she was trying to keep her husband moving. When a friend asked her about the appropriateness of some appearance, Gloria glared at him and said, "It got him out of the house for a few hours, didn't it?"

Even though most conversation beneath the decibel range of a yell was lost to Jim, he was always polite to everybody. He was careful to wear his hairpiece in public, but didn't bother with it at private social occasions. One observer noticed that he looked younger without the toupee.

He had reached that stage of life where he was forced to reminisce, even though it was a double-edged sword — on the one hand, he was remembering great times. On the other, everybody he was talking about was dead. Even Hank.

"This friendship with Fonda over the years was tremendous," he said. "I valued it so much. Tremendous friendship, tremendous admiration for him. He was good at his job if anybody was ever good at his job. It was a terrible thing to lose him. Which happens so much, you know. I think about it every once in a while — I try *not* to think about it. I've lost so many — I've lost so many people. You think of somebody and then you think, 'When did she die?' "

He would get a little moist around the eyes then, but he was far too dignified to cry in public, so would quickly close the subject: "But Fonda was a wonderful, close friend."

At one party, the author and screenwriter John Gregory Dunne asked him about the difference between flying the B-17 Flying Fortress and the B-24 Liberator. "The most amazing thing happened," reported Dunne. "Thirty-five years just vanished from his demeanor, and his hearing seemed to return. He was a young colonel again, as he tried to explain to me which one was the easiest to fly, and the difference in trim and configuration between the two planes. He held his hands out the way pilots do — and said, this one was more stable, you could not smoke in that one because fuel fumes built up in it. . . .

"What was astonishing was his immediate and glowing transformation from an elderly gentleman and semi-retired motion picture star to a combat officer in his 30s."

■ ■ ■ ■

In the fall of 1993, Gloria Stewart was diagnosed with lung cancer. She had been a smoker for most of her life, while Jim would borrow a cigarette only when he was nervously watching a preview of one of his films. Moments like that aside, he didn't smoke.

"Her reaction," said her daughter Kelly, "was not to think too much about it. She knew something was deeply wrong, she knew it was called cancer and she knew she didn't have all that long. We knew she knew, but we also knew that Mom did not want to sit down and have it spelled out. She did not really want to discuss it."

As for Jim's reaction to his wife's illness, "He couldn't deal with it," said Kelly. "He was there in the house with Mom and doing all the daily routines they had always done, but he did not deal with the logistics of her treatment or discuss what lay ahead. He just couldn't bear to really see it. I think that was fine with Mom. They were both just there together, with each other, one day at a time."

Gloria flipped a mental switch and began to live completely in the present, not thinking about the future, not even the next day. She would reminisce freely, and every once in a while she would stop and say, "You know, I've had a really good life." It was not a veiled request for confirmation; rather, it was a statement of fact.

Gloria discussed possible treatments with her children, and decided to try a round of chemo after radiation. Other than her hair falling out, the chemo wasn't atrocious, but she was tired all the time and made a decision to forgo a second round if the doctors suggested it. Gloria got through Thanksgiving and Christmas of 1993 in decent shape, surrounded by family, friends, and laughter.

Gloria Hatrick McLean Stewart died on February 16, 1994. She was seventy-five years old.

It was a stunning blow that Jim had never imagined — wasn't Gloria fully ten years younger than he was? As his hearing had slowly disappeared, Gloria had functioned as his lifeline, his conduit to the world. At the funeral, he kept repeating, "It's just wrong, it's absolutely wrong that it happened this way."

Gloria's death precipitated Stewart's final, definitive retreat from the world. He had always assumed that he would die first, and she probably had as well — men usually do. But now Gloria was gone; what was he supposed to do without her?

"He was lost," said Bill Hayward. "He took it very hard, and understandably so. She was a remarkable woman."

President Bill Clinton called to offer his condolences, but even with his hearing aid Jim couldn't hear Clinton. He grew irritated and hung up. Anne, his housekeeper, and the woman he would grow to depend upon, scolded him. "You just hung up on the President of the United States!"

He thought about that for a moment, then said, "W-w-well, I've never done that before!" He was touched by Clinton's gesture and the rock-ribbed Republican grew rather conciliatory about the president, and even went so far as to suggest that "I think Bill Clinton deserves a chance."

"Dad withdrew from the world after Mom died. He didn't know what to do with himself," said Kelly. "He was sad and empty. He wasn't there anymore." People who had been close friends for decades — Lew Wasserman, Dorothy McGuire — tried to see him, but their phone calls were not returned. If they showed up at the front door they were gently turned away. Burgess Meredith, one of the few old friends left from the University Players era, wrote him several times after Gloria died, but Jim didn't respond. Dinner invitations arrived, but he didn't want to go anywhere.

And so the house at 918 Roxbury became unnaturally quiet.

Jim Stewart had never really submitted to anyone or anything in life but his father, and then only in matters he didn't regard as crucial. His ambition and his resolve had taken him to the heights of Hollywood and of the military, but with his wife's death he was defeated. He was a man in mourning and would remain that way for the rest of his life.

He mostly stayed in his bedroom, with Anne or someone else bringing him his meals. For years he had been saying that he would die at the age of eighty-nine, just as his father had, and now he was content to wait for that eventuality. The clinical depression was obvious, but the reality was that after war and a venturesome life that had taken him to the furthest reaches of his imagination, Jim's emotional and physical resources were spent.

"People thought he should see a counselor, but the people that thought he would do that didn't know him at all," said Kelly. "He was the most stubborn person I've met

541

in my entire life. You couldn't make him do *anything* he didn't want to do. Well-meaning people would say we should get him a personal trainer or take him out for a drive to see the sunset. They didn't understand. Dad was going to do what he wanted, and that's all he was going to do."

Occasionally there was a hint of the actor. Anne, the housekeeper, constituted the primary fabric of his life, and he would occasionally try to pluck her heartstrings by slightly overdoing the trembling old man routine. She would call him on it every time.

He would see his children, and a friend named Tom Jones (not the singer) and he would be alert and interested, but only up to a point. After a while his attention would flag, and it became clear that it was time for his visitors to leave. He was waiting.

James Maitland Stewart died in his home of a heart attack brought on by an embolism on July 2, 1997. The last thing he said was "Anne." Just as he had foretold, he was eighty-nine years old — the same age as his father. He was buried next to Gloria at Forest Lawn, far from Indiana, Pennsylvania.

A few days before, Henry Nicklas, the barber at the Bel-Air Country Club, had stopped by to shave his favorite client, just as he had been doing for years. Stewart had a small bandage on the left side of his face. "Shall I take it off to shave your face?" Nicklas asked.

"Henry," replied Stewart, "don't worry about the left side of my face. God will take care of it."

In 1999, a bust of Stewart was unveiled at the Eighth Air Force Heritage Museum outside Savannah, Georgia. The plaque states:

JAMES MAITLAND STEWART

Brigadier General, Air Force Reserve —
Retired

1908–1997

The Comrades-in-Arms of
General Stewart of the 445th, 453rd
and 389th Bombardment Groups (Heavy)
and the Second Combat Wing, are proud
to recognize his outstanding record of
exemplary achievements while serving
with these combat units during
World War II.

PRESENTED TO THE EIGHTH AIR
FORCE HERITAGE MUSEUM AS A

LABOR OF LOVE BY THE
MEMBERSHIP OF THE 453RD BOMB
GROUP MEMORIAL PROJECT.

EPILOGUE

In the spring of 1998, Jim and Gloria's house was sold for $5.6 million to the founder of an online discount brokerage. He pronounced the house "a dump," and tore it down in order to build a faux Italian villa.

Shirlee Fonda continued to live in the house in Bel-Air after her husband died, refusing all offers for the land, even when they cascaded past $20 million. "They'll just tear the house down, and I don't want it torn down," said Shirlee. "I'll leave this house when they carry me out."

The Bel-Air house had been carefully preserved as it was when Hank died — a museum of Shirlee's life with a painfully shy man who needed to escape into other people. Hank's paintings still hung where he had put them, his needlepoint pillows still lay in the corners of the thickly upholstered chairs.

The two friends live on in their best work, in the affections of their audience, and in the memories of the people who knew them. Even now, decades after his death, Henry Fonda comes to his daughter in a recurring dream. He steps out from behind a tree and she can sense that he is radiantly happy. He tells her that she doesn't have to worry about him. Not anymore.

One day, Jane Fonda realized with some astonishment that she was older than her father was when he died. Shortly afterward, she was asked what she understood about him that she could not have known when she was younger.

"That he suffered from undiagnosed depression," she said. "Prozac would have changed everybody's life. But the most important thing is forgiveness. I've *studied* him. I've read books that have helped me understand him. Like him, I'm a loner, I tend to be depressed, and I have to work every day to keep myself on an even keel.

"His acting? Absolute integrity. Purity. Not a smidgen of indicating. He so internalized those characters because he so wanted to be like them. He couldn't teach me directly because he didn't talk much, but he taught me through his films, through his acting."

In so many ways, the lives of the younger generation were as bound together as their parents — by choice, by heredity, by love. Bill Hayward grew up to strongly resemble his father, produced *Easy Rider* and *The Hired Hand* for his best friend Peter Fonda. He came to appreciate his mother only when he produced a film of his sister's book *Haywire,* and watched all of Margaret Sullavan's movies.

"My mom only did thirteen movies," he said, "and I suddenly realized, 'God, she is good.' Not just because she was my mother. She was a *good* actress. She was a phenomenally *interesting* actress. She had a wonderful voice. It was very distinctive. Most people would probably think of it as a husky voice, which it probably was. . . . And onstage she was a spectacular actress."

Bill was in the commissary at Columbia working on *Easy Rider* with Dennis Hopper when they encountered William Wyler — Sullavan's second husband. "How's Brooke?" asked Wyler of Hopper. Unfortunately, Hopper's marriage to her had just broken up, a fact of which Wyler was unaware. Hopper was embarrassed and said quietly, "Well, Willy, we're getting a divorce."

Wyler was completely deaf in one ear and

didn't hear Hopper, so he repeated the question, a little louder. Hopper said, "We're getting a divorce, Willy," a little louder in return.

The Abbott and Costello routine went on a few more times, and Wyler still hadn't heard the answer, so now he finally yelled "HOW'S BROOKE?" and half the commissary yelled, "THEY'RE GETTING A DIVORCE, WILLY!"

At which point Wyler said, "Oh. Guess you couldn't hold on to her any better than I could her mother."

Like his mother, like his sister Bridget, Bill Hayward would ultimately commit suicide. So the world of Brooke Hayward and Jane and Peter Fonda grew a little smaller. To an unusual degree, Jane and Peter, Michael McLean, Kelly Stewart Harcourt and Judy Stewart were left to live their lives looking forward and backward simultaneously, forging their own friendships and careers while simultaneously analyzing their parents' enduring bond.

"I see them more clearly now," said Peter Fonda,

> and it's all for the good. My father and Uncle Jimmy had this code. It was not spoken, it was embodied. It had to do with

showing, not telling. It was something they shared.

I think the core of the relationship was their professionalism. They both saw life as a series of jobs and they were determined to do them to the best of their ability. There's a sense in which they were both Boy Scouts — literally and metaphorically.

I look back on it, and I see that we grew up in an unbiased house. My father was completely without bias. One day I came home from school and asked my father, "What does 'nigger' mean?"

He just exploded. He *screamed* at me. It was as if I had invented the word and what it represented. I never said the word again. And he never did explain what the word meant. For that, I had to ask our neighbors.

I obviously didn't learn my lesson about asking him questions about the meaning of words, because the next word I brought home was "kike." Once again there was a deafening apoplectic outburst but no explanation. I got back on my bike and rode to my friend's house — we had both been running away from other boys who were throwing rocks at him and yelling that word. The family was gathered around him and were surprised to see me. I asked them what "kike" meant. They gasped and said it was a terrible thing to call someone who was a Jew.

"What's a Jew?" I asked.

In retrospect I can see that my father had a fabulous underpinning of character. I have never said those words again, and I have walked away from people who spoke like that for the rest of my life.

Michael McLean felt that Hank and Jim were held together by shared history and a mutual sense of privacy, which in most cases left them alone with each other, which was more or less the way they liked it.

"Dad was very happy when he and Hank lived together," said Michael McLean, "and besides the friendship, I was always conscious of the fact that they had a deep and abiding respect for each other."

So they never discussed Frances's suicide, or Ronald McLean's death, or Jane's flirtation with the Vietcong. They didn't have to. Jim knew what Hank felt, and vice versa.

"What you learn is never what's said," said Jane.

It's what's done. It's what you do that gets passed along. And I guess what my father did was always remain true to himself even when it wasn't particularly fashionable.

Katharine Hepburn said that a star's job was to be fascinating. . . . My father could not have cared less about being fascinating. He would sit in his chair reserving his energy and he would wait until the director was ready. I really respected his quiet professionalism.

I wouldn't have wanted to be the daughter of Katharine Hepburn. I'm glad I was his daughter.

"No explanation was required for almost anything," Stewart explained. "When we were both away doing pictures or something, and then we'd see each other, get our wives and go off and have dinner, there was never any reason to say, 'Well now, let's catch up. Let's catch up on all that you've been doing and everything.' It is just as though we'd never been parted. . . . The only bringing up to date was how many jokes we had, how many stories."

It was only when they grew too old to be fashionable that it became clear that they were also too good to be fully appreciated — two tall men united by shared loves, shared passions, a shared concern with what can only be called moral purpose. And there was something else, something that can be called honor, which was reflected in the characters they played.

They were two loners who went off to see the world and remade component parts of it into their own images, two fiercely private men who were quite capable of confounding their own families. "You can't build . . . with nice, polite people," said Josh Logan, who loved them both. "They're too round. What you need are concrete blocks."

Acting allowed them to express emotions neither of them could have otherwise expressed, use experiences that they would normally have blocked. Although their styles were quite different, they shared an internal sense of true north that was effectively analyzed by Dorothy McGuire: "He has this extraordinary thing inside of him," she said of Fonda, although it applied to Stewart as well. "It's buried and he has it. And it's *cleansed.* It's purified. The chaff has all fallen away and it's *true.* It's on course and it's on its beam. And people recognize it. It has an intangible vibration."

Neither of them was particularly introspective; indeed, they may have been afraid to analyze themselves too deeply lest they expose their creative mainspring to corro-

552

sion. They spent more time thinking about their characters' internal lives than their own. Fictional lives gave them an excuse to avoid thinking about their own.

"They were both consummate artists who cared about the work they did," said Edwin Sherin. "Because they had standards about what they did, they never developed that contempt for the audience that becomes contempt for themselves, which destroys many actors."

In their friendship they created a safe place for themselves, away from the fears and frustrations of their careers, their domestic problems, the responsibilities of their legendary status. When they were together, they were just Hank and Jim, a couple of actors unaccountably grown old. When they were together, they could chortle over their shared youthful misadventures. When they were together, they were still young.

After John Swope died, Hank wrote a letter to Dorothy McGuire. It is full of loss, memory, time, long-delayed self-awareness as well as that thing he was only comfortable displaying in his work: emotion.

"I never feel that I have really expressed my great feeling about John," he wrote.

But then, that's the story of my life. For reasons that are too deeply buried for me to understand, I have never been able to articulate my emotions. Only recently, Peter has been ending his phone calls by saying, "love you, dad." And of course, it has forced me to say, "And I love you, son." He knew I did. But he was making me say it. And now it's coming easier.

I loved John. I truly did. I was just 23 when we first became friends and I don't think I originally appreciated how much his outgoing, giving, resounding personality affected me in a positive way. . . . I have never known a man to so thoroughly enjoy life as John did, and to live it as fully. His enthusiasms were contagious. You always felt better for having been with John.

And then in closing, he cast himself back to Falmouth, to the University Players, to the windswept days and nights when Maggie had bewitched them all, when a midnight swim led to passion and marriage, when their talents surged at flood tide and the world waited for them to make their grand entrances.

"Just last night, he was with me in the most realistic dream, surrealistic, really. A rowboat, a beautiful rocky coastline, a majestic, pounding surf. We were both young and strong and unafraid.

"I think it will always be like that . . ."

ACKNOWLEDGMENTS

My wife and I were having dinner with John Sacret Young and his wife. "What are you doing next?" he asked. We were in Los Angeles on a promotional tour for my biography of John Wayne. I was exhausted, and the next book was the last thing on my mind. I told him I had no idea but that something would turn up.

"I've always wanted to read a book about the friendship between Henry Fonda and Jimmy Stewart," John said.

Something turned up.

To John and Claudia, my gratitude for their friendship and their ideas. Keep 'em coming.

John gave me the concept, but without Robert Osborne this book wouldn't exist. Bob was a magical presence in my life. With Bob in your corner, you were never alone, never outgunned. His death left an irreparable hole in the fortifications of the people who loved him, which was nearly everybody who ever met him.

Bob, this one's for you.

He thought this book was a great idea and made my problems his problems. He picked up the phone and called Shirlee Fonda, Henry Fonda's widow. Shirlee hadn't talked to a writer in more than thirty years, but she also thought the book was a great idea, as did Rob Wolders. Shirlee opened her house to me for hours of honest conversation, then asked her stepchildren Jane and Peter to lend their memories to the project.

While all this was going on, my dear friend Robert Wagner, with whom I've written three books, called Kelly Stewart Harcourt. Kelly brought her brother and sister into the project. Without the input of their families, I could never have recreated the lives of Henry Fonda and James Stewart.

At Turner Classic Movies, Charlie Tabesh has filled his roster with people who know movies and care about people. People like Scott McGee and Darcy Hettrich. Darcy and Scott made it possible for me to talk to Kim Novak, which was a glorious experience.

Brooke Hayward agreed to talk to me about her father and the deeply intertwined lives of her godfathers. Maria Cooper Janis spoke of her parents and their friends with her typical fond acuity. Norman Lloyd is the most remarkable centenarian I've known and talked eloquently of his friend John Swope. Jane Alexander and Edwin Sherin brought the trained eye of brilliant theatrical professionals to the style and technique of my subjects. Sue Lloyd, the granddaughter of Harold Lloyd, shared very specific experiences of growing up in Beverly Hills. Mark Swope told me about his father's friendship with Fonda and Stewart and gave me access to his photographic archive. He also showed me John Swope's home movies of the wedding of Henry Fonda and Margaret Sullavan. Mark's death in December 2016 deprived the world of a true gentleman.

Henry Fonda and James Stewart inevitably came up in my interviews with other actors, writers, and directors, and I have used insights from Sandra Dee, Bob Hope, Dan Ford, Shirley Jones, Jack Lemmon, Fess Parker, Jack Valenti, William Wellman Sr., William Wellman Jr., Billy Wilder, and Stuart Woods.

My fellow authors came through when I needed them: Pat McGilligan, Tracey Goessel, John McElwee, Robert Matzen. Dennis Doros and Amy Heller of Milestone Films have been part of my life for more than thirty years, and I continue to rely on their humor and good sense.

The mother lode for the research consisted of the thousand single-spaced pages of interview transcripts with Henry Fonda and his circle in the Teichmann collection at the Library of Congress — material gathered for Fonda's autobiography.

And then there are the librarians. At the New York Public Library, John Calhoun never let me down, guiding me through the thickets of the Leland Hayward and Brooke Hayward collections. At USC, Ned Comstock has spent decades shipping me documents I didn't know enough to ask for. Ned is not only a spectacular librarian, he's a great and loyal friend. At the Museum of Modern Art, thanks go to my old friend Dave Kehr and to Ashley Swinnerton, the keeper of the Film Study Center.

At the University of Miami, Christina Lane gifted me with an unexpected but deeply gratifying second — or is it third? — career. And thanks to Gregory Shepherd, the dean of the School of Communications, who agreed with Christina that I just might have the makings of a teacher. Captain Robert Beck used his thirty-two years of piloting experience to help me understand confusing elements of WWII aviation.

Finally, there is the posse at Simon & Schuster, who have been putting up with me for, I'm proud to say, a quarter century: my editor, Bob Bender, usually gentle but firm when he needs to be; publisher Jon Karp; publicist Amanda Lang; and Johanna Li, who is not only adorable but manages to never lose her sense of humor. Last but certainly not least, Fred Chase proved yet again that he is the world's best copy editor.

In the conclusion of his memoir, Charlie Chaplin wrote, "I have the good fortune to be married to a wonderful wife. I wish I could write more about this, but it involves love, and perfect love is the most beautiful of all frustrations because it is more than one can express."

I don't know if my love for Lynn Kalber is perfect, but I do know that marrying her was the smartest thing I've ever done. She's been the making of me, as well as of our life together. My love for her is boundless.

— Scott Eyman
April 2014–August 2017
Los Angeles, Santa Monica, Aspen, New York City, St. Maarten, San Juan, Nice, Monte Carlo, Vallarius, Barcelona, Santa Fe, Fort Sumner, West Palm Beach.

NOTES

Unless otherwise indicated, all quotations from Shirlee Fonda, Jane Fonda, Peter Fonda, Brooke Hayward, Michael McLean, Kelly Stewart Harcourt, Judy Stewart, and Mark Swope derive from their interviews with the author.

MOMA: Museum of Modern Art

USC: University of Southern California Cinematic Arts Library

LOC: Library of Congress

NYPL: New York Pubic Library for the Performing Arts

LOC, Teichmann papers: Unless otherwise indicated, these are the interviews Howard Teichmann conducted with Henry Fonda and his circle in 1979 and 1980.

Prologue

The cancer had moved into the bone: LOC, Teichmann papers, tape 37, p. 1080.

"Retire? I wouldn't know what to do": Ibid.

"anger over affirmation": McKinney, p. 75.

One actress said that if you happened: Sandra Dee to SE.

"People say Hank and I are living in the past": MOMA, James Stewart file, Aljean Harmetz, "James Stewart Says He's 'Fortunate Fellow,' " New York Times, 3-1-80.

"You don't get to know Jimmy Stewart": Dewey, p. 27.

"I made a pact with myself": MOMA, Henry Fonda file, Time, 3-18-82.

One

"Dr. Roeder reports": McKinney, p. 28.

By that time: 1920 census.

"I was assigned to an ambition": LOC, Teichmann papers, Henry Fonda letters, box 6, f. 2.

"When it was all over": McKinney, p. 340.

"land-based morality": Jane Fonda, p. 38.

"They had rehearsed": Ray Hagen, "Henry Fonda in His Own Words, Part One," Films of the Golden Age, Issue 63, Winter 2010–11.

"got the smell": Ibid.

"My mother was the diplomat": Ibid.

"Well, from that moment": Ibid.

"I remember his father": LOC, Teichmann

papers, Joshua Logan interview, part one.

"I don't intend to make acting": LOC, Teichmann papers, Henry Fonda letters, box 6, f. 1.

"The thing that I was getting": LOC, Teichmann papers, tape 1, p. 10.

"Only when I grew up and moved away": McKinney, p. 31.

Girls had to pursue him: Jane Fonda to SE.

Fonda learned that the one sure way: LOC, Teichmann papers, tape 1, p. 17

"Prospects for future work": Fonda on Fonda, Turner Broadcasting, 1992.

"I didn't make $100 a week": LOC, Teichmann papers, tape 2, p. 26.

"Don't swing your ass": Logan, p. 12.

"I had to be in that club": Ibid., p. 18.

"He was the best-looking human being": NYPL, Brooke Hayward papers, Joshua Logan interview, box 7, f. 10.

"Benign anarchy": Logan, pp. 25–26.

"I can't imitate it": LOC, Teichmann papers, Joshua Logan interview, part one.

"I loved him from that minute on": Ibid.

"First loves are so strong": Jane Alexander to SE.

"Fonda wiped us all": Logan, p. 28.

"She was not exactly beautiful": Houghton, p. 48.

She began acting: NYPL, Margaret Sullavan papers, "Sore Throat Started Star on Film Career," *Atlanta Constitution*, 12-17-39.

"She had from the very beginning": Logan, p. 32.

One night someone: LOC, Teichmann papers, tape 3, p. 7.

"She was a character": NYPL, Leland Hayward papers, box 7, f. 6.

Two

"Hank wasn't in the show": LOC, Teichmann papers, James Stewart interview.

The atmosphere Swope photographed: I am indebted to the late Mark Swope for sharing these remarkable home movies with me.

"Hank Fonda could be": Norman Lloyd to SE.

"In a company": Logan, p. 34.

"He had great convictions": LOC, Teichmann papers, Joshua Logan interview, part one.

"He had them": Ibid.

"I didn't like them": LOC, Teichmann papers, tape B8, p. 7.

"to appreciate the furnishings": Logan, p. 29.

"nearly seven years of unparalleled plenty": Watkins, p. 15.

Between 1865 and 1920: Watkins, p. 42.

"Seven or eight years ago": Watkins, p. 60.

"like particles in liquid suspension": Watkins, p. 60.

"Working in Falmouth": Dewey, p. 102.

"Offstage she was a true": Henry Fonda with Howard Teichmann, p. 58.

Fonda declared himself: NYPL, Leland Hayward papers, box 1, f. 8.

"Sullavan had an atrocious voice": LOC, Teichmann papers, Joshua Logan interview, part one.

He didn't know the play: Logan, p. 67.

"We've got many people": LOC, Teichmann papers, Joshua Logan interview, part one.

"He was my friend": LOC, Teichmann papers, Joshua Logan interview, part one.

"He was the most outstanding": LOC, Teichmann papers, Joshua Logan interview, part one.

"I think she probably": Ibid.

"I never knew I had a temper": Henry Fonda with Howard Teichmann, p. 64.

"It was just hot and cold": LOC, Teichmann papers, tape A1, no page.

"I don't remember it": LOC, Teichmann papers, tape A4, p. 4.

"They fought like cats and dogs": LOC, Teichmann papers, Joshua Logan interview, part one.

"I'd stand there and cry": Henry Fonda with

Howard Teichmann, p. 65.

"I'm ready to kill myself": Gottfried, pp. 147–49.

"Oh, no," Stewart protested: Ibid., p. 68.

"he was swept into the theater": NYPL, Brooke Hayward papers, "A Broadway Drama," *Pageant,* June 1953, box 21, f. 21.

Three

"full to the rafters": Dewey, p. 56.

"I wouldn't say he was a loner": Eliot, p. 17.

"We celebrated Halloween": Michael Wilmington, "Small Town Guy," *Film Comment,* March–April 1990.

Jim had a dog: Michael McLean to SE.

Jim remembered that his mother: MOMA, James Stewart file, Cleveland Amory, "The Man Even Hollywood Likes," *Parade,* 10-21-84.

"Jimmy had an interesting": Smith, p. 20.

The admission was one cent: Dewey, p. 66.

"The stuttering and the stammering": Wilmington, "Small Town Guy."

"He'd go to a movie": Dewey, p. 83.

Neff was a magician: Ibid., p. 91.

"He was good": Smith, p. 25.

"The enthusiasm of Leatherbee": Dewey, p. 105.

"Amateur work is fun": Lanahan, p. 121.

His favorite building: MOMA, James Stewart file, Judy Klemesrud, "Today's Kids Should Laugh More," *New York Times,* 2-22-70.

"That got me into it": Wilmington, "Small Town Guy."

"It was clear on that night: Michael Buckley, "James Stewart," *Films in Review,* June 1991.

"I think it was because": MOMA, James Stewart file, Joyce Haber, "The Rise and Rise of Jimmy Stewart," *Los Angeles Times,* undated.

"I forget who found the place": LOC, Teichmann papers, James Stewart interview.

"a soot colored bedroom": Logan, p. 71.

"Those were great days": Fonda on Fonda, Turner Broadcasting, 1992.

"I wasn't smart enough": LOC, Teichmann papers, tape B2, p. 19.

"We'd get a job and open": LOC, Teichmann papers, Henry Fonda, *Good Morning America,* 1978, transcript.

"Hank just went about his work": LOC, Teichmann papers, James Stewart interview.

He would call his mother: Shirlee Fonda to SE.

"Since childhood": Logan, p. 73.

"*Fonda had tremendous humor*": LOC, Teichmann papers, James Stewart interview.

"*I was barely aware of it*": McKinney, p. 79.

Lugging the tree: LOC, Teichmann papers, James Stewart interview.

"*letting a great deal hang out*": Dewey, p. 115.

"*I brought my accordion*": Wilmington, "Small Town Guy."

One night they both: Henry Fonda with Howard Teichmann, p. 78.

"*Hank was crazy*": LOC, Teichmann papers, James Stewart interview.

"*It was very hot*": Ray Hagen, "Henry Fonda in His Own Words, Part One," *Films of the Golden Age,* Issue 63, Winter 2010–11.

"*Names were his priority,*": Laurents, p. 376.

"*He couldn't stand a bad deal*": Shorris and Bundy, p. 109.

"*The pickings were so easy*": Ogden, pp. 271–72.

"*I got in touch with him*": LOC, Teichmann papers, Marc Connelly interview.

Herberta Jaynes Fonda: LOC, Teichmann papers, tape 19, p. 598.

Her death notice: Herberta Jaynes Fonda obituary, *Lincoln Star,* Lincoln, Nebraska, 10-8-34.

"*He was playing the son*": Dewey, p. 127.

One of the backstage people: Ibid. p. 113.

"By then": Henry Fonda with Howard Teichmann, p. 92.

Fonda was wearing three hats: LOC, Teichmann papers, tape 19, p. 586.

"He called me every once in a while": Wilmington, "Small Town Guy."

"He wanted me to wait": LOC, Teichmann papers, James Stewart interview.

"My dad made a box for it": Wilmington, "Small Town Guy."

Jim stopped to admire: "V-8 Times," March–April 2010, p. 34.

Four

"Grapes of Wrath I saw": LOC, Teichmann papers, Henry Fonda *Good Morning America,* 1978, transcript.

"Was he a comedian": Dewey, p. 136.

Written by an interesting: USC, Universal collection, *Next Time We Love,* box 272, f. 8655.

In May 1936: "Miss Graham Dines with Two Leading Men," *Hartford Courant,* 5-20-36.

"I was just wrapped up": LOC, Teichmann papers, James Stewart interview.

"He had this sort of way": Ibid.

They were living in a rented house: 1936 voter registration for Henry Fonda.

Years later, Josh Logan mentioned: LOC,

571

Teichmann papers, Joshua Logan interview, part one.

He said that the sight: Westmore with Davidson, p. 102.

"Bullshit": LOC, Teichmann papers, tape B2, p. 6.

John D. Stewart: Dewey, p. 135.

"One of the first": Henry Fonda with Howard Teichmann, p. 103.

Hoagy Carmichael would stop by: LOC, Teichmann papers, tape 28, p. 811.

"In a way": LOC, Teichmann papers, tape 3X, p. 10.

They dreamed up a movie melodrama: Henry Fonda with Howard Teichmann, p. 107.

"I thought these two guys: Dewey, p. 181.

Louella Parsons wrote: "Angel Picture Trimuph for Dramatic Team," *Los Angeles Examiner,* 8-26-38.

"I've always felt": Michael Wilmington, "Small Town Guy," *Film Comment,* March–April 1990.

"If you detested some idea": Dewey, p. 141.

"I'm going to begin": NYPL, Leland Hayward papers, Stewart to Hayward, 9-9, no year, box 206, f. 12.

"Jimmy was respectful": Dewey, p. 163.

"Now, don't paw the ground": James Stewart: A Wonderful Life, PBS Great Performances, 1987.

Stewart just looked at him: To his credit, Stewart told this story on himself in ibid.

"Humor. She had great humor": Dewey, p. 190.

"This is a mistake": Henry Fonda with Howard Teichmann, p. 106.

"Women wanted to": MOMA, James Stewart file, Dwight Whitney, "Conversation with a Non-Talker," *TV Guide,* 5-16-70.

"I reacted badly": LOC, Teichmann papers, tape B1, p. 24.

"He had his share": LOC, Teichmann papers, James Stewart interview.

"Peggy My Dear": NYPL, Margaret Sullavan papers, box 1, f. 8.

"This is not in the nature of an explanation": Ibid.

"She was always in love": NYPL, Margaret Sullavan papers, box 7, f. 6.

"My baby blues": Technicolor Corp. interview with Henry Fonda, courtesy of David Pierce.

"Delightful . . . wonderful": Technicolor Corp. interview with Henry Fonda, courtesy of David Pierce.

"Do you think Wyler": Herman, p. 179.

"Get me out of this picture": Ibid., p. 181.

"I ADMIRE YOUR PICTURES": Ibid.

"He didn't shoot a hundred thousand feet": LOC, Teichmann papers, tape 1x, p. 3.

"What a performance, Toots": Fonda on *Fonda,* Turner Broadcasting, 1992.

"We became such a family": Technicolor Corp. interview with Henry Fonda, courtesy of David Pierce.

"a sensitive man": Ibid.

"1:18 pm. Went ashore": Eyman, p. 136.

"From then on": LOC, Teichmann papers, Joshua Logan interview, part one.

Marion Davies was not one to hold a grudge: Swope, p. 18.

"Jimmy had the ability": Michael Buckley, "James Stewart," *Films in Review,* June 1991.

"The long, shy, former architecture student": Logan, p. 131.

"that mumbling baby-faced beanpole": Riva, p. 486.

"After a week's work": Bach, p. 253.

"You're trying to look me in the eyes": Buckley, "James Stewart."

Fifty years later: Bach, p. 253.

"The main thing about Jimmy's relations": Dewey, p. 187.

"I had to stop going with Olivia": MOMA, James Stewart file, Bill Davidson, "Wal, You See, I'm an Actor," *TV Guide,* 10-2-71.

"He was a press agent's nightmare": Meredith, p. 101.

"You're like a bird up there": Smith, p. 28.

"He likes to chew his cud": Meredith, p. 102.

"She was wonderful": Buckley, "James Stewart."

"Once you got to know Swope": Swope, pp. 18–19.

"Dad was so emotionally distant": McKinney, p. 95.

Fonda felt: LOC, Teichmann papers, tape A7, p. 20.

"Talk to me, Hank": Jane Fonda, p. 50.

"Jim's spoiled and always has been": LOC, Joshua Logan papers, Ginnie Stewart to Logan, undated, but 1940.

"stricken for weeks": LOC, Teichmann papers, tape A7, p. 27.

"I hear you won something": MOMA, James Stewart file, *Modern Maturity*, December–January 1976–77.

"My impressions of Hank": Herman, p. 72.

"Fonda has no sex appeal": Viertel, p. 298.

"I told him that I never get great comedies": Curtis, *Between Flops*, p. 145.

Sturges would write: Sturges, p. 294.

"I adore that woman": LOC, Teichmann papers, tape 29, p. 832–33.

"If she hadn't been married": MOMA, Henry Fonda file, Thomas Thompson, "Fonda at 69," *McCall's*, 9–73.

"It looks like you are definitely": NYPL,

Leland Hayward papers, box 206, f. 12.

Five

"shy, intense, not much of a talker": Smith, p. 31.

"You know when I felt really lonely?": MOMA, James Stewart file, *Modern Maturity,* December–January 1976–77.

More importantly, it was estimated: Ibid., p. 321.

A little over a month after: MOMA, James Stewart file, Beirne Lay Jr., "Jimmy Stewart's Finest Performance," *Saturday Evening Post,* 12-8-45.

"A fundamental trait": Ibid.

"There must be some hitch": Ibid.

Among the pilots: Don Moore, War Tales, "Jimmy Stewart Taught Englewood Man How to Fly," *Charlotte* (Florida) *Sun,* 10-22-06.

he ran into a test pilot: MOMA, James Stewart file, Lay, "Jimmy Stewart's Finest Performance," 12-8-45.

Jim wrote a letter to Sullavan: NYPL, Margaret Sullavan papers, undated but 1943, box 1, f. 12.

"My dear Jim boy": Smith, p. 71.

Wellman was getting punchy: Wellman Sr. to SE.

They had been friendly: Wellman Jr., p. 379.

He talked to Joel McCrea: Wellman Jr. to SE.

"Henry Fonda was not an extrovert": Wellman Jr. to SE.

"I think everybody in the company": LOC, Teichmann papers, tape A6, p. 28.

Lieutenant Charles Cassell, who was executive officer: Wise and Rehill, p. 35.

His superior officer wrote: McKinney, p. 113.

"It was an awesome sight": Henry Fonda with Howard Teichmann, p. 147.

"Mister Fonda?": Ibid., p. 149.

"Can you barely remember": LOC, Teichmann papers, "Aunt Jayne and Uncle John," Fonda letters, undated, box 60, f. 6.

"I think about working": LOC, Teichmann papers, Fonda letters, box 60, f. 6, Henry Fonda to Peter Fonda, 10-10-44.

"Nobody would believe: LOC, Teichmann papers, Fonda letters, box 60, f. 6, Henry Fonda to Jane Fonda, 10-24-1944.

Six

B-24 crews: Bloomfield et al., p. 288.

"He . . . spent quite a bit of time": Ibid., p. 293.

The Eighth was taking East Anglia airfields: Overy, p. 103.

From the beginning of 1942: Stout, p. 99.

In 1943, as the Eighth: Miller, p. 266.

By December 1943: Overy, p. 124.

A bombing mission could include: MOMA, James Stewart file, Beirne Lay Jr., "Jimmy Stewart's Finest Performance," *Saturday Evening Post,* 12-15-45.

"Formation bombing like that": MOMA, James Stewart file, Cleveland Amory, "The Man Even Hollywood Likes," *Parade,* 10-21-84.

"thorough, deliberate, unspectacular": MOMA, James Stewart file, Lay, "Jimmy Stewart's Finest Performance," 12-15-45.

Damaged but intact: Ibid.

"The flight surgeon": Miller, p. 267.

"Well, fellows, we are sure glad": Smith, pp. 67–68.

"Anyone who doesn't want to go: Ibid., p. 82.

Lear was a scrounger: Lear, p. 76.

noted how the other men: James Stewart: A Wonderful Life, PBS Great Performances, 1987.

"It was cold": Zuckoff, p. 45.

"most crew on a tour": Overy, p. 164.

Stewart remembered his feelings: Smith, p. 131.

"brutality and the danger": Jack Valenti to SE.

"Jimmy Stewart came into our hut": Smith, p. 105.

"Well, this black English beer": Ibid., pp. 106–8.

"You keep on going: Stout, p. 362.

"Everybody's scared": James Stewart: A Wonderful Life, PBS Great Performances, 1987.

Seven

Among other refugees from Hollywood: Bloomfield et al., p. 248.

"I have never seen a greater exhibition": Ibid., p. 259.

"our doctor has had to order him": McKinney, p. 115.

Climbing down a ladder: Wise and Rehill, p. 39.

"For distinguishing himself": Ibid., p. 43.

"My former group commander": Smith, pp. 146–53.

"B-24's and B-17's seem to excite an affection": Miller, p. 441.

"Jimmy Stewart was a very good B-24 pilot": Smith, p. 125.

"Morale was unusually high": Dewey, p. 250.

"He was so popular": Don Moore, "He Flew with Jimmy Stewart in WWII," *Charlotte* (Florida) *Sun,* undated clipping.

"Stewart showed a ripping temper": Smith, 128.

Germany diverted two million workers: Miller, p. 483.

On the morning of D-Day: Overy, p. 396.

"This is it for you guys": Don Moore, "Jimmy Stewart Taught Englewood Man How to Fly," *Charlotte* (Florida) *Sun,* 10-22-2006.

"We had faith in him": Smith, 105.

"Sergeant, somebody sure": Dewey, p. 247.

He was carefully extricated: MOMA, James Stewart file, Beirne Lay Jr., "Jimmy Stewart's Finest Performance," *Saturday Evening Post,* 12-15-45.

"If the war had gone on": Smith, p. 16.

Newsboys sold condoms: Stout, p. 253.

On May 8 Stewart was awarded: MOMA, James Stewart file, Cleveland Amory, "The Man Even Hollywood Likes," *Parade,* 10-21-84.

"You have displayed: MOMA, James Stewart file, Lay, "Jimmy Stewart's Finest Performance," 12-15-45.

Between 1942 and the end of the war: Stout, p. 238.

"Never marry a musician": Jane Fonda, p. 23.

"I came home with a hangover": LOC, Teichmann papers, tape 33, p. 974.

"I couldn't stand it": Henry Fonda with Howard Teichmann, p. 163.

"Peter lost it": McKinney, p. 120.

"Much greater": Smith, p. 261.

Eight

"[Hayward] was forever on the phone": NYPL, Brooke Hayward papers, box 1, f. 2.

When Wasserman walked into his office: Bruck, p. 75.

"I want to be able": Ogden, p. 275.

"He had a childlike instinct": NYPL, Brooke Hayward papers, George Axelrod interview.

"the best story": NYPL, Leland Hayward papers, Leland Hayward to Billy Wilder, 7-10-51, box 208, f. 26.

"Having returned to the ranks": NYPL, Leland Hayward papers, box 206, f. 12.

"It was just the most successful party": LOC, Teichmann papers, tape 35, p. 1024.

"There was an infinite number": Dewey, p. 260.

"Instead of talking about it": Miller, p. 648.

"I can remember long car rides": Henry Fonda with Howard Teichmann, p. 187.

"I'm not difficult to anger": Ibid., p. 179.

"And I looked out": LOC, Teichmann papers, James Stewart interview.

Nine

"Lew was one of the smartest guys": Jack Valenti to SE.

"She really manipulated him": Dewey, p. 295.

"like a tranquil hobo": MOMA, Henry Fonda file, David Thomson, "Henry Fonda, 1905–1982," *Boston Phoenix,* 8-24-82.

"in the moment": LOC, Teichmann papers, tape 28, p. 818.

"You've got your raise": LOC, Teichmann papers, Charles Bidwell interview.

"Wasserman present": Basinger, p. 5.

"I didn't know what the hell": Cox, p. 72.

"Frank, if you want to make": MOMA, James Stewart file, Joyce Haber, "The Rise and Rise of Jimmy Stewart," *Los Angeles Times,* undated.

But as documents in Capra's papers prove: The document specifying Stewart's contract is dated July 2, 1947, from W. H. Clarke, treasurer of RKO Radio Pictures, to Ross Hastings. It's reproduced in Basinger, p. 61.

"I felt when I got back to pictures": Dewey, p. 266.

"It's a skill, you know": Cox, p. 104.

"What Lionel did": Ibid., p. 76.

It's from Stewart to Capra: The check is reproduced without comment by an obviously amused author, in Basinger, p. 47.

He saw Wellman regularly: Wellman Jr. to SE.

"It had Jimmy Stewart and Fonda": McGilli-

gan, *Film Crazy,* p. 89.

"It was just pure joy": LOC, Teichmann papers, tape 18, p. 554.

it managed $1.2 million: Financial figures courtesy of John McElwee.

"He's the most professional actor": LOC, Teichmann papers, Charles Bidwell interview.

"I needed him": James Bawden, "Henry Hathaway," *Films in Review,* 3–84.

"Why don't you bastards": Michael Buckley, "James Stewart," *Films in Review,* June 1991.

"It was hard to see": Dewey, p. 280.

"the McLean family were friends": Maria Cooper Janis to SE. All further quotes from Mrs. Janis derive from our interview.

They were dancing: MOMA, James Stewart file, Cleveland Amory, "The Man Even Hollywood Likes," *Parade,* 10-21-84.

"You know, I eat too": Buckley, "James Stewart."

It looked like urine: Bruck, p. 468.

Much of their honeymoon: Dewey, p. 319.

Jim also invested in a surplus P-51 Mustang: Smith, p. 190.

"It's as comfortable as Jimmy": A. Scott Berg, "Jimmy Stewart: The Star of *It's a Wonderful Life* and *The Philadelphia Story* in

Beverly Hills," *Architectural Digest,* April 1998.

"Jim Stewart phoned your house": NYPL, Leland Hayward papers, box 206, f. 12.

"The thing I like best about Jimmy": MOMA, James Stewart file, Amory, "The Man Even Hollywood Likes."

"About 15 minutes": Sue Lloyd to SE.

"I, too, am very glad about Stewart": NYPL, Leland Hayward papers, Hayward to Logan, 9-25-50, box 30, f. 3.

Ten

"I know it's crazy": Logan, p. 258.

"My mother was everything": Truman Capote, "The Duke in His Domain," *The New Yorker,* 11-9-57.

"The world is only made up": LOC, Teichmann papers, Jocelyn Brando interview.

"I'm not trying to help you": Logan, p. 263.

"Fonda has within him": Ibid., p. 264.

Josh Logan was in for 3 percent: NYPL, Leland Hayward papers, Backers box 31, f. 4; Finances box 31, f. 10.

"the most electric party": LOC, Teichmann papers, Nedda Logan interview.

"Every performance" Fess Parker to SE.

"I know what I want to achieve": LOC, Teichmann papers, Henry Fonda, *Good Morn-*

ing America, 1978, transcript.

"All of them were playing": LOC, Teichmann papers, Joshua Logan interview, part one.

"If that goddamned Logan": Logan, p. 327.

"She was a beautiful": LOC, Teichmann papers, Joshua Logan interview, part one.

"Fonda was . . . a stoic": Henry Fonda with Howard Teichmann, p. 192.

At its peak, the Anti-Nazi League: Cogley, p. 39.

"If we were going to stay friends": LOC, Teichmann papers, Henry Fonda, *Good Morning America,* 1978, transcript.

"I told Ward [Bond] off": LOC, Teichmann papers, tape A6, pp. 9–10.

"I choose to believe: NYPL, Brooke Hayward papers, Peter Fonda interview, box 7, f. 7.

"Henry Fonda," he insisted: Zollo, p. 297.

"the ridiculous side of Fonda": LOC, Teichmann papers, Joshua Logan interview, part one.

"He's a really unique character": Zollo, p. 297.

"Don't you ever": Jane Fonda, p. 68.

"Darling children": NYPL, Leland Hayward papers, box 206, folder 19.

"Are you going to do right": LOC, Teichmann papers, Joshua Logan interview, part one.

Frances asked her daughter: Jane Fonda, p. 14.

The latter read: Henry Fonda with Howard Teichmann, p. 202.

"We were all stunned": LOC, Teichmann papers, Jocelyn Brando interview.

"Frances had been away so long": LOC, Teichmann papers, tape 30, no page.

"I survived [Sullavan]": LOC, Teichmann papers, tape 19, p. 602.

"I hear myself telling these stories": LOC, Teichmann papers, tape 3, p. 27.

Jane never told her father: Jane Fonda, p. 19.

"I was never impressed": Grissom, p. 224.

"I talked to Fonda this morning": NYPL, Leland Hayward papers, Hayward to Logan, 5-1-50, box 30, f. 3.

"You know how mean Fonda can be": NYPL, Leland Hayward papers, box 30, f. 3.

She was devastated: Jane Fonda to SE.

"Do we really have to finish this?": NYPL, Leland Hayward papers, Fonda to Hayward, 1-7-53, box 45, f. 8.

"I'm a zoo freak": LOC, Teichmann papers, tape 38, p. 1105.

Eleven

The two men bonded: Peros, p. 75.

"I didn't think that Jimmy Stewart": Bob Hope to SE.

"My father always had a horse": Michael Buckley, "James Stewart," *Films in Review,* June 1991.

"My father had taught me how to behave": MOMA, James Stewart file, Cleveland Amory, "The Man Even Hollywood Likes," *Parade,* 10-21-84.

"I just fell in love with the horse": Ibid.

"Throughout the picture": Michael Wilmington "Small Town Guy," *Film Comment,* March–April 1990.

In April 1953, Universal donated: USC Cinema Arts Library, Universal Collection, Daily Minutes, committee meeting, Tuesday, April 21, 1953.

"Hitch is the champion eater: MOMA, James Stewart file, Bill Davidson, "Wal, You See, I'm an Actor," *TV Guide,* 10-2-71.

Lay cobbled together: Suid, p. 220.

"I'm in the boob business": McGilligan, *Backstory 3,* p. 62.

"His big point": USC, Jack L. Warner collection, *Spirit of St. Louis,* file 2.

"That was rather disconcerting": Sikov, pp. 378–79.

"It is needless for me to tell you what I think": NYPL, Leland Hayward papers, Warner to Hayward, 3-23-56, box 162, f. 11.

"I liked the book very much": Billy Wilder to SE.

"I myself had known": Dewey, p. 380.

"My all-time favorite man": Kim Novak to SE.

"We would sit on the set": Ibid.

"He closeted himself": Fujiwara, p. 242.

Jim told Gazzara: Gazzara, p. 104

"Coop didn't waste many words": MOMA, James Stewart file, Dwight Whitney, "Conversation with a Non-Talker," *TV Guide,* 5-16-70.

"Jimmy Galanos and Dior": Maria Cooper Janis to SE.

"After the glamour and glitter": Farkis, p. 220.

"I understand it's dirty": MOMA, James Stewart file, Whitney, "Conversation with a Non-Talker."

"I have a very soft and pleasant job": NYPL, Leland Hayward papers, box 206, f. 12.

"I would've died and been out of work": LOC, Teichmann papers, Henry Fonda *Good Morning America,* 1978, transcript.

"Jim is a man who became an actor": MOMA, James Stewart file, Amory, "The Man Even Hollywood Likes."

"The fact is that once we'd decided": Ibid.

"Jimmy was Jimmy": Dewey, p. 480.

"He is a priest": NYPL, Brooke Hayward papers, Joshua Logan interview box 7, f. 10.

"Josh could remember": Zollo, p. 297.

"I remember we did it one night": LOC, Teichmann papers, tape 37, p. 1098.

"Life with John": Norman Lloyd to SE.

"John Swope was elegant": Swope, p. 9.

"Your father is the kind of man": Henry Fonda with Howard Teichmann, p. 221.

"I don't think": LOC, Teichmann papers, Joshua Logan interview, part one.

The story derives: Simon Callow to SE.

"It was a wonderful": LOC, Teichmann papers, tape 29, p. 851.

"crisis after crisis": Wouk, p. 41.

"On those nights": LOC, Teichmann papers, Wouk to Teichmann, 10-23-80.

"Fonda never let down": Garner with Winokur, pp. 35–37.

Twelve

he felt Fonda's performance was definitive: NYPL, Leland Hayward papers, box 30, f. 3.

"With your cast insurance problems": NYPL, Leland Hayward papers, Brando to Hayward, 3-7-54, box 157, f. 5.

"Logan would always do": USC, Jack L.

Warner collection, *Mister Roberts,* box 26, phone conversation between Trilling and Ebenstein, 11-17-53.

"I don't know if he will": NYPL, Leland Hayward papers, Hayward to Bert Allenberg, 3-26-54, box 159, f. 6.

It was too broad": Ray Hagen, "Henry Fonda in His Own Words, Part Two," *Films of the Golden Age,* Issue 64, Spring 2011.

"windmilling": Jack Lemmon to SE.

On October 16: USC, Eric Stacey to Jack Warner, 10-16-54.

"Mervyn take precedence": USC, Hayward to Warner, 12-20-54.

"I think it is very fine": MOMA, Henry Fonda file, Bill Kelley, "Henry Fonda: On Peter, Jane, Movies Past and Present," *The Acquarian,* December 26, 1979–January 2, 1980.

"an extrovert": LOC, Teichmann papers, Nedda Logan interview.

"He really was a husband": LOC, Teichmann papers, Afdera Fonda interview.

"I thought this was a play": Segaloff, p. 80.

"an unattractive version": McKinney, p. 199.

"We went into production": Segaloff, p. 79.

"I'll take you through it": Grant, p. 121.

"They were bush league," LOC, Teichmann papers, Fonda interview.

Hayward took Brooke: Ogden, p. 278.

"Whatever you do: Ibid., p. 280.

"Sullavan is strictly compromise": Williams, pp. 107–9.

"Dear Maggie": NYPL, Leland Hayward papers, box 206, f. 19.

"How do you know it's suicide?": Ogden, p. 300.

"Love and luck, Hank": NYPL, Brooke Hayward papers, box 2, f. 28.

"was almost desperate": Spoto, p. 149.

"natural, unself-conscious, beautiful": LOC, Teichmann papers, tape 14, p. 448.

"We would go a couple of years": LOC, Teichmann papers, James Stewart interview.

"Jim and Hank": Dewey, p. 480.

"I hear Fonda": LOC, Joshua Logan papers, Stewart correspondence.

Alex then informed his son: MOMA, James Stewart file, Dwight Whitney, "Conversation with a Non-Talker," *TV Guide,* 5-16-70.

"He climbs on that nag": MOMA, James Stewart file, Pete Martin, "Jimmy Stewart, Mr. Hollywood," *Saturday Evening Post,* 3–78.

"Gloria was fantastic": Zollo, p. 298.

"Just remember always to be nice": Dewey, p. 24.

Thirteen

"Imagine a man so professional!": Earl Wilson, "Bald Is Beautiful Man Reminisces," *Hartford Courant,* 12-19-71.

"Garson can write": LOC, Teichmann papers, tape 34, p. 1009.

"The play is absolutely fascinating,": NYPL, Leland Hayward papers, box 206, f. 12.

"Take as much as you want": Bruck, p. 468.

"They had a flippant kind of relationship: Dewey, p. 410.

"I always had great respect for John Ford": Michael Wilmington, "Small Town Guy," *Film Comment,* March–April 1990.

One running gag: Peros, p. 175.

"It was the first time": MOMA, Stewart, Bill Davidson, "Wal, You See, I'm an Actor," *TV Guide,* 10-2-71.

"What the hell are you doing?": Classic Images, July 2015, p. 10.

"We hunted for one year": MOMA, James Stewart file, Aljean Harmetz, "James Stewart Says He's 'Fortunate Fellow,' " *New York Times,* 3-1-80.

"not one word": Kramer and Heeley, p. 230.

"Mr. Fonda, my name is Mae Clarke": Curtis, *Featured Player* p. 255.

"mostly silent and mysterious": Phillips, p. 160.

He was like a metronome: John Sacret Young to SE.

He hired his old friend: NYPL, Leland Hayward papers, contract dated 11-1-63, box 148, f. 32.

"Hayward seemed lost": Stuart Woods to SE.

"I don't do any exercise": MOMA, Henry Fonda file, Thomas Thompson, "Fonda at 68," *McCall's,* 9-73.

"Hank loved Shirlee deeply": Edwin Sherin to SE.

"I grow anything that is possible to grow": MOMA, Henry Fonda file, Thompson, "Fonda at 68."

"Duke Wayne was like that too": MOMA, James Stewart file, Cleveland Amory, "The Man Even Hollywood Likes," *Parade,* 10-21-84.

"I don't think I was ever ready": LOC, Teichmann papers, tape 22, p. 664.

he wrote: Ogden, pp. 283–84.

In 1967, he had a small stroke: Ibid., p. 293.

"I tried to kill Jim Stewart": LOC, Teichmann papers, tape 22, p. 957.

"Pay no attention to the script": Frayling, p. 269.

"The vice presidents of the companies": Ibid., p. 271.

"Sergio really directed that one, too": MOMA, Henry Fonda file, *The Acquarian,* Decem-

ber 26, 1979–January 2, 1980.

"We've got to get back": Gottfried, p. 242.

"I was fascinated with the care": MOMA, Henry Fonda file, *Premiere,* June 2005, p. 112.

"Why don't you imitate somebody good?": Garner with Winokur, p. 36.

"I'm very bad": Ray Hagen, "Henry Fonda in His Own Words, Part Two," *Films of the Golden Age,* Issue 64, Spring 2011.

"Aversion wouldn't be the word": Ibid.

"He said it was important": Kramer and Heeley, p. 305.

Kanter had to recast: Dewey, p. 454.

"What struck me": MOMA, Henry Fonda file, *Premiere,* June 2005, p. 112.

"Fonda called me up": Michael Wilmington "Small Town Guy," *Film Comment,* March–April 1990.

Whenever Jones met him: Jones with Leigh, p. 164.

"I don't really like myself": Henry Fonda with Howard Teichmann, p. 297.

"great to work with": Shirley Jones to SE.

"maybe a little intimidated": Ibid.

"Jim tried hard": Henry Fonda with Howard Teichmann, p. 309.

"You learn not to look at something like this": MOMA, James Stewart file, *Modern Maturity,* December–January 1976–77.

"These are patriotic kids": MOMA, James Stewart file, Judy Klemesrud, "Today's Kids Should Laugh More," *New York Times,* 2-22-70.

"I have seldom seen": LOC, Joshua Logan papers, James Stewart file, Logan to Stewart, April 27, 1970.

"Jimmy is lazier": LOC, Teichmann papers, Nedda Logan interview.

Fourteen

Bill Hayward was sitting: NYPL, Brooke Hayward papers, William Hayward transcript, box 7, f. 9.

Ford never slagged Fonda: Dan Ford to SE.

"Elephants never forget": Ibid.

"How can you say anybody's better": LOC, Teichmann papers, tape B10, p. 7.

"What am I supposed to do?": Dewey, p. 460.

"Why not Henry Fonda": Richard L. Coe, "An American 'Home,' " *Washington Post,* 8-13-72.

"I hate them!": MOMA, James Stewart file, *Modern Maturity,* December–January 1976–77.

"Saw The Graduate": MOMA, James Stewart file, Dwight Whitney, "Conversation with a Non-Talker," *TV Guide,* 5-16-70.

"We found ourselves sitting around: MOMA,

James Stewart file, Judy Klemesrud, "Today's Kids Should Laugh More," *New York Times,* 2-22-70.

his favorite novel: LOC, Teichmann papers, tape A6, p. 22.

"I won't have a gun": LOC, Teichmann papers, tape 33, p. 973.

"Maybe one ejaculation": LOC, Teichmann papers, tape A6, p. 26.

"Unlike Stewart": LOC, Teichmann papers, first part, tape 18, p. 565; second part, tape 33, p. 982.

"His whole life opened:" LOC, Teichmann papers, Nedda Logan interview.

"I am better with Shirlee": LOC, Teichmann papers, tape 34, p. 986.

"It makes me sound pretty dull": Dewey, p. 478.

"I've always felt that the way to learn:" MOMA, James Stewart file, Rob Lardine, "Not the Retiring Type," *New York Sunday News,* 6-21-70.

"I love this play": LOC, Joshua Logan papers, James Stewart file, Logan to Stewart, 12-22-82.

"This has been a wonderful evening": Kenneth Turan, "A Win for the Other Jimmy," *Washington Post,* 3-1-80.

"Hank my Love": LOC, Teichmann papers, Fonda letters, box 60, f. 6.

"You don't stumble into this": LOC, Teichmann papers, James Stewart interview.

"I felt so badly about the phony make-up: LOC, Teichmann papers, Henry Fonda to Peter Fonda, undated, but 1978, Fonda letters, box 60, f. 6.

When he got to the room: McKinney, p. 291.

"This is the most amazing boy": LOC, Teichmann papers, tape 33, p. 973.

"At first, I was intimidated": Jane Alexander to SE. All further quotes from Alexander derive from this interview.

After biopsies and X-rays: LOC, Teichmann papers, Edward A. Newman M.D. to R.A. Boyer, 5-1-79.

"I used to have a house": MOMA, James Stewart file, Joyce Haber, "The Rise and Rise of Jimmy Stewart," *Los Angeles Times,* undated.

Fifteen

"Fonda is a loner": MOMA, Henry Fonda file, Thomas Thompson, "Fonda at 68," *McCall's,* 9–73.

"I've had a good deal of satisfaction": Ray Hagen, "Henry Fonda in His Own Words, Part two," *Films of the Golden Age,* issue 64, Spring, 2011.

"Well, Henry Fonda won't": MOMA, Henry

Fonda file, Diana Maychick, "Hank's Greatest Night: The Oscar," *New York Post,* 4-7-82.

"I don't think there was ever any sense": Dewey, p. 477.

He never received a reply: Peter Fonda to SE.

"I don't need to see your eyes": Jane Fonda, p. 422.

"With her energy": Ibid., p. 437.

"Henry Fonda was the hardest": Ibid.

"It was in the wind": MOMA, Henry Fonda file, "For Jane Fonda, Those Days on Golden Pond Brought Her and Her Dad Together At Last," *People,* 4-12-82.

"I just feel so lucky": LOC, Teichmann papers, tape 33, p. 975.

Hank's will instructed: MOMA, Henry Fonda file, "Wife and Adopted Daughter to Share Henry Fonda Estate," *New York Times,* 8-22-82.

"Just who are you working for": James D'Arc to SE.

"As a kid": MOMA, James Stewart file, "It's Still a Wonderful Life for Jimmy Stewart as Indiana, Pa. Welcomes Home the Boy Who Made Good," *People,* 6-6-83.

"I know I'm forgetful": MOMA, James Stewart file, Aljean Harmetz, "James Stewart Says He's Fortunate Fellow," *New York*

Times, 3-1-80.

"So many actors nowadays": MOMA, James Stewart file, Michael Blowen, "Looking in on Jimmy Stewart," *Boston Globe,* 10-27-83.

"The frail old man": Kramer and Heeley, p. 202.

"But don't fuck with him": Dewey, p. 207.

"This friendship with Fonda": MOMA, James Stewart file, unsourced clipping.

"The most amazing thing happened": MOMA, James Stewart file, John Gregory Dunne, "Goodbye Mr. Stewart," *New York Times,* 7-5-97.

Epilogue

"My mom only did thirteen": Zollo, p. 296.

"How's Brooke?": Ibid., p. 300.

"What you learn is never what's said": First part, LOC, Teichmann papers, Henry Fonda *Good Morning America,* 1978, transcript; second part, MOMA, *Premiere,* June 2005, p. 134.

"No explanation was required: LOC, Teichmann papers, James Stewart interview.

"You can't build": Itzkoff, p. 242.

"He has this extraordinary thing": LOC, Teichmann papers, Dorothy McGuire interview.

"I never feel that I have really expressed": LOC, Teichmann papers, Dorothy McGuire interview.

BIBLIOGRAPHY

Bach, Steven. *Marlene Dietrich: Life and Legend.* New York: Morrow, 1992.

Basinger, Jeanine. *The It's a Wonderful Life Book.* New York: Knopf, 1986.

Brady, John. *Frank and Ava: In Love and War.* New York: St. Martin's, 2015.

Bruck, Connie. *When Hollywood Had a King.* New York: Random House, 2003.

Caine, Michael. *The Elephant to Hollywood.* New York: Holt, 2010.

Clarke, Gerald. *Capote: A Biography.* New York: Simon & Schuster, 1988.

Cogley, John. *Report on Blacklisting: Movies.* Fund for the Republic, 1956.

Coldstream, John. *Dirk Bogarde: The Authorized Biography.* London: Weidenfeld & Nicolson, 2004.

Cox, Stephen. *It's a Wonderful Life: A Memory Book.* Nashville: Cumberland Press, 2003.

Curtis, James. *Between Flops.* New York:

Harcourt Brace Jovanovich, 1982.

———. *Featured Player: An Oral Autobiography of Mae Clarke.* Lanham, MD: Scarecrow Press, 1996.

Dewey, Donald. *James Stewart: A Biography.* Atlanta: Turner, 1996.

Eliot, Marc. *Jimmy Stewart.* New York: Crown, 2006.

Eyman, Scott. *Print the Legend.* New York, Simon & Schuster, 1999.

Farkis, John. *Not Thinkin' . . . Just Rememberin' . . . : The Making of John Wayne's The Alamo.* Albany, GA: BearManor, 2015.

Fonda, Henry, with Howard Teichmann. *Fonda: My Life.* New York: New American Library, 1981.

Fonda, Jane. *My Life So Far.* New York: Random House, 2005.

Frayling, Christopher. *Sergio Leone: Something to Do with Death.* Minneapolis: University of Minnesota Press, 2012.

Fujiwara, Chris. *The World and Its Double: The Life and Work of Otto Preminger.* New York: Faber & Faber, 2008.

Garner, James, with Jon Winokur. *The Garner Files.* New York: Simon & Schuster, 2011.

Gazzara, Ben. *In the Moment.* New York:

Carroll & Graf, 2004.

Gottfried, Martin. *Jed Harris: The Curse of Genius.* Boston: Little Brown, 1984.

Grant, Lee. *I Said Yes to Everything.* New York: Blue Rider Press, 2014.

Grissom, James. *Follies of God: Tennessee Williams and the Women of the Fog.* New York, Knopf, 2016.

Helmick, Paul A. *Cut, Print, and That's a Wrap!: A Hollywood Memoir.* Jefferson, NC: McFarland, 2001.

Herman, Jan. *A Talent for Trouble: The Life of William Wyler.* New York: Putnam,

Houghton, Norris. *But Not Forgotten.* New York: Sloane, 1957.

Itzkoff, Dave. *Mad as Hell: The Making of Network and the Fateful Vision of the Angriest Man in Movies.* New York: Times Books, 2014.

Jacobs, Diane. *Christmas in July: The Life and Art of Preston Sturges.* Berkeley: University of California Press, 1992.

Janis, Maria Cooper. *Gary Cooper Off Camera: A Daughter Remembers.* New York: Abrams, 1999.

Jones, Shirley, with Wendy Leigh. *Shirley Jones: A Memoir.* New York: Gallery Books, 2013.

Kramer, Joan, and David Heeley. *In the*

Company of Legends. New York: Beaufort Books, 2015.

Lally, Kevin. *Wilder Times: The Life of Billy Wilder.* New York: Holt, 1996.

Lambert, Gavin. *Natalie Wood: A Life.* New York: Knopf, 2004.

Laurents, Arthur. *Original Story By.* New York: Knopf, 2002.

Lear, Norman. *Even This I Get to Experience.* New York: Penguin, 2014.

Logan, Joshua. *Josh: My Up and Down, In and Out Life.* New York: Delacorte, 1976.

McGilligan, Patrick. *Backstory 3: Interviews with Screenwriters of the '60s.* Berkeley: University of California Press, 1997.

———. *Film Crazy.* New York: St. Martin's, 2000.

McKinney, Devin. *The Man Who Saw a Ghost: The Life and Work of Henry Fonda.* New York: St. Martin's, 2012.

Meredith, Burgess. *So Far, So Good.* New York: Little, Brown, 1994.

Meyers, Jeffrey. *Gary Cooper: American Hero.* New York: Morrow, 1998.

Miller, Donald L. *The Story of World War II.* New York: Simon & Schuster, 2001.

Ogden, Christopher. *Life of the Party: The Biography of Pamela Digby Churchill Hay-*

ward Harriman. New York: Little, Brown, 1994.

Overy, Richard. *The Bombers and the Bombed: Allied Air War over Europe, 1940–1945.* New York: Viking, 2013.

Peros, Mike. *Dan Duryea: Heel with a Heart.* Jackson: University Press of Mississippi, 2016.

Phillips, Stevie. *Judy & Liza & Robert & Freddie & David & Sue & Me.* New York: St. Martin's, 2015.

Riva, Maria. *Marlene Dietrich.* New York: Knopf, 1992.

Rogers, Clifford, Ty Seidule, and Steve Waddell, eds. *The West Point History of World War II,* Vol. II. New York: Simon & Schuster, 2016.

Segaloff, Nat. *Arthur Penn: American Director.* Lexington: University Press of Kentucky, 2011.

Shorris, Sylvia, and Marion Abbott Bundy. *Talking Pictures.* New York: New Press, 1994.

Siegel, Don. *A Siegel Film.* London: Faber & Faber, 1993.

Sikov, Ed. *On Sunset Boulevard: The Life and Times of Billy Wilder.* New York: Hyperion, 1998.

Slide, Anthony. *A Special Relationship:*

Britain Comes to Hollywood and Hollywood Comes to Britain. Jackson: University Press of Mississippi, 2015.

Smith, Starr. *Jimmy Stewart: Bomber Pilot*. St. Paul: Zenith Press, 2005.

Spoto, Donald. *A Girl's Got to Breathe: The Life of Teresa Wright*. Jackson: University Press of Mississippi, 2016.

Stein, Jean. *West of Eden: An American Place*. New York: Random House, 2016.

Stephens, George, Jr. *Conversations with the Great Moviemakers of Hollywood's Golden Age*. New York: Knopf, 2006.

Stout, Jay A. *Hell's Angels: The True Story of the 303rd Bomb Group in World War II*. New York: Berkley, 2015.

Sturges, Preston. *Preston Sturges by Preston Sturges*. New York: Simon & Schuster, 1990.

Suid, Lawrence H. *Guts and Glory: The Making of the American Military Image in Film*. Lexington: University Press of Kentucky, 2002.

Swope, John. *Camera Over Hollywood*. New York: Distributed Art Publishers, 1999.

Viertel, Peter. *Dangerous Friends*. New York: Doubleday, 1992.

Vinciguerra, Thomas. *Cast of Characters: Wolcott Gibbs, E. B. White, James Thurber, and the Golden Age of The New Yorker.* New York: Norton, 2016.

Wallach, Eli. *The Good, the Bad, and Me.* Orlando, FL: Harcourt, 2004.

Watkins, T. H. *The Hungry Years.* New York: Holt, 1999.

Wellman, William Jr. *Wild Bill Wellman: Hollywood Rebel.* New York: Pantheon, 2015.

Westmore, Frank, with Muriel Davidson. *The Westmores of Hollywood.* New York: Lippincott, 1976.

Williams, Tennessee (edited by Albert J. Devlin). *The Selected Letters of Tennessee Williams,* Vol. II, 1945–1957. New York: New Directions, 2004.

Willian, Michael. *The Essential It's a Wonderful Life.* Chicago: Chicago Review Press, 2006.

Wise, James E. Jr., and Anne Collier Rehill. *Stars in Blue: Movie Actors in America's Sea Services.* Annapolis, MD: Naval Institute Press, 1997.

Wouk, Herman. *Sailor and Fiddler: Reflections of a 100 Year Old Author.* New York: Simon & Schuster, 2016.

Zollo, Paul. *Hollywood Remembered.* New York: Cooper Square, 2002.

Zolotow, Maurice. *Billy Wilder in Hollywood.*

New York: Putnam, 1977.

Zuckoff, Mitchell. *Robert Altman: The Oral Biography.* New York: Knopf, 2009.

ABOUT THE AUTHOR

Scott Eyman is the author or coauthor of fifteen books, including the bestseller *John Wayne* and (with actor Robert Wagner) the bestsellers *Pieces of My Heart* and *You Must Remember This*. Among his other books are *Empire of Dreams: The Epic Life of Cecil B. DeMille*, *Lion of Hollywood: The Life and Legend of Louis B. Mayer*, and *Print the Legend: The Life and Times of John Ford*. Eyman also writes book reviews for *The Wall Street Journal* and has written for *The New York Times*, *The Washington Post*, and the *Chicago Tribune*, as well as practically every film magazine extinct or still extant. He teaches film history at the University of Miami and lives in West Palm Beach with his wife, Lynn.